OBJECTS OF SURVIVANCE

OBJECTS OF SURVIVANCE

A MATERIAL HISTORY OF THE AMERICAN INDIAN SCHOOL EXPERIENCE

LINDSAY M. MONTGOMERY AND CHIP COLWELL

Denver Museum of Nature & Science
University Press of Colorado

Published by the Denver Museum of Nature & Science and University Press of Colorado

2001 Colorado Boulevard
Denver, Colorado 80205

245 Century Circle, Suite 202
Louisville, Colorado 80027

 The University Press of Colorado is a proud member of
The Association of American University Presses.

The University Press of Colorado is a cooperative publishing enterprise supported, in part, by Adams State University, Colorado State University, Fort Lewis College, Metropolitan State University of Denver, Regis University, University of Colorado, University of Northern Colorado, University of Wyoming, Utah State University, and Western Colorado University.

∞ This paper meets the requirements of the ANSI/NISO Z39.48-1992 (Permanence of Paper)

ISBN: 978-1-60732-992-3 (hardcover)
ISBN: 978-1-60732-993-0 (ebook)
https://doi.org/10.5876/9781607329930

Library of Congress Cataloging-in-Publication Data

Names: Montgomery, Lindsay M. (Lindsay Martel), author. | Colwell, Chip (John Stephen), 1975– author.
Title: Objects of survivance : a material history of the American Indian school experience / Lindsay M. Montgomery, Chip Colwell.
Description: Louisville : University Press of Colorado, [2019] | Includes bibliographical references and index.
Identifiers: LCCN 2019032796 (print) | LCCN 2019032797 (ebook) | ISBN 9781607329923 (hardcover) | ISBN 9781607329930 (ebook)
Subjects: LCSH: Bratley, J. H. (Jesse H.)—Photograph collections. | Indians of North America—Cultural assimilation. | Indigenous peoples—Cultural assimilation—United States. | Off-reservation boarding schools—United States. | Indians of North America—Education—History. | Indigenous peoples—Education—United States.
Classification: LCC E98.C89 M66 2019 (print) | LCC E98.C89 (ebook) | DDC 970.004/97—dc23
LC record available at https://lccn.loc.gov/2019032796
LC ebook record available at https://lccn.loc.gov/2019032797

COVER ILLUSTRATIONS. Front, Top: Cartoon of Turning Eagle attempting to kill Jesse H. Bratley (DMNS AC.11680); front, bottom: S'Klallam children in Western clothes, S'Klallam Reservation, ca. 1893–1895 (DMNS BR61-494); Back: Hopi rabbit stick, Hopi Reservation, 1902 (DMNS AC.5576).

1

A MAN AND WORLD IN BETWEEN 3

2

BRATLEY'S COLLECTION IN CONTEXT 36

Indian Schools 37
Collecting Cultures 41
Corners and Fairs 53

3

THE PIONEERING LIFE OF JESSE H. BRATLEY 68

Port Gamble Day School, 1893–1895 73
Lower Cut Meat Creek Day School, 1895–1899 81
Cantonment Boarding School, 1899–1900 91
Havasupai Day School, 1900–1901 95
Polacca Day School, 1902 98
Kansas and Florida, 1903–1948 110

4

THE CIVILIZING MACHINE 116

Work Conquers All 117
Resistance 144
Persistence 156

5

OBJECTS OF SURVIVANCE 189

Acknowledgments 213
References 215
Index 237

Contents

OBJECTS OF SURVIVANCE

By 1890, the end seemed very near. The Indian Wars had drawn to a close, with the US military the undisputed victor. America's Western frontier was opened to endless waves of settlers, taking land, water, forests, wildlife, minerals for their own. Native Americans, once numbering in the millions, were now less than 250,000. Confined to reservations, a fraction of their traditional homelands, Native Americans continued to lose land throughout the early twentieth century through a process called allotment, which assigned small homesteads to tribal members and sold "excess" land to non-Indians. No longer dependent on their own subsistence, Native people were forced into a labor economy that was foreign and alienating—or were left as supplicants to government handouts. Long-standing religious practices were attacked and outlawed. Many were forced into clothes and homes that were considered by their conquerors to be "civilized."

After centuries of colonialism, the extinction of Native Americans now seemed certain. This fact obliged the US government to determine how to handle the twilight of the continent's first people. With peace, the government could not so simply eradicate the Indians who remained. The only real choice left was assimilation—to force Native Americans to adopt the beliefs, attitudes, tastes, habits, and work of good Anglo-Americans.[1]

But how?

Education.

School was quickly determined to be the avenue by which Native Americans would sojourn into an assimilated future. By transforming the next generation of Indians into good citizens, the government could swiftly sever Indians from the deep roots of their culture. Although Native Americans had long been the focus of educational efforts—Harvard University and William and Mary College began educating Indian youth in the 1600s—this strategy of advancement took on a fresh urgency.[2] Four hundred years after Christopher Columbus made landfall, the work of American colonialism was not quite over. The resources that were used in the old war were needed for a new one—a seamless transformation, often literally, of barracks into boarding schools (figure 1.1).

The new battle required new soldiers. Schools required educators willing to run these outposts dedicated to civilizing the savages at the gates of America's future.

Jesse H. Bratley was one such man.

1

A MAN AND WORLD IN BETWEEN

FIGURE 1.1. Cheyenne
and Arapaho students
pose in front of the Can-
tonment Boarding School.
Before Cantonment was an
Indian school, it was a US
Army barracks. Cheyenne
and Arapaho Reserva-
tion, 1899–1900. (DMNS
BR61-375)

A MAN AND
WORLD IN
BETWEEN

4

▼ ▽ ▼

Born in 1867, Jesse Hastings Bratley was an unlikely candidate to become an Indian schoolteacher. The son of pioneers Joseph and Mary Hastings Bratley, Jesse spent much of his early life helping his impoverished family merely survive (figure 1.2). When he was three years old, the family moved from Wisconsin to Kansas, lured by the promise of the frontier. Kansas proved just as difficult; the family owed a large debt for its new land and constantly faced poverty, poor harvests, inclement weather, wildfires, and Indian attacks. Jesse spent his childhood laboring on the family farm and, for only three months a year, attending school. As a student, Jesse struggled. He especially loathed arithmetic and grammar.

When he was nineteen, Bratley began his peripatetic work life—by turns a farmer, janitor, accountant, homesteader, traveling salesman, teacher, postal worker, and realtor. In 1893, Bratley saw an ad for positions at federally funded Indian schools. Attracted by the possibility of steady employment, he applied. Bratley was soon headed to teach the S'Klallam at the Port Gamble Day School, northwest of Seattle, Washington. Over the next decade, he taught at four more schools across the United States.

Yet this new opportunity would become more than a job; living among Native Americans permanently changed the direction of Bratley's life. He began an ad hoc anthropological

survey of Native communities, ultimately taking more than 500 glass-plate photographs and collecting nearly 1,000 artifacts—images and things that would last beyond his lifetime and form the foundation of his legacy (figure 1.3).

The Jesse H. Bratley collection, as it came to be known, however, has more to teach us than about one man's life. Because Bratley occupied a perfect gray zone—a supporter of Indian schools but not their architect, a collector with only vague aspirations to anthropological seriousness, a photographer variously motivated by entrepreneurship, documentary voyeurism, and romantic dreams—he gives us an unusual visual and material testimony of one of the most profoundly important moments in the history of contemporary Native America. Bratley's story allows us to witness Native Americans' dramatically shifting way of life—the tangled processes of civilizing, resistance, and persistence—as the nineteenth century surrendered to the modern age.

After finishing his career as an Indian schoolteacher, Bratley and his family moved to Florida in 1910. Bratley dreamed of building his own museum in Miami where he could display the hundreds of objects he had collected. Unable to marshal the time or resources, Bratley never realized his dream. Following his death in 1948, Bratley's extensive collection

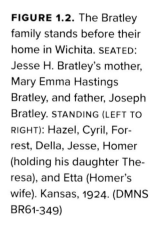

FIGURE 1.2. The Bratley family stands before their home in Wichita. SEATED: Jesse H. Bratley's mother, Mary Emma Hastings Bratley, and father, Joseph Bratley. STANDING (LEFT TO RIGHT): Hazel, Cyril, Forrest, Della, Jesse, Homer (holding his daughter Theresa), and Etta (Homer's wife). Kansas, 1924. (DMNS BR61-349)

FIGURE 1.3. Bratley sits with pride next to a small portion of his collection. Florida, date unknown. (Children of Dr. Forrest G. Bratley)

was divided among his four children: Homer, Hazel, Cyril, and Forrest. In 1961, Hazel sold her share of the collection, along with Homer's and Cyril's portions, to the Southeast Museum of the North American Indian, located in Marathon, Florida. In selling Bratley's collection, Hazel earnestly hoped to fulfill her father's lifelong wish to stimulate "interest in and appreciation for the North American Indian among the many visitors who will see these treasures through the years."[3]

The Southeast Museum was owned and operated by Mary and Francis Crane. The Cranes, as wife and husband, structured their retirement around a passion for collecting Native American artifacts.[4] They had come to believe in the educational value of Native American collections and set about acquiring thousands of ethnographic and archaeological objects over the course of a seventeen-year shopping blitz. In 1958, the Cranes used their private collections to open the Southeast Museum, advertising it as "the largest and finest collection of artifacts south of the Smithsonian."[5] Although the Southeast Museum's holdings were sweeping, many considered the museum a tourist trap; it also remained relatively obscure among professional researchers and curators. The lack of professional attention was amplified by the museum's remote location and the public's recreation focus in the Florida Keys.

As a result of chronically low attendance, the Southeast Museum closed its doors in 1968 and the Cranes donated their extensive 12,000-piece collection to the Denver Museum of Nature & Science (then the Denver Museum of Natural History).[6] When the Denver Museum received the collection from the Cranes, it contained roughly 1,500 ethnographic and archaeological objects, documents, and photographic items that Bratley had amassed. Before the Denver Museum took control of the collection, the Cranes invited the Smithsonian Institution to duplicate Bratley's photographs. The Smithsonian made prints of 243 glass plates and copies of 200 original photos and stereopticon views.[7]

Although the majority of the Bratley collection found its way to the Denver Museum, about a quarter of it remained with Forrest G. Bratley, the youngest of Jesse's children. In 1983, Forrest donated 47 ethnographic objects, primarily from the Plains and Southwest—including an impressive Lakota Winter Count (figure 1.4)—to the National Cowboy & Western Heritage Museum in Oklahoma City, Oklahoma, and another small portion to the Robinson Museum in Pierre, South Dakota.[8] Forrest bequeathed the remainder of his collection to his own children, Jesse's grandchildren.

The Denver Museum of Nature & Science has long touted the Bratley collection as one of its prized possessions. Bratley's photographs have been used extensively in exhibits and programs; a number of the collected artifacts have been on permanent display at the museum. Yet despite the prestige accorded to the collection, it has never been the focus of sustained study.

In 2015, we had the chance to embark on a research project. Montgomery had joined the Denver Museum for a one-year postdoctoral fellowship, and Colwell, as a curator on staff, had long set his sights on the Bratley collection. Soon after beginning the work, we saw the Bratley collection's immense significance. The collection was widely used but little understood—images and objects more often employed as decoration than as an analytical lens. Jesse had written an autobiography, which had never been published. He left behind a paper trail in archives that could be followed. The Bratley family held more pieces, which had never been studied. For all its prominence, Bratley's life work was essentially unknown.

We considered it an imperative to document what Bratley had left behind. Even more, we saw the potential for a great and important story.

But what exactly did we see? What is the meaning of these hundreds of objects and images, which Bratley collected from 1893 to 1903? What should we make of them—and of him? Why do Bratley's collections of the S'Klallam, Lakota Sioux, Cheyenne, Arapaho, Havasupai, Hopi, and Seminole a century ago matter today?[9]

▼ ▽ ▼

FIGURE 1.4 (above and facing page). The Chief Swift Bear Winter Count is now curated at the National Cowboy & Western Heritage Museum. Recounted by the Swift Bear family, the Winter Count uses ideographs to depict the major events that occurred each year from 1800 to 1898. (National Cowboy & Western Heritage Museum)

Swift Bear's Winter Count

1800–1801 First Good White Man Comes Winter

Position of the hand indicates good. First White man recorded by this Winter Count. First White man to live and trade with the Dakota Indians; however, White men had traded with them before this time but did not live among them.

1801–1802 First Good White Man Returns with Gun to Trade Winter

1802–1803 Chief Big Elk Killed Winter

1803–1804 White Trader Come Built House Winter

Probably this man is Little Beaver, so called by Indians and whose house burned down with the trader in it.

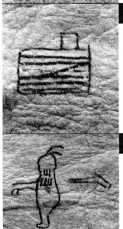

1804–1805 Seven Pawnees Came to Dakota Camp All Killed Winter

Had one gun from first White man.

1805–1806 Eight White Traders Come Winter

Other Counts call this winter "Eight Dakotas killed winter"; Hat counts one.

A MAN AND
WORLD IN
BETWEEN

continued on next page

1806–1807	Dakotas Killed Three Pawnees Winter

Pawnees and Dakotas both on the warpath and met, had a battle; three Pawnees killed, and two Dakotas wounded, one shot in throat.

1807–1808	Many Flags Flying for Medicine Winter

The material used was red flannel procured through trade with first good White man. Indians were troubled with a bad cough this winter.

1808–1809	Pail Killed by Falling Tree Winter

Pail in His Hand is his name totem. The Indian was outing the tree when it fell on him and crushed him as the red on his body indicates.

1809–1810	Little Beaver's (White Trader) House Burned Winter

Burning is indicated by red on the rectangle, which indicates the house, and by the black marks above, which is fire and smoke, respectively.

1810–1811	Swift Horse with Feathers Tied in His Tail Winter

This was an extra fine horse with his tail so decorated that was in a herd of horses that was taken on the South Platte River. Some of the Indians say that the horses were stolen from the Pawnees and some say that they were wild.

1811–1812	Many Dakota Starve Winter

Buffalo meat was scarce as the empty drying pole indicates.

continued on next page

	1812–1813	White Man (Yellow Face) Comes Trade Provisions Winter

1813–1814 A Crow Went on a Visit and Was Scalped Winter

He was killed by Sioux. He made no resistance. His scalp is tied to a stick, as shown in the picture.

1814–1815 A Shoshone with One Arrow Came to Dakota Lodge to Make Peace Was Killed with Dakota Tomahawk Winter

The one arrow is noticed in front of the Indian, which indicates that he had come to treat for peace. The tomahawk is sticking in the Shoshone's head. Other Winter Counts call this a Kiowa, others an Arapahoe.

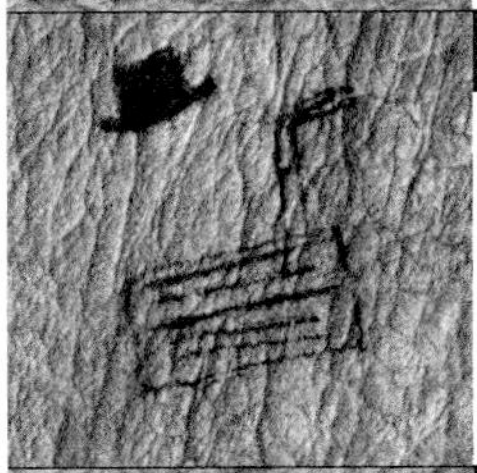

1815–1816 White Man Made House Winter

Boke is the name as nearly as I can understand it, which is not an Indian word.

1816–1817 Wounded Heel Went on Warpath Got Shot in Heel Winter

As the enemy outnumbered him, on first sight of the enemy he turned and started to run away when he was shot in the heel by an arrow. This man's name was changed after he was shot.

1817–1818 Crooked Wrist Killed Winter

This warrior's wrist was crooked from infancy.

1818–1819 Smallpox Killed Dakota Winter

The red spots on the body show the disease.

A MAN AND
WORLD IN
BETWEEN

continued on next page

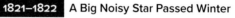

| **1819–1820** | Many Old Men Died Winter |

1820–1821 Two Utes Killed Winter

Red on the head of the first one shows that the scalp was taken. The other one has a round head; the Dakotas thinking him an African American, did not scalp him. The long hair is shown, which he had, they likely thinking at that early day that the African American's hair would grow long. Single Wood says they found out later that he was not an African American.

1821–1822 A Big Noisy Star Passed Winter

The streaks show that it let off particles of light in its passage. Red Cloud was born this winter. Much whiskey winter; Red Cloud's father died of drunkenness.

1822–1823 Wa-sku-pi Broke Leg Off Winter

While chasing buffalo his pony stopped suddenly, throwing the rider off, and at the same time, Single Wood says, his leg at the knee joint was taken entirely from his body.

1823–1824 White Man Taught Dakotas Plant Corn Winter

Corn growing is represented by a single stock of corn. The hat indicates a White man.

1824–1825 Killed One Buffalo Winter

The head on tipi indicates the one buffalo killed and also shows that the Indians made buffalo medicine in this tipi over the one buffalo head, after which many buffalo came.

A MAN AND
WORLD IN
BETWEEN

continued on next page

Swift Bear's Winter Count—*continued*

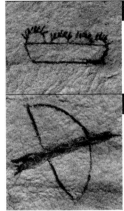

1825–1826   Many Dakotas Drowned in Great Flood Winter

They were camped at some point in a valley on the Missouri River, and as the ice was going out in the spring, there was an unusually large rise in the water, which overtook the Indians by surprise and many were drowned and crushed to death. All counts mention this.

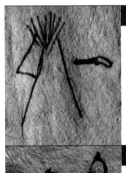

1826–1827   Dragged Goods up River on Ice Winter

This was a very severe winter, which killed most of the ponies, and the Indians wished to move up the river as there was much timber further up and wished to visit another band of Sioux. So they dragged their tipis and all their goods on the ice. The road they made is plainly marked, showing that there were many of them, which wore the ice considerably. They used their saddles for sleds. Yellow Robe was born this year. They went upstream instead of across, as indicated by drawing on pictograph.

1827–1828   Crows Killed Dakotas in Lodge Winter

1828–1829   Dakotas Killed Three Crows Winter

Crows are indicated by the pompadour.

1829–1830   Swift Bears Father Made Medicine Winter

This man began the Winter Count.

1830–1831   Killed Ten White Buffalo Cows Winter

All were killed with arrows.

1831–1832   Broken Toe Winter

A warrior was sent out on a morning to a hill, by the Dakotas, to look for Crows, when out from the camp but a little way he was surprised by a band of Crows and in running from them he stubbed his toes (of one foot) on a rock, which broke them all back, indicated by red spots on foot. As he did not return that night, his people went out the next morning to hunt him. They found him alive as the Crows did not find him. This is the winter in which this happened.

continued on next page

A MAN AND
WORLD IN
BETWEEN

1832–1833   Grey Eagle Tail Died Winter or Tie Knot in His Penis Died Winter

Chief Grey Eagle Tail of Lower Cut Meat camp was named for this man.

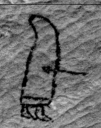

1833–1834   Many Stars Fall Winter

The circle represents a lodge or tipi with a shower of stars over or around it. Spotted Tail was born this year. (All counts mention this shower of stars.)

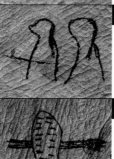

1834–1835   Man Came with Gray Cap on Killed Winter

The Dakotas saw a stranger wearing a gray cap and leaning against one of their lodges. Knowing that none of their people had such caps, they took this man to be an enemy and shot him through the body with an arrow. This was a Shoshone. He probably came to steal horses, or to kill the Sioux. His cap was like With-Horns, made up with a cape.

1835–1836   Two Cree Chiefs Went on Warpath Killed Winter

The pipe indicates the leader of a war party; or rather the pipe is carried by the leader of a war party.

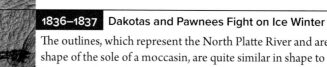

1836–1837   Dakotas and Pawnees Fight on Ice Winter

The outlines, which represent the North Platte River and are very much the shape of the sole of a moccasin, are quite similar in shape to a portion of the figures in 1826–1827, 1811–1812, 1856–1857, although the first and last do not indicate rivers at all, but the former a death circle and the latter a high bank or bluff. The Pawnees had come from the South and were in camp as the Dakotas came from the North. The battle took place on the ice. There were only ten of the Dakotas killed and nine of the Pawnees, as indicated by the death marks on the respective sides. In 1899, Pawnee Tom told me at Cantonment that White Wolf, Old Hawk, and Standing Bull were among the Pawnees killed. Pawnee Tom says he is the only man that was with Custer that escaped alive.

1837–1838   Paints the Lower Half of His Face Red and Family Killed Winter

This man and family were moving from place to place and camping alone while hunting for buffalo. The entire family was killed by Pawnees. Sitting Bull was born this year. Willow Creek, North Dakota. Jumping Bull was his father.

continued on next page

1838–1839	Many Mad Coyotes Winter

There were a great many mad coyotes and two Dakota men were bitten by a mad coyote. The men both died very shortly after being bitten.

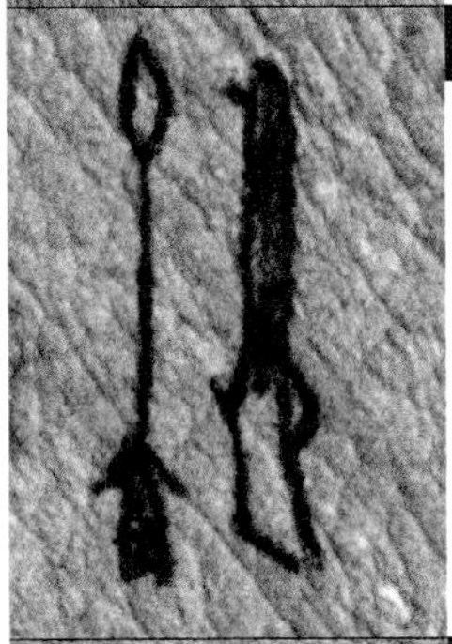

1839–1840	All Dakota Tribes United and Made War on the Pawnees Winter

They killed 100 Pawnees. The arrow and guns show that they used both weapons and forces were united.

1840–1841	Pawnees Killed Five of Little Thunder's Brothers Winter

1841–1842	Bear Hand Brought Striped Blankets to Trade Winter

Bear Hand is the name given to the White man who probably brought the first Mexican blankets to trade to the Dakotas.

1842–1843	Spotted Penis Died Winter

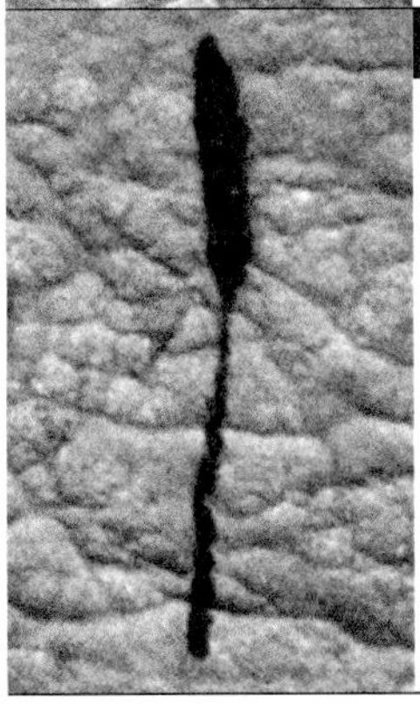

1843–1844	Brought Home the Cheyenne Medicine Arrow Winter

The arrow seemed to have some magic power. It had been stolen from the Cheyennes by the Pawnees, and the Dakotas in turn captured it from them. It was used to make medicine for the three Dakota bands that were together at this time. Mr. Fowke says that the Cheyennes had a bundle of arrows, which they regarded as the Jews did the Ark of the Covenant. In 1890, the writer found this arrow in charge of Chief Little Man of the Cheyenne at Cantonment, Oklahoma. The Cheyenne gave 100 Ponies to the Sioux to redeem the arrows.

A MAN AND
WORLD IN
BETWEEN

continued on next page

1844–1845 Mules Father Died Winter

1845–1846 Smallpox Again Winter

1846–1847 Dakota Woman Killed Winter

This was a married woman who had slept with another man other than her husband. The Dakota punishment for such a deed is death to the woman. She was stripped of all clothing, her hands were tied, and then she was shot with a gun as the drawing indicates.

1847–1848 Paints Himself Yellow Died Winter

This was a good Dakota man, so Single Wood says.

1848–1849 Killed Half Man and Half Woman Winter

This person was a Crow, drawing indicates in woman's dress, who was captured by the Dakotas but as the person proved to be a hermaphrodite, it was killed.

1849–1850 Shoshone Man Killed Winter

The red on his head indicates that his scalp was taken.

continued on next page

1850–1851	Big Smallpox Used Them Up Winter

The large-sized figures of a person and large red spots show that the epidemic was severe and that it killed a great many persons.

1851–1852	First Goods Issued Winter

This is a gray blanket, which is a symbol for many kinds of goods that were issued at this time, such as blankets, calico, guns, powder flour, sugar, tobacco, and everything as Single Wood says. These issues were to continue annually for fifty-five years, during which time the Dakota understood that he would not have to work. The number of issues was possibly changed in the treaty of 1868 and the one of 1877.

1852–1853	Crows Stole Many Dakota Horses Winter

1853–1854	Brave Bear Killed Winter

This Indian was killed by the Blackfeet Indians.

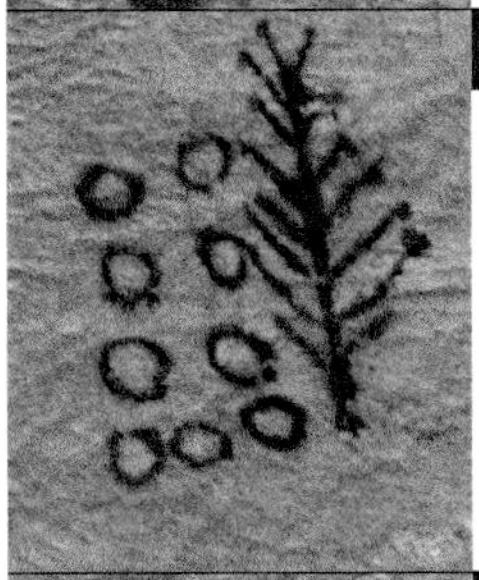

1854–1855	Red Leaf Went to Washington Winter

The red-tipped leaves of the pine tree indicate his name; the nine yellow circles represent the money.

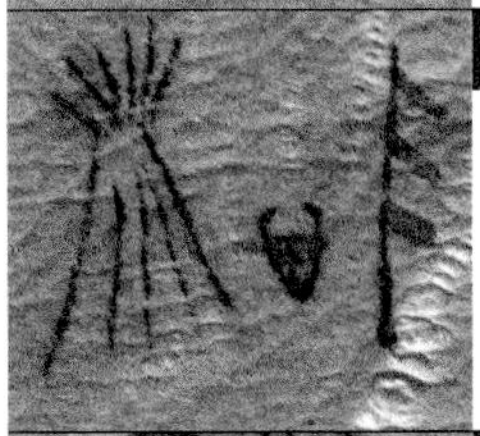

1855–1856	Swift Bear's Father Made Medicine Again Winter

The buffalo head shows that it was buffalo medicine that was made, probably on account of the scarcity of that animal.

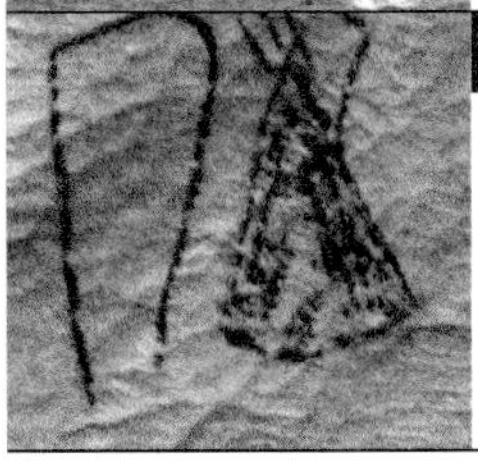

1856–1857	Camp under White Bluff Hunting Buffalo Winter

This was at or near the head of Little White River.

A MAN AND
WORLD IN
BETWEEN

continued on next page **17**

Swift Bear's Winter Count—*continued*

| 1857–1858 | Buffalo Bull Meat Winter |

This shows that the Indians were hard pushed for food, as they never ate buffalo bull meat if other could be had.

| 1858–1859 | Many Ceremonial Flags Winter |

This appears to be a form of worship in which all this people took part. Many flags were put on the hills around the Indian villages.

| 1859–1860 | Big Crow Killed Winter |

A Dakota chief was killed by the Crow Indians. He had received his name from killing a Crow Indian of unusually large size.

| 1860–1861 | Cooking Utensils Died Winter |

This man was a Dakota brave. He was a very large man, especially large around the body, as the drawing indicates. The circle indicates cooking utensils.

| 1861–1862 | Killed Spotted Horse Winter |

Spotted Horse and three other Crows came and stole many horses from the Dakotas, who followed them, killed them, and recovered their horses. The red on his head shows that they were scalped.

| 1862–1863 | Crow Scalped Dakota Boy Winter |

The knife blade above his head shows that he was scalped. The boy had gone just across the river to visit at some other lodges; he did not start home until after dark, and when crossing the river on the ice, some Crows that were in hiding scalped the boy. The next morning the Dakotas, after finding the boy, followed the Crows but on coming up with them decided not to attack as there were many Crows.

| 1863–1864 | Rattlesnake Elk Killed Winter |

This is probably one of the eight Dakotas that other winter counts refer to as being killed on this date. The rattlesnake and the elk horns on its head is the name totem.

continued on next page

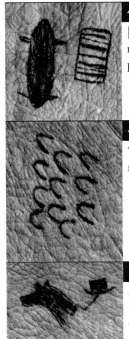

1864–1865 White Man Brought Navajo Blankets Winter

[Single] Wood pronounces the name "Long Dum Husk." The drawing is the medicine sack made from the entire skin of a mink or weasel, as will be seen in a photo of it.

1865–1866 Crows Stole Many Horses Again Winter

This is the time Yellow Robe told me about in February 1899. He was thirty-nine years old when this happened.

1866–1867 Bear Head Killed by Soldiers Winter

Some emigrants passing through left a worn-out cow by the roadside near where the Goose River empties in the Platte River. A Miniconjou (who plants by the water) named Pompadour (his hair stood up) shot the cow with an arrow. Thirty soldiers came for him; he refused to go although his friends tried to persuade him to go. On his refusal an officer came in the tipi, the other Indians in the tipi came out and started to run off when the soldiers opened fire and wounded Red Leaf; then the Indians turned in and killed all the soldiers. The soldiers had two cannons. Search the Enemy Out and Chauncey Yellow Robe were born this year.

1867–1868 Thorney Went to Cree Camp Was Killed Winter

He was a young Dakota warrior and was killed by the Cree with a gun, as blood is shown and no arrow, lance, knife, or tomahawk is shown but only the bullet mark. He went to Cree camp to get something to eat as they had but little meat this winter.

1868–1869 Traded Mules to White Men for Corn Winter

The Dakotas were in a starving condition and traded a mule for only one or two sacks of corn or flour.

1869–1870 Tree Fell on and Killed Woman Who Was Cutting Wood Winter

This drawing is similar to the one in 1808–1809. According to Indian custom, it is the woman's place to get the wood; consequently, it seems strange that Pail (a man) should have been getting wood. This woman is the mother of High Back Bone, who was killed the next year.

continued on next page

A MAN AND
WORLD IN
BETWEEN

Swift Bear's Winter Count—*continued*

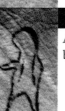

1870–1871 High Back Bone Killed Winter

He was killed by the Shoshone. William Yellow Robe was born this year.

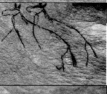

1871–1872 Show Prophesied Many Buffalo Winter

A Dakota whose name is Show is shown pointing to a buffalo head, but the buffalo did not come.

1872–1873 Issue Horses Winter

Horses first issued to Dakotas but only one horse to a family.

1873–1874 Killed Indian Agent's Son Winter

A Dakota named Bear Kicks knocked at the door of the agent's house; as the son opened the door, Bear Kicks shot the boy with a gun, as the drawing indicates. This took place at the Red Cloud Agency. Curtis, a soldier, says it was Appling and not the agent's son who was killed.

1874–1875 Turning Eagle Stole Spotted Mule Winter

Turning Eagle now lives in Lower Cut Meat Camp. The mule was stolen from the Omaha Indians by Four Ways, who now has charge of the Upper Cut Meat Omaha house. Turning Eagle was the chief or was party leader, hence the honor to him, to be chosen to mark a winter.

1875–1876 Spotted Bear or Buffalo Head Killed Winter

This man has two names and will be seen in the drawing. He and two other Dakotas were killed by the Shoshone.

1876–1877 Soldiers Drove Away Dakotas Horses Winter

The tracks of the horses indicate that the horses went to the White man. These horses belonged to Red Cloud's band. There was $200,000 paid in 1891 to the Indians for these horses. I believe $40 a piece for each pony was allowed.

continued on next page

1877–1878 Crazy Horse Killed Winter

Spotted Tail, Red Cloud, and other Indian leaders were taken East, probably concerning the 1877 treaty, and Crazy Horse was wanted to [go] also, he had not promised the soldiers that he would go but came to his Indian friends and asked their advice. They said "don't go" so he decided not to go. Some soldiers were sent for him; they were putting him in the guardhouse at Ft. Robinson when he made a dash to get by the soldiers and out of the open door when a soldier bayoneted him. The instrument by the wound has the appearance of a sword. The horse head with a wavy line from its forehead is the name totem.

The millions of buffalo that supplied the Sioux with good, clothing and shelter, thousands of horses, and hundreds of miles of free range made them, up to the year 1868 (time of first treaty with the Sioux), the richest most prosperous, the proudest, and withal, perhaps, the wildest of all the tribes of the Plains. According to the treaty of 1868 a reservation that includes all the present state of South Dakota west of the Missouri River was set aside for their absolute and undisturbed use and occupation. At one stroke of the pen they were reduced from a free nation to dependent wards of the government. In eight years the buffalo were nearly exterminated by White hunters and then followed the rush of gold hunters to the Black Hills, which was the direct cause of the Indian's Massacre of Custer and his men in 1876.

As the White man wanted the Black Hill country, another treaty of 1877 was made by which the Sioux was shorn of one third of their reservation, the Black Hills County. As Elk Stands Looks Back said last Monday (March 20, 1899) on his return from Deadwood, "That it made me have a very bad heart to see the White man's town, with electric lights, in what was once our home where there were plenty of wood, deer and bear."

The Treaty of 1868 gave each male person over fourteen years of age a suit of good, substantial woolen clothing, consisting of coat, pantaloons, flannel shirt, hat, and a pair of homemade socks. For each female over twelve years of age, a flannel skirt or the goods necessary to make it, a pair of woolen hose, twelve yards of calico and twelve yards of cotton domestics. For boys and girls under the ages named, such flannel and cotton goods as may be needed to make each a suit aforesaid, with a pair of hoses for each. These goods were to be delivered by August 1 each year.

The Treaty of 1877 allowed for each individual 1½ pounds beef or ½ pound bacon, ½ pound of flour, and ½ pound of corn for a day's rations and for every one hundred rations, 4 pounds of coffee, 8 pounds of sugar, and 3 pounds of beans.

1878–1879 Wagons Issued to the Dakotas Winter

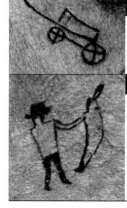

1879–1880 Boys Girls Taken Dakota School Winter

October 1879 Major Pratt took eighty-two Sioux children to school; but one could speak any English and but one wore garments of our civilization. The others wore blankets and wore in their Indian dress. Clarence Three Stars was one of the number.

A MAN AND WORLD IN BETWEEN

continued on next page

1880–1881 White Man's Son Stands on Prairie Killed Winter

This boy was the son of a squaw man who lived a few miles west of Rosebud Agency. The boy was standing near the house when an Indian was passing who was lamenting his sister's death and upon seeing the boy took his bow and an arrow and shot the boy.

1881–1882 Spotted Tail Killed Winter

He was a friendly Dakota to the White[s] and was killed by Crow Dog, a Dakota who was jealous of Spotted Tail. The government built a large two-story house near the agency for Spotted Tail and also gave him a very large flag, all as a reward.

1882–1883 Sitting Bull and Many Dakotas Put in Steamboat and Taken to Yankton Agency Winter

The smokestack with smoke issuing from it is the most nearly like a steamboat and, in fact, the only part of the boat that is recognizable.

1883–1884 Iron Horse Made Medicine Winter

He made medicine about three miles up Cut Meat from the schoolhouse.

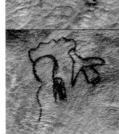

1884–1885 White Cloud Killed Winter

He lived four miles below the schoolhouse and was killed by Lightning Hawk. Notice the hawk with a crooked line running from its mouth: lightning. Lightning Hawk had threatened to steal White Cloud's wife, which kept up a quarrel. Finally the Indians called a council in which the peace pipe played its part. The Indians gave many ponies to the injured parties and got their promise to have no more trouble but finally Lightning Hawk did steal White Cloud's wife and later killed White Cloud.

1885–1886 Ten Crows Come to Dance Winter

The Crows cut their hair off across the forehead while the other hair hangs down and is kept smooth and streaked with horizontal bars of white earth, as shown in the picture. The dance was held on Scabby Creek, eight miles northwest of the agency.

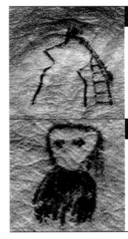

1886–1887 Six More Crows Come to Dance Winter

His drawing does not look like that of the year before.

continued on next page

Swift Bear's Winter Count—*continued*

1887–1888   Dakota Visit Crows Winter

Sitting Bear, Fast Dog, and Turning Eagle, with others from Rosebud and Pine Ridge, went to visit the Crows to learn about the Indian Messiah but were turned back by the Crow police on Agent Wright's orders.

1888–1889   Children Had Measles Winter

1889–1890   Issue Horses Again Winter

1890–1891   Spotted Female Elk Killed Winter

The crooked line from the mouth indicates that this is the name. This war leader is known to the White people as "Big Foot," who together with his band or most of his band were killed by the soldiers during the Ghost Dance craze, which ended in the Wounded Knee fight at Pine Ridge. The cost to the government for breaking faith with the Indians was about $1.2 million and forty-nine Whites and others, one church, two schoolhouses, and one bridge, while the Indians' loss was about 300 or more. There was much suffering from hunger and cold and fifty-three Indian dwellings burned.

At the Wounded Knee engagement, three officers and twenty-eight privates were mortally wounded and four officers and thirty-eight privates were less severely wounded, several of these dying later. The Indian loss, according to the best estimates, was at least 250 Indians killed and died from exposure. The writer has the deer antler saddle that Big Foot used during this campaign. It bears bullet marks.

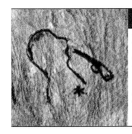

1891–1892   Rolls Off Shoots Himself Winter

He was one of Chief Yellow Robe's sons, who was a policeman in Lower Cut Meat camp. Cause of his rash act is not known, but supposes the drinking of two Indians, Raymond Steward and Pulls the Arrow Out, who was arrested by this policeman, taken to the Agency and the[n] sent to the U.S. Court at Deadwood, where they were punished had something to do with this.

A MAN AND
WORLD IN
BETWEEN

continued on next page

1892–1893 | Issue Cows Winter

1893–1894 | Dakota Policeman Killed Winter

This occurred at the issue house near the Lower Cut Meat Creek School.

1894–1895 | Lightning Hawk Killed a Woman Winter

This woman lived in Big Turkey's camp, which is Southwest of Rosebud Agency. Lightning Hawk caught the woman out and, after sleeping with her, killed her. This is the same man who killed White Cloud 1884–1885. The Indians say that he was hung but for what is not known.

1895–1896 | Blue Lightning Froze to Death Winter

The Dakota believe that the thunder and lightning are the cry and look of a large bird; which they call thunder bird, hence the thunder bird with a blue line from his mouth is the name totem.

1896–1897 | Indian Collect Much Money Winter

The red disk above the Indian's head indicates collecting money. They had meetings in every camp just before annuity payment and took pledges for money and in this way a great deal of money was raised to use in celebrating the Fourth of July, at which time the agent allowed the Indians to indulge in old Indian ceremonies and dance some of which they were told that they would never be allowed to practice again. Indians from several reservations were visitors during the first week of July. The Indians followed the old custom of arranging their tipis in a circular fashion, making a circle nearly three miles across. It was a sight worth beholding.

1897–1898 | Bear Looking Died Winter

1898–1899 | One Ear Horse Died Winter

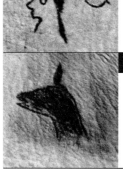

Jesse H. Bratley's role as an educator first defined his time in Indian country. It was his job to help enact the annihilation of Indian cultures ordered by the US government—or, from another viewpoint, to ensure that Native peoples were brought into the twentieth century as dutiful citizens and moral Christians. This he would do. Bratley taught his students English, arithmetic, and history. He showed them how to farm and garden. He cut their hair. He dressed them in neat clothes and crisp uniforms. He lined them up like soldiers. Bratley was little different from the thousands of other Indian schoolteachers and government agents of his era.[10]

Yet unlike many of his colleagues, Bratley was curious enough to attend ceremonies and enjoy local foods. He learned some Chinook and took notes on the Hopi language. He journeyed to sacred places. He amassed hundreds of objects. He took hundreds of photographs of the people he lived among. Looking back across the distance of time, Bratley does not always seem to be a perfectly devout disciple of the assimilationist creed he pledged to uphold.

Neither was Bratley an advocate for Native peoples. There is no documentary evidence that he fought for Native American rights or even acknowledged the validity of their traditional ways of life. Nor was Bratley a full student of Indian culture; he was not an avocationalist who managed to segue the unplanned opportunity to be among Indians into a reputation as a respectable near-anthropologist, like John G. Bourke, a US Army captain who published academic volumes and came to sit on the board of the Washington Anthropological Society.[11] In some ways, Bratley was just a more earnest apprentice of the flowering market in Indian crafts at the end of the twentieth century—a man consumed by the so-called Indian craze.[12]

Bratley did aspire to be associated with the burgeoning field of anthropology. He corresponded with the Bureau of American Ethnology—the government agency, which was then among the premier institutes for anthropological research—at times seeming eager to understand the people he now found himself among. He offered his objects for display at international expositions. He lectured on his experiences and clearly cherished his time—so unexpected, given his humble family origins—living among tribal people. Bratley perhaps saw his photographs as a method of anthropological inquiry, which the "father" of American anthropology, Franz Boas, and other scholars of this age had begun to deploy for research, publications, and the field's popularization.[13] One reading of Bratley's efforts is that he was sincerely curious about Native Americans and held a genuine appreciation for their history and arts—a paradoxical esteem for the very traditions his work required him to eradicate.

Another view would be that his vocation and collection were not a contradiction at all. Perhaps he collected objects and took photographs precisely because the things and images were evidence—positive evidence, in Bratley's mind—of a Native America fast fading. Most of Bratley's images do not present a romantic vision but instead an everyday reality, one that does not glimpse backward but rather gazes into the future. The images do not say *this is what was* so much as *this is how it will be*. As we will discuss, the world's fairs, which were hugely transformative for turn-of-the-century America, are one way to understand what might otherwise appear to be paradoxical about Bratley: a fascination with Native Americans as caught between the old and the new, traditional and modern, "savage" and "civilized."

The juxtaposed exhibits at the world's fairs—as well as the reenacted battles in Wild West shows—provided a public stage on which Native people could act out a myth of their gradual disappearance.[14] In one area of the fairs, Native Americans wore traditional clothing and performed demonstrations of traditional arts and crafts; in the next area were Native American school students newly steeped in Euro-American clothing, behavior, language, and learning. In the same way the world's fairs paired tradition and education side by side to illustrate both Native America's past and its future, perhaps Bratley—who visited the famous 1893 Chicago World's Fair and other expositions—hoped to embody this vision of Native Americans before and after the arrival of "civilization."

Perhaps Bratley's entire collection can be understood as an echo of George Catlin's famous 1837–1839 painting *Wi-jn-jon, Pigeon's Egg Head (the Light) Going to and Returning from Washington*, a kind of split-screen image of the Assiniboine leader before and after his 1832 journey to the nation's capital—in traditional dress on one side of the canvas and in fancy Euro-American duds on the other.[15] A photographic version of this genre was used to great effect by those seeking to promote the Carlisle Indian School, the first major boarding school, depicting a student's evolution from savagery to civilization.[16] Bratley took several photographs that imitated this tableau. In one photo, a man decked out in tribal attire is standing beside another man dressed in a police uniform (figure 1.5). Another Bratley photo featured a Carlisle graduate dressed in a three-piece suit standing beside his "traditionalist" father (figure 1.6).

Bratley's ultimate aims as a photographer are just as elusive. He was generally like most of his generation even as he was precisely like none of them. Historian William E. Farr has described five categories of photographers that bridged the end of the 1800s and the start of the 1900s.[17] First, there were the romantics, men like Walter McClintock and Edward Curtis who purposefully mourned the swiftly vanishing Indian (figure 1.7). Second, there were businessmen like N. F. Forsyth, J. H. Sherburne, and Thomas B. Magee who tried to make a living selling "Indian views"—images of the exotic, barbaric Indians. Third were the transformers: government officials, missionaries, and teachers trying to prove that Indians were progressing into a brighter future. Fourth were the snap shooters, Whites living near reservations and tourists who thought they were experiencing the authentic frontier and wanted to preserve the moment (figure 1.8). (This was possible because in the late 1800s, Kodak produced cheap, easy-to-use cameras. The rise of commercial photography equipment companies converged with mass tourism and the final colonization of Native Americans.)[18] Fifth are the self-portraits, which Indians wanted to have for themselves (figure 1.9).[19] While some of these photographers embraced multiple aims—Curtis was

FIGURE 1.5 (left). Bratley
took this photo of two
young Lakota Sioux
men—one a policeman,
the other dressed in
traditional courting blanket and headdress. The
contrast between "civi-
lized" and "savage" was
likely intended to draw
the viewer into questions
about Native America's
past and future. (DMNS
BR61-292)

FIGURE 1.6 (right).
Chauncey Yellow Robe,
dressed in Euro-American-
style clothing, poses next
to his father, Chief Yellow
Robe, who is wearing a
mix of clothing styles.
Chauncey Yellow Robe
was among the first
children taken to Carlisle
Indian School in Pennsyl-
vania. After graduating
from Carlisle in 1895,
Chauncey held various
positions in the Indian
School Service. Rosebud
Reservation, 1895–1899.
(DMNS BR61-325)

both a romantic and (albeit struggling) a businessman—for the most part these stances were fairly delineated.[20]

For Bratley, all of these motivations propelled his work, but he never fully subscribed to one of them (figure 1.10). Some Bratley images do present a kind of wistful nostalgia, an effort at aesthetically capturing the cultural precipice on which Native Americans then stood. He also invested in expensive equipment to sell images, including to Indians themselves (combining Farr's types two and five). Dozens of photographs of school-children lined up military style, classroom scenes, and images of agricultural and out-door labor also point to his role as a government official. Still other shots are clearly snapshots—opportune images little different from those of other travelers, such as the Hopi Snake Dance ceremony, which tourists attended and photographed in the early 1900s (figure 1.11).[21]

Many of Bratley's images help show why he escapes easy categorization. Like a select few of his generation, the photographs in Bratley's oeuvre "chart a continuum of encounters."[22] Consider Bratley's image of Sam Powiky, a Hopi who delivered mail on the Star Route, walking 35 miles each day (figure 1.12). Which of Farr's types would have taken this image? Surely not the romantic Edward Curtis—the image is not one that *simulates* Indianness.[23] This would not be a bestselling "Indian view." A government bureaucrat would take this image to show the progress of civilization, but the delivery of mail on foot—of a man sporting a traditional Hopi haircut and with tracks of a wagon visible

FIGURE 1.7. Bratley likely posed Goes-to-War for this portrait in his ceremonial clothing and feather headdress. This image plays on the romantic image of the proud Plains warrior and fits neatly within the nostalgic genre of photography, which both professional and amateur photographers often used during this period. Rosebud Reservation, 1895–1899. (DMNS BR61-272)

behind Powiky—would hardly be suitable proof of modernity's advent. Neither would Powiky be a good shot for tourists and an unlikely one anyway, since the tourist would have to happen upon Powiky during his long walks. And there's no evidence that Bratley sold the image to Powiky or any other Hopis while in Arizona.

In short, the image of Powiky—everyday, impromptu, and unlike his contemporaries who constructed images of the barbarous Indian, noble Indian, or spiritual Indian—epitomizes many of Bratley's photographs.[24] They are thus special because they touch on all of the categories we have come to understand of Bratley's generation, and yet they cross all boundaries and frequently escape them.

This is in part the power of Bratley's photos, as much as the act of photographing is an act of power. "To photograph people is to violate them," the essayist Susan Sontag famously and astutely wrote, "by seeing them as they never see themselves, by having knowledge of them they can never have; it turns people into objects that can be symbolically possessed."[25] The art historian John Tagg similarly noted: "Like the state, the camera

FIGURE 1.8 (above). A group of mounted onlookers watch as a Lakota Sioux man rides a bucking bronco. Throughout Bratley's photographic career, he snapped many pictures of Native people's everyday life. Rosebud Reservation, 1895–1899. (DMNS BR61-263)

FIGURE 1.9 (left). Bratley took this portrait of Chief Mud Hole attired in traditional dress. He is wearing a beaded bandolier bag over one shoulder and holds a cane quirt. Similar to his picture of Goes-to-War (DMNS BR61-272), this image is representative of the posed style of portraiture Bratley and his contemporaries commonly deployed. Rosebud Reservation, 1895–1899. (DMNS BR61-175)

FIGURE 1.10 (left). This photograph captures the way Bratley's images moved between photographic genres. The Western hat in the background of the image as well as the man's clothing suggest that the image was posed, with Bratley providing the Indian artifacts for the subject to wear and hold—a supposition further supported by the pipe bag, which appears in other Bratley images. Yet this image defies easy classification. It seems to show that Native people were increasingly taking on the Western style of dress while also referencing the romantic image of the proud Plains warrior. Rosebud Reservation, 1895–1899. (DMNS BR61-312)

FIGURE 1.11 (right). According to Bratley, Shuplo—pictured here—was the oldest living snake chief at Hopi, and his wife, Sololk, was the only woman who knew how to make the medicine to cure snakebites. Hopi Reservation, 1902. (DMNS BR61-149)

is never neutral. The representations it produces are highly coded, and the power it wields is never its own."[26] Bratley and his collection take on this power by epitomizing the churning uncertainty and the convergences of multiple interests—governmental, political, social, economic, scientific, voyeuristic—on Native America at the turn of the last century.

Bratley also matters because the historical moment he found himself in—namely, 1893 to 1903—was utterly pivotal for Native Americans and even the United States as a whole. Would the continent's first peoples wither and evaporate like a dying spring? Or would they persist and survive? And even if they survived, would it be in any recognizable form as Indians—or would they fully meld into Anglo-American society?

Just as Bratley himself was a man in between worlds, so, too, were Native Americans, ensnared between their traditional loyalties and the prospects of a terrifying modernity. More than a century later we know that those who were to vanish did not: instead, they endured. However, the US government's cruel mathematics of cultural subtraction and the equation of Native people's survival must be remembered. For in this story are planted the seeds of understanding why one group of people seeks to extinguish another and how those victims may oppose and outlast the forces of their destruction.

In the end, we suggest that the collection Bratley made consists of "objects of survivance." Survivance is an inelegant word that elegantly unpacks the complexities of the colonial moment. Coined by Anishinaabe scholar Gerald Vizenor, he uses the term *survivance* to recast Native history so that it does not merely dwell on loss and surrender but rather on survival and resistance. Survivance, Vizenor writes, "is more than survival, more than endurance or mere response . . . survivance is an active repudiation of dominance, tragedy, and [victimhood]."[27] Vizenor acknowledges the power of colonialism to reshape lives and

entire nations. But he is saying that the subjects of colonialism have a power of their own. In survivance stories, Native actors become the protagonists who refuse to see their condition as tragic and refuse to be the victim. In this way, "Survivance emphasizes creative responses to difficult times, or agentive actions through struggle."[28]

The photographs and things in the Bratley collection can be interpreted as objects of survivance—objects made in the crucible of colonialism but with the full agency of Native Americans. These objects thus not only reflect decision points of adaptation and accommodation, survival and resistance, but also continue on today as material memories that can help Native peoples overcome, persevere, inspire, change, persist. Seeing these objects as embodied memories that connect the past to the present helps us reframe the collection, turning it away from a story of preserving the dying Indian. In many ways, the tribal members we worked with reconnected to these objects and images, embracing them as part of their past and reclaiming them as part of their contemporary identities.

The goal of disappearing Indian peoples was not at all haphazard. It was a fundamental and purposeful part of American colonialism. But today, these acts of cultural genocide have too often been rendered invisible.[29] Few outside Native communities grasp how much they have borne. Bratley's legacy—his captured images and collected objects—force us to visibly and tangibly confront America's attempted annihilation of its first inhabitants and its aftermath for the survivors.

FIGURE 1.12. A Hopi mail carrier named Sam Powiky delivered mail on the Star Route from Keams Canyon to Oraibi, stopping at Toreva on Second Mesa and Polacca at First Mesa. The mail carrier would typically travel the 35-mile route into the canyon in one day and back the next. Hopi Reservation, 1902. (DMNS BR61-135)

A MAN AND
WORLD IN
BETWEEN

▼ ▽ ▼

FIGURE 1.13. Lindsay
M. Montgomery shares
images of the Bratley
collection with Hopi elder
Elidia S. Chapella and
her family in 2016. (Chip
Colwell)

The story of the convergence of American Indian education, collecting, and the life of
Jesse H. Bratley is based on the 500 photographs and nearly 1,000 objects currently held
at the Denver Museum of Nature & Science. We also depended on an unpublished autobiography that Bratley wrote sometime after his retirement in 1932. Although never formally published, several excerpts from Bratley's autobiography were publicly circulated by
Forrest after Jesse's death in 1948.[30] Further, we draw on several archival sources, most notably records held by the Denver Museum, National Archives, National Anthropological
Archives, and National Cowboy & Western Heritage Museum. In addition, the children
of Dr. Forrest G. Bratley have served as an excellent steward of Jesse's legacy; they have
protected a substantial collection as well as a number of documentary sources, and they
generously allowed us access to their holdings. Finally, we reached out to representatives
of the five tribes Bratley worked with and invited their participation in the project. Four
of the tribes—we were unable to connect with the Havasupai—generously agreed to col-
laborate with us; their assistance and interpretations have been irreplaceable (figure 1.13).

This book aspires to be a kind of biography of Bratley and a history of Native American
survivance between 1893 and 1903 on five reservations. However, we do not want this
work to be five ethnographies of five Native communities or an all-encompassing history of Indian education in the United States; there are enough of both and of far greater

quality and depth than we could provide here. What we hope to add to this rich field of study is a new way of looking at this dynamic period in Native North American history. Through the collection—the visual and the material—we cannot just conceptually contemplate this moment, but we can also picture it in concrete terms. A photograph of children lined up like soldiers, a metal Western-style fork with a beaded handle, a ceremonial drum made when traditional religion was outlawed, and more all give a kind of testimony that otherwise may be abstract or found only in words on a page (figure 1.14). Written for a broad readership while grounded in academic research, this book explores what evidence the Bratley collection gives to scholarship that has revealed the US government's attempt to "civilize" Native Americans and, in turn, Native Americans' struggle to persist. The book is a case study that examines how these concepts are proven through the past's material remnants.

From the collection, we have picked a series of objects and images that help us consider three key themes—civilizing, resistance, persistence—for the five tribes Bratley worked among during this period. This is an expansive history we seek to tell through the

FIGURE 1.14. Bratley collected this decorated rawhide drum, suggesting one means by which Lakota Sioux culture continued in the face of cultural extermination. Rosebud Reservation, 1895–1899. (DMNS AC.5727)

narrow lens of Bratley and his collection—a biography of "intimate colonialism"—to give us focus on the immediate and everyday means by which Indians withstood this colonial moment.[31] For objects, inspired by an object-based learning approach, we undertake a close "reading" of them, focusing on their form, function, sensory qualities, aesthetics, significance (symbolic and otherwise), provenience (original context), provenance (history of collection), and our reaction in a reflexive mode.[32] We aim to consider how these objects are not passive products but how "individuals seek to influence others through the production of material objects," how "objects are imbued with the intentions and agency of their originators."[33] Rather than passive objects, we see each item in Bratley's collection as holding stories and having readable meanings.

For Bratley's photographs, we similarly sought to "read" them, considering the subjects' poses, clothing, context, and gaze. Like other photographs of this period, Bratley's images can be seen as a "manifestation of an oppressive colonial process," but also the people in the photographs can exude "defiance, pride, and nonconformity with US norms at a time when it was extremely difficult and unpopular to be Indian."[34] Where the subject can be linked to documentary evidence, we particularly pause to make these connections. In addition, we depended on an analytical framework that approaches images not as perfectly "true" representations but as crafted ones that reveal as much about the photographer and us the viewer as about the subject captured in time. The book is thus also a kind of museum catalogue—necessarily selective and personal, as much a springboard for future research as a statement of its own.

Throughout the book, we include the voices of living Native Americans. This was deeply important to the project because it links the past to the present, allowing an interpretation of the past grounded in the experiences of the generations that followed in the path of those Bratley taught, photographed, and collected from. We traveled to four of the reservations where Bratley worked, and our tribal colleagues showed us where Bratley lived and photographed so we could have a firsthand understanding of how these places are part of a living cultural landscape rather than places frozen in the past.

For our Native colleagues, as in other photo-based projects, the images allowed them to learn about their past and look for clues about what has been gained and lost, to see how images shape the contours of what it means to be an American Indian.[35] But more, historical images, as William Farr learned with the Blackfeet, do not so much as "explain the past" to community members as allow them to literally "picture it."[36] In turn, it is Native community members who can help interpret the images for outsiders less familiar with the people, places, and events crystallized on glass plates.[37] The qualitative, open-ended interviews we conducted with thirty-six people from four tribes provided added layers of meaning to the objects and the places and people ensnared in Bratley's images.

The interviews also allow us to further reflect on the possible need to seek reconciliation and forms of restorative justice for those who were harmed through the US government's policies. In Canada, a Truth and Reconciliation Commission on the Indian residential school system has allowed for a public airing of history and the opportunity, however imperfect, for healing.[38] In the United States, considering such an approach should begin with the victims and their descendants. Most basically, by consulting directly with contemporary tribes, we have worked toward a collaborative methodology to ensure that Native American voices and their values and viewpoints are not drowned but are saved from the wreckage of the American Indian school experience at the turn of the last century.

Notes

1. Hoxie 1984.
2. Adams 1997; Lomawaima 2006; Miller 1996; Reyhner and Eder 2004; Szasz 2007.
3. Bratley 1961:2.
4. Herold 1999:259.
5. Herold 1999:285.
6. Colwell-Chanthaphonh et al. 2013.
7. Dolan 1977.
8. Bratley 1992.
9. We have aimed to use the tribal names related to us by tribal officials; however, we retain the tribal names given when used in a quote.
10. Cahill 2011; Collins 2004; Duncan 1990; Riney 1999:167–192.
11. Turcheneske 1979.
12. Hutchinson 2009.
13. Edwards 2001; Gmelch 2008:7; Jacknis 1984.
14. Gram 2016:255.
15. Eisler 2013:106.
16. Bernadin et al. 2003:8.
17. Farr 1984:188–193.
18. Hoelscher 2008:9; Southwell and Lovett 2010:10; West 2000:24.
19. Jones et al. 2011; Strathman 2002.
20. Egan 2012.
21. Shannon 2015:104.
22. Bernadin et al. 2003:2.
23. Vizenor 1998:11.
24. Blackhawk 2004:29.
25. Sontag 1977:14.
26. Tagg 1993:63.
27. Vizenor 1998:15.
28. Silliman 2014:59.
29. Grinde 2004.
30. Reutter and Reutter 1962.
31. Cahill 2011:98.
32. https://www.peabody.harvard.edu/sites/default/files/Guide%20to%20Looking-2017.pdf, accessed July 14, 2017.
33. Jordan 2012:20.
34. Riding In 2004:52.
35. Katakis 1998; Lippard 1992.
36. Farr 1984:xi.
37. Farr 1984:xv.
38. http://www.trc.ca/websites/trcinstitution/File/2015/Findings/Exec_Summary_2015_05_31_web_0.pdf, accessed July 4, 2017.

2

BRATLEY'S COLLECTION IN CONTEXT

It is time to embalm that odious expression "The only good Indian is a dead one," and substitute "The only good Indian is the educated one."

—A visitor at the 1898 Great American Exposition[1]

In the early fall of 1893, only two days after beginning his career as a teacher at the Port Gamble Day School on Puget Sound, Jesse H. Bratley was ready to quit. Each morning Bratley faced a mostly empty classroom: the S'Klallam children refused to attend classes. In any case, Bratley could not converse with the few kids he managed to wrangle. He spoke neither S'Klallam nor the simplified local Chinook Jargon; they, in turn, refused to speak English. In light of the S'Klallam community's long history of contact with Euro-Americans, the children's choice to not speak English to Bratley strongly suggests that this was a deliberate act of refusal rather than simply a lack of understanding. Bratley, the farmer and failed student turned teacher, was totally unprepared for the job he had just started.

Bratley's doggedness in adapting to the challenges of living and teaching in a community in which he was an outsider was inspired by his fiscal straits. He would later conclude that "this is one time that not having money was a blessing" because it forced him to persevere.[2] Eventually, he devised a way to communicate and compel attendance. Bratley grew to embrace his charge; he proved to be an inventive, hardworking, and dedicated instructor. Over the next decade, he worked his way up the administrative ladder and across the country, moving on to four other schools among the Lakota Sioux, Cheyenne and Arapaho, Havasupai, and Hopi.

Bratley's adventure had nearly ended before it began. But his obstinacy gave Bratley the chance to explore new worlds and to play a part in the transition of American Indian communities in the wake of decades of violent confrontation and colonial negotiations.

Although Bratley was seemingly unaware, his response to the Native communities he worked in was part of and a reflection of much broader systems, institutions, and social trends. Bratley's story weaves together multiple threads: the US government's intense focus on using schools to forcibly transform Native Americans, the emergence of anthropology as a discipline (which itself was tied to artifact collecting), documentary photography, and the wild popularity of world's fairs, which were venues to showcase both anthropology and Indian education and to feed the public's fascination with Native Americans, now that they were conquered and on their way to joining the privileged ranks of the "civilized."

Indian Schools

Bratley embraced the federal government's vision of assimilating the Indian. As a small boy growing up in Kansas, Bratley came into contact with Indians through his occasional visits to the Greiffenstein's Trading Post and through newspaper articles detailing the violence of the Indian Wars. Reflecting on these childhood encounters, Bratley later stated that he "thought them [Indians] too dirty to be people. In fact I despised them."[3]

This negative opinion was firmly rooted in the widespread prejudices of White settler society during the nineteenth and twentieth centuries. As impediments to American settlement and progress, the growing number of Euro-Americans colonizing the West detested and distrusted Indians. Underlying the enmity toward Native people was a perception of Indians as inherently savage—a debased condition that entitled civilized Americans to take their land and resources. The disregard, at least, was largely mutual. At most of the schools Bratley taught at, parents refused to send their children. Among the Lakota Sioux he was attacked. Among the Cheyenne and Arapaho he was pushed down a flight of stairs and knifed by a student's grandmother.

Such animosity and antagonism only emboldened nineteenth-century government administrators to accelerate efforts to assimilate Native Americans.[4] Although Indian education did not become an official component of federal policy to control them until the 1870s, throughout the colonial period independent citizens as well as colleges attempted to educate individual Indian youth.[5] In 1775, the Continental Congress expanded these pedagogic enterprises when it passed a bill appropriating $500 for the education of Native adolescents at Dartmouth College in New Hampshire.[6] Amid the turmoil of the Revolutionary War, the government's support of Indian education was temporarily suspended, but it resumed in 1794 with added vigor. The eighteenth century's closing years were defined by a series of treaties with the Oneida, Tuscarora, Stockbridge, and Kaskaskia Nations, which included promises to support the education and employment of those Native Americans "who had faithfully adhered to the United States and assisted them with warriors during the Revolution."[7]

A congressional bill passed in 1819 helped fulfill the promise of education for loyal tribes by appropriating $10,000 and authorizing the president to employ teachers to instruct Native people.[8] Labeled the "Civilization of Indians," this law marked the first time the US government viewed education as a means of mitigating Indian defiance toward colonialism on its Western frontier. Following the bill's passage, the United States entered into a long line of treaties with Native nations, which often allocated government funding for the creation and maintenance of Indian schools.[9]

Over the decades, education increasingly became a cornerstone in America's interior affairs. Even amid the endless wars with tribes, education helped shift the national policy from an overt military program to one with loftier purposes. In 1824, the Bureau of Indian Affairs (BIA) was opened, and within years the US government was spending thousands of dollars annually on Indian education, distributed among forty schools controlled by Christian missionaries who taught nearly 1,200 Indian pupils, primarily from the northern and southeastern United States.[10] In the 1840s, the government formed the Civilization Division to promote the moral, intellectual, and social improvement of Native Americans—and then the BIA was transferred from the Department of War to the Department of the Interior.[11] These bureaucratic changes foreshadowed the federal government's shifting approach to Native Americans—a movement away from brute force and toward cultural assimilation.[12]

In 1870, the US Congress authorized an annual appropriation of $100,000 for schooling Indians, a sum that increased steadily during the 1880s and 1890s.[13] The federal government's increasing investment in education was informed by a broader shift in America's approach toward Native people following the Civil War. Under President Ulysses S. Grant, Christian reformers were increasingly given influence over the structure and vision of federal Indian policy. Recognizing the failures of previous, more violent policies, the explicit aim of what became known as Grant's peace policy was to encourage Native Americans to appreciate the benefits of Christian civilization and willingly take up the duties of citizenship.

This goal was to be accomplished with the guidance of Christian organizations and the federal government.[14] A central feature of the president's 1873 policy was the creation of schools staffed by church-appointed agents to teach. Although the practice of church-nominated teachers was on the decline by the late 1870s, the peace policy's emphasis on the importance of both Christian and civic education became an ingrained feature of federal Indian policy for the next fifty years. Importantly, Grant's initiative was intimately informed by a particularly American version of Protestantism, which emerged over the course of the 1850s and emphasized lay leadership, interdenominational cooperation, and the importance of moral behavior.[15]

To manage the growing education enterprise, the BIA created the position of superintendent of Indian schools in 1882.[16] Reporting directly to the commissioner of Indian affairs, the superintendent of Indians schools conducted school visits, appointed teachers, directed policy, and allocated resources. The superintendent was assisted by six field superintendents who visited and inspected schools.[17] (To further confuse matters, many schools had a position titled superintendent, which was a kind of school principal who oversaw the staff and programs.) By 1890, the superintendent of Indian schools had codified a set of standardized rules guiding the curriculum and structure of Indian education. This curriculum's ultimate goal was to incorporate Native people into mainstream American society so that the federal government would no longer be responsible for their financial care. The 1885 annual report of the superintendent of Indian schools nakedly stated the role of education in achieving this purpose: "It is an understood fact that in making large appropriations for Indian school purposes, the aim of the Government is the ultimate complete civilization of the Indian. When this shall have been accomplished the Indian will have ceased to be a beneficiary of the Government, and will have attained the ability to take care of himself. Hence national selfishness, as well as a broad philanthropy calls for the earliest possible achievement of the end in view."[18]

In 1889, Commissioner of Indian Affairs Thomas J. Morgan established that Indian schools' primary purpose was to change the Indian character. "The fear of God and respect for the rights of others; love of truth and fidelity to duty; personal purity, philanthropy, and patriotism," Morgan wrote, were to be achieved by clothing children in Western clothes and forcing them to speak English.[19] The central problem, though, was the Indians' perceived aversion to work. Morgan ordered that schools were to turn Indians away from "indolence and indifference" and in their place inculcate "habits of industry and love of learning."[20] In accordance with America's new approach to colonization, the BIA intensified its efforts to educate Indian children, generating an extensive network of federally supported schools.

After 1884, the Civilization Division was renamed the Education Division.[21] An expansion in the types of schools the government supported accompanied this administrative transition. In addition to reservation day schools, government funds were used to finance on- and off-reservation boarding schools and industrial schools. These schools were in session ten months of the year—including a five-day Christmas vacation—with the standard school day running from 9:00 a.m. to 4:00 p.m.[22] Schools provided support for many of the students' needs, including meals (figure 2.1). Conditions at the schools, however, were often abysmal. Outbreaks of disease were common; in Virginia, during the Hampton Institute's first decade, one of every eleven students died.[23]

Up until 1897, the network of federally operated schools was supplemented by a contract program, which provided government funds to Indian schools that various Christian denominations operated.[24] Within this swelling organization of schools, administrators increasingly viewed education as broadly empowering the Indian pupil for life. As Estelle Reel, the superintendent of Indian schools, wrote in 1901: "The value of education must be measured by its contribution to life interests . . . It is the privilege of the elementary school to awaken the child's capacities and quicken his interest, giving him an appreciation of his own power, awakening his interest in and appreciation of things about him, cultivating a desire to cooperate with his fellow-men in the pursuit of knowledge and its achievement."[25]

The totalizing mission of the Indian education system was deemed so valuable that annual government spending on Indian education had increased from less than $10,000 at its start to more than $2 million by the close of the century.[26] By 1900, this funding supported the daily operation of 307 schools educating over 26,000 Indian pupils across the United States.[27]

▼ ▽ ▼

FIGURE 2.1. The dining room of the Cantonment Boarding School was necessary to support children away from their families and served as an integral part of the school system's civilizing mission. Cheyenne and Arapaho Reservation, 1899–1900. (DMNS BR61-374)

By the second half of the 1800s, as the United States became increasingly urban and ethnically diverse, school administrators wanted to provide "all children of whatever origin a basic education to form them into good Americans, which meant civically engaged, patriotic, English-speaking Protestants."[28] Government officials worried about what would happen to Indians when they were finally free from tribal authority but also about what would happen to the rush of new immigrants from southern and eastern Europe and East Asia.

To ease these fears, educational policy became sharply focused on training new citizens. In this mode, US citizenship was understood as absorption for *all* groups—one that "demanded total adaptation to a homogenous national culture."[29] In many ways, the treatment of Native Americans at Carlisle and other boarding schools was little different from that of African American students at the Tuskegee Institute.[30] It is thus unsurprising that a school such as the Hampton Institute would educate American Indian and African American youth together.[31] In fact, the education of non-White children—from curricula to corporeal punishment—during this period was not entirely dissimilar from that in schools provided for White children.[32]

This is not to say that all children were treated equally—or that the outcomes of education were expected to be equal.[33] In the late nineteenth century, American policymakers were committed to assimilation but battled between theories of universalism and social Darwinism. They argued, Do all people have equal potential, or are some races destined to inferiority or superiority? Some educators like Carlisle's Richard Pratt contended that Indians *could* be made equal to Whites. Others claimed that White children would necessarily stay atop humanity's evolutionary chain. American Indians could hope to evolve out of barbarism but would never be the equal of Whites; meanwhile, African Americans would always dwell in an unbridgeable social and intellectual chasm.[34] Such views prompted, for example, California in 1924 to pass a law "to establish separate schools for Indian children, and for children of Chinese, Japanese, or Mongolian parentage."[35] In short, for those students who were not Anglo-American, this strain of evolutionary thinking helped "solidify their positioning on the bottom rungs of a hierarchical class structure once they entered mainstream US life."[36]

In many ways, the government achieved its aims for Indian students. In 1898, an official survey was conducted to evaluate the Indian school curriculum. Indian school agents canvassed returned pupils living on reservations and assessed "their efficiency as men and women in the ordinary relations of everyday life."[37] Returned students were placed on a scale ranging from good to bad, with "good" denoting individuals who were "capable of dealing with the ordinary problems of life and taking their places in the great body politic of our country."[38] Although fundamentally racist and highly subjective, the survey classified 73 percent of pupils who attended any type of Indian school as "good," while only 24 percent were considered bad or "worthless."

In 1903, Superintendent Reel remarked on the continued progress of the Indian education system, stating that 25 percent more Indians were self-supporting compared to the previous ten years, twice as many spoke English, and comparatively few received rations from the federal government.[39] Indian savagery was conceptualized as a disease that could spread from one generation to the next; Anglo-American civilization was viewed as the cure.

Fears over Indian pupils relapsing into savagery pervaded the reports of Indian schoolteachers and administrators. Reel articulated this concern in her 1898 report, stating that government officials must keep the Indian "above and free from the debasing influences of the camp by keeping him away from it. There is no other way. Send someone else as a missionary to the tribe to elevate the old. The schoolboy or girl cannot do it. The down pull of the tribe is greater vastly than the uplift of a few unassisted boys and girls."[40]

Although some students did ultimately return to their traditional practices, these anxieties were tragically unfounded. By 1903, when Bratley and his wife left the Indian Service, the US government had successfully stripped untold thousands of Native students of their Indigenous language and culture.

Collecting Cultures

Bratley's interest in collecting Native American objects was sparked as a young boy in Kansas. During the spring planting season, the family's plow would turn up arrowheads and stone axes that young Bratley would pick up and collect. Fascinated by the beautiful

symmetry of these flint points, Bratley collected them and daydreamed about how long ago the arrow was shot and if it had killed an antelope, a buffalo, or an Indian enemy. Although it is uncertain if any of these early relics survived into Bratley's later collection, the annual harvesting of artifacts marked the beginning of a lifelong fascination with the material culture of Native people (figure 2.2).

It was during Bratley's first year among the S'Klallam Indians of Puget Sound that he began collecting the Native objects that comprise the Denver Museum's current Bratley collection. Shortly after he arrived in Washington, a missionary who was developing a collection of Indian curios came to visit the Port Gamble Day School; he asked Bratley to buy him an Indian hammer that he would pick up when he returned in two weeks. Bratley agreed. He bought the missionary a granite hammer for fifty cents, also acquiring one for himself (figure 2.3).[41] Years later, when writing his autobiography, Bratley offered a precise account of how the hammer was made, its use, and its physical characteristics. This descriptive language suggests Bratley's aspirations for his collection to be seen in anthropological terms:

The hammer was made out of granite, pecked and chipped out with granite and flint rocks. It took an Indian two months to chip out one hammer and polish it as smooth as glass. In the long ago, the hammer would buy or pay for two slaves. The Siwash used these hammers to make canoes by burning the side of a log and pounding the charcoal out.[42] The hammer is somewhat in the shape of an hourglass, six to seven inches tall, two and one half inches in diameter across the top end and one inch wider at the bottom end. It weighs three and one half pounds.[43]

FIGURE 2.3. A large S'Klallam granite grinding tool was all it took to spark Bratley's interest in collecting Native American tools, artifacts, arts, and crafts. (Children of Dr. Forest G. Bratley)

Enthused by his first collecting experience, Bratley became an avid collector. By the time his family moved to Miami in 1910, Bratley had acquired 1,800 pounds of Indian curios.[44]

Bratley's first teaching assignment in Washington coincided with the formation of anthropology as a formal scholarly discipline. In the previous decades, anthropological museums and collections were slowly gaining momentum: the Smithsonian Institution was founded in 1846, the Harvard Peabody Museum in 1856, and the American Museum of Natural History in 1869.[45] Among the most important anthropological institutions to emerge at this time was the Bureau of Ethnology (later renamed the BAE: the Bureau of American Ethnology), established in 1879. The US federal government operated and funded the BAE in an effort to support the scientific research of humanity.

Under the direction of a one-armed former Civil War hero and adventurer, John Wesley Powell, the BAE was primarily concerned with collecting Native American objects to devise "a practical classification of the Indian tribes."[46] The perceived degradation and contamination of Native societies by Western civilization in the late 1800s further underpinned the emerging science of anthropology. Anthropologists and museum collectors flocked to remote reservations, hoping to preserve what remained of traditional cultures—those "authentic," essential aspects of social life that were considered "uncontaminated" by modernizing forces such as education.[47]

As a result, a "salvage paradigm" informed much of early anthropology, which in part sought out Indian-made things and swept them away to museums in distant cities where they could be preserved as "specimens."[48] Bratley's own pursuit of an Indian collection fell right in the middle of the great age of anthropological collecting, which lasted from 1860 to 1930.[49]

The emergence of anthropology as a professional discipline coincided with the closing of the Indian War period and the introduction of an assimilationist agenda among federal administrators. In March 1879, the Smithsonian Institution formally created the Bureau of

Ethnology, marking the formalization of anthropology as a professional discipline. Native people quickly became the primary subjects of the bureau's inquiry, for several reasons.

On the one hand, following their military defeat, Native people offered the perfect balance between diversity—various different cultures were represented across the continent—and exoticism, and they were geographically close. On the other hand, by government standards, Native Americans were considered a comparatively benign subject of inquiry. In contrast to other non-White populations, such as African or Asian Americans, scientific investigations of Native people were unlikely to upset any key political constituencies.[50]

By the early 1900s, American anthropology's interest in studying and theorizing about Native Americans united four previously distinct fields: linguistics, archaeology, ethnology, and physical anthropology.[51] As a unified discipline, anthropology was characterized by a basic set of attributes: fieldwork and language competence, scientific training, astute powers of observation, focus on particular societal elements (such as kinship, religion, subsistence), and a theoretical framework with which to synthesize observations that would lead to publications.[52] While scholars within this newly emerging profession came from many different backgrounds, they all embraced social evolution as the best framework for understanding human development and explaining variance across racial and ethnic groups.

Led by the work of Lewis Henry Morgan among the Haudenosaunee and Anishnaabe, American ethnologists sought to categorize human societies into one of three stages—savagery, barbarism, and civilization.[53] Significantly, for Indian policymakers, Morgan believed that change was part of a universal process of evolution and that the principal means of achieving advancement was through the private ownership of property.[54] Although some groups advanced more quickly than others, advancement was inevitable. Morgan's perspective came to define anthropological thought for a century and directly informed the assimilationist agenda of the federal government. For many administrators, there was a clear link among allotment, which would introduce private property to tribal nations, education in the arts of civilization, and social advancement.

Although Bratley was not an anthropologist, in some measure he would seek to mimic this emerging discipline. But as an outsider with no training, institutional support, focused study, or published work, there was little chance for him to be accepted within the ranks of the new field. Still, as an Indian schoolteacher for a decade, Bratley had access to a diverse array of Native American objects and practices. Bratley often referenced his credentials as a firsthand observer of Native culture when lecturing about or displaying his collection of curios (figure 2.4). In 1902, Bratley requested a short endorsement from the superintendent of Indian schools to be used in an advertisement poster for his lecture titled "J. H. Bratley's Indian and Western Scenes."[55]

The "salvage paradigm" of the discipline influenced Bratley's collecting practices as an amateur anthropologist. As Bratley once commented in a journal entry, "Civilization, edu-

FIGURE 2.4. During an educational slide show presentation, Bratley provided the following information on Hopi corn-grinding practices to accompany this image: "In every Moqui [Hopi] home there is a set of at least three grinding stones and sometimes more, enclosed in small pens or boxes made of stone slabs. The large stones are set in the pens at angles of about 45 degrees. The rub stones have very much the appearance of a baker's loaf of rye bread. The operator seated on her knees behind one of the boxes or pens begin[s] to rub the smaller stones over the larger one with about the same movement a woman would make in using a washboard. On the first stone the corn is simply crushed: It is then swept together by the aid of this stub broom and placed on the next stone which is of finer grit in the adjoining pen and upon this the crushed corn is ground much finer and so on until it is passed over the last stone. After that it is nearly as fine as our flour." Hopi Reservation, 1902. (DMNS BR61-240)

cation, and 'fire water' are fast eradicating the individuality of these savages."⁵⁶ Such statements indicate that Bratley was aware he was documenting Native American culture as it was waning—that he likely believed he was preserving Native America's past by collecting the things discarded in the wake of an assimilated future (figure 2.5). If so, Bratley never seems to have come to terms with a central paradox of his life: given his job as civilizer and educator, Bratley was salvaging aspects of the very cultures he was helping to dismantle.

Along with collecting objects, Bratley was a dedicated photographer. He took hundreds of pictures, documenting his life among the Indians. Bratley's lifelong passion for photography began during his tenure on the Rosebud Reservation. In part inspired by his desire

FIGURE 2.5. Bratley collected these shaped eagle feathers on the Cheyenne and Arapaho Reservation. He documented how the feathers were given as war honors and how each type of notch signified different accomplishments in battle. Yet, as the Indian Wars had ended, these honors would no longer be awarded; they would no longer have the same significance. (DMNS AC.5719A-H)

to send photographs to his family in Kansas of his unique experiences, a love of photography was hard labor.[57] "No one will ever know the hardships and hours Mrs. Bratley and I spent making our pictures," Jesse once said, "when we had no dark rooms and had to carry water into the house in washtubs and then out again after washing our negatives and prints, etc., at night time."[58]

In addition to spending eighty-two dollars—more than the cost of several months of groceries—on a 5 × 7 stereoscopic camera sent from New York, Bratley's account books document that, for example, in just one month he spent an additional fifty-seven dollars setting up his photo studio by buying a tripod, printing and developing trays, brushes, dry plates, and printing paper.[59] Bratley would come to photograph not just his own life but all aspects of life on the reservations he lived on, taking portraits and landscapes and documenting a wide range of intimate, religious, and everyday scenes (figure 2.6).

Over the course of his four years on the Rosebud Reservation, Bratley established a lively business as the community photographer, selling photos to tribal members and neighboring teachers as well as trading his images for curios.[60] (The idea that some tribal members loved photographs of themselves and their families should not be surprising but is evidenced by how Native photographers emerged by the mid-twentieth century.)[61] Between March 20, 1897—when he bought his first camera—and June 6, 1900, Bratley earned $208 while paying out $200 in supplies and remuneration, leaving a net gain of $8.[62]

As not only a collector but also an observer of Indian life who flirted with anthropological pretense, Bratley supplemented his photographs and curios with detailed (though unsystematic) notes on various traditional cultural practices. For example, in one personal journal entry, Bratley documented a S'Klallam oral history, which contends that "at

first snow among the Clallam's their tradition say [*sic*] they emptied their baskets of dried salmon out with the waste and filled them with snow which was set overhead in their communal houses, but to their sorrow soon melted away."[63] In the same journal, Bratley claimed to know a commonly held cultural practice among the Hopi, stating that "Hopis do not kill one of a pair of twins as the other twin would die—Hopi believe that twins die on same day" (figure 2.7).[64] Adopting the comparative and classificatory approach of early ethnographers, Bratley drew comparisons

across the diverse area of cultures he observed, as seen in a journal entry in which Bratley notes that "Clallam fish and clamed, Sioux beef fed, Hopi and Havasupai corn fed Indians" (figure 2.8).[65] In addition to taking notes on cultural practices, Bratley actively recorded traditional terminology—particularly among the Hopi—listing the Native words for foods and cultural objects (figures 2.9 and 2.10).

Although Bratley readily accepted his work of assimilating Native peoples and the overarching assumption of Native savagery, at a few points we see a complex layering of alternate attitudes.[66] After his time in the Indian Service, Bratley clearly felt compelled to share his experiences, at least in part to inspire a sense of admiration for Native peoples. A *Miami Herald* article recounting Bratley's time as an Indian schoolteacher articulates this sentiment, stating that Bratley has an "eradicable esteem for the red man. He rates him high as a human being."[67]

FIGURE 2.8. In this photograph, a group of forty-five Hopi men (not all seen here) work together to plant corn. Bratley wrote that each man used a stick to create a hole approximately 16 inches deep in which he dropped a handful of corn. Holes were spaced about 9 feet apart, and each hole produced as many as thirty-seven ears of corn. Hopi Reservation, 1902. (DMNS BR61-198)

FIGURE 2.9. This entry in Bratley's personal journal documents the names of Hopi katsina and basketry. (DMNS Archives)

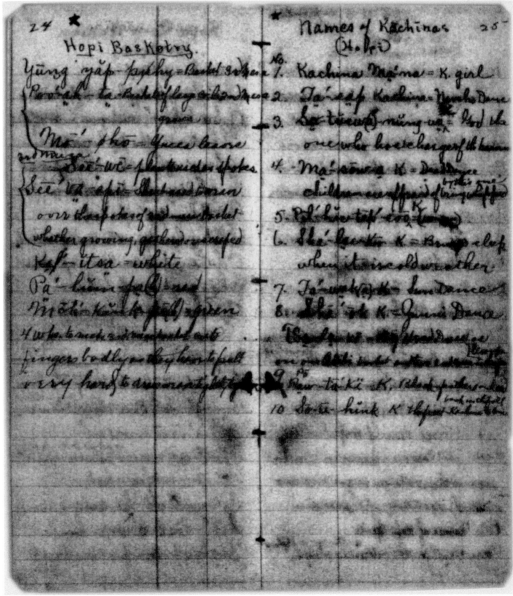

Bratley also seemed motivated by the opportunity to share—and sell—pieces from his collection. After retiring from the BIA and returning to Wichita, Bratley often exhibited his collection on Douglas Avenue and sold many of his artifacts as a special attraction at the annual Kansas State Fair.[68] Bratley pivoted from his personal experience to claim a kind of quasi-expertise. He frequently gave lectures to school and church groups on Native American culture, dressing up in war bonnet, leather coat, leggings, and moccasins.[69] Wearing the outfit drew from a long tradition of Anglo-Americans "playing Indian," which would have allowed Bratley to claim a kind of authenticity and insider knowledge (figure 2.11).

It seems that the community relished these lectures, as indicated by the accolades Pastor J. L. Hoyt heaped on Bratley in 1902: "Mr. J. H. Bratley who lectured by the aid of a first-class stereocopticales at our Open House last night on Indian and Western scenes, exceeded all other lecturers who have come to us in Educational value. His nine years' experience as an educator of the Indians in various parts of the West has equipped him

FIGURE 2.10. Katsina—which Bratley listed in a journal entry—are the ancestral spirits of the Hopi and are honored through their depiction in multiple media, even subtly woven into basketry designs. (DMNS AC.5656)

as few others to give reliable information on the dying race, and the territories still inhabited. I therefore heartily recommend him to all desiring all educational and high[ly] interesting entertainment."[70]

In addition to these demonstrations and lectures, Bratley occasionally wrote articles sharing his experiences with and knowledge of Native Americans. For example, in 1938, Bratley wrote a letter to the editor of the *Herald* titled "Indian's Belief." In the article, Bratley discusses the concept of the "happy hunting grounds" in response to an article from *Bulletin 30* of the Bureau of American Ethnology. In the *Herald* article, Bratley draws on his experiences among the Havasupai to discuss Native American spirituality and death taboos, concluding: "We may doubt that the red man's horse, dog, bow and arrow accompanied him to the 'happy hunting ground,' but this concept of a future life in the Indian's mind was strongly rooted. We love the old happy hunting ground fable, even though we know it is not true."[71]

Bratley supplemented the knowledge of Native culture he gained as a firsthand observer with insights from professional anthropologists and published ethnological research (figure 2.12). Between 1898 and 1906, Bratley regularly corresponded with the Bureau of American Ethnology regarding his artifact collection. During this time Bratley sought to display his collection through various avenues, such as contributing photographs to the bureau's annual report and displaying his growing collection in the BAE's Indian exhibit at the 1898 Trans-Mississippi and International Exposition in Omaha, Nebraska (figure 2.13).[72]

The exhibit presented over 545 Indian delegates, many of whom were photographed, which might have been a further source of inspiration for Bratley's own work.[73] In addition to sharing his knowledge and collections with this academic institution, Bratley also relied on professional anthropologists to enhance his own understanding of Native culture more generally. An avid reader, Bratley consumed a variety of anthropological texts published by the BAE during this time on reservations, such as Victor Mindeleff's "Pueblo Architecture," Stephen Riggs and John Wesley Powell's *Contributions to North American Ethnology*, and Thomas Donaldson's "Moqui Pueblo Indians of Arizona and Pueblo Indians of New Mexico."[74]

In addition to archaeological and anthropological texts, Bratley was interested in the larger historical context of North America, diligently recording details of Spanish colonization from J. H. Beadle's *Five Years in the Territories* as well as the following notes on Euro-American colonization as outlined in the *18th Annual Report of the Bureau of Ethnology*: "The sovereigns of the Old world therefore found no difficulty in convincing themselves that they made ample compensation to the nations by bestowing on them the benefit of civilization and Christianity in exchange for control over them and their country."[75] The

FIGURE 2.11. Bratley dressed in this headdress, breastplate, and beadwork he had acquired while on the Rosebud Reservation. Florida, date unknown. (Children of Dr. Forrest G. Bratley)

methods, descriptions, and interpretations offered in these publications inevitably influenced Bratley's perceptions of Native people as well as informing what objects he collected and photographs he took.

Bratley's quest for a better understanding of North American history and its inhabitants is exemplified in a letter he wrote to the BAE in which he asks the following questions:

1. Of what linguistic are the Pueblo Indians of Arizona and New Mexico?
2. Are albinos known among any other Indians than the Pueblos, if so what tribes?
3. a. Is it a fact that the Zunis have "Winter Counts"? b. Do any other tribes make Winter Counts besides the Sioux and Kiowas? c. Which is considered to be the most complete?
4. Is anything known about the tumuli of cool cinders and fragment pottery scattered along the sides of the mesas in Hopi land?[76]

Bratley asks a similar set of questions regarding the Havasupai in a letter to the secretary of the Smithsonian Institution, in which he requests information regarding their family "stock" (meaning their racial lineage), language, and migration patterns.[77] These correspondences reveal Bratley's thirst for at least some anthropological knowledge to better understand the Native people among whom he had by then labored for nine years.

In addition to studying Native cultures, Bratley was fascinated with the North American landscape. This passion is reflected in the plethora of books Bratley read on American

FIGURE 2.12. Bratley observed many Native ceremonies and rituals, such as this Cheyenne dance ring in Watonga. Oklahoma, 1899–1900. (DMNS BR61-365)

geography and landmarks, including David M. Warren and W. H. Brewer's *New Physical Geography*, Francois E. Matthes's *New Survey of the Grand Canyon*, and John Wesley Powell's *Geological Survey Report for 1880–1881*.[78] In a personal journal entry, Bratley meditates on the splendor and mystery of the American landscape:

> When I attempt to philosophize or geologize on mountain scenery, or speculate on the age of such peaks or canyons, or the cause that brought them about, I soon drift out of science and into mystical imaginings. Such scenery will never let me philosophize; it will have me muse. We may go back, back, from one geologic age to another; from cosmic process to cosmic process, from the warming period to the glacial period, and thence to the cooling period, and the gaseous period, and come at last to a mighty void, which the mind can only reach out to "In the beginning, God..."[79]

These comments are a striking contrast to Bratley's anthropological queries. While he states that studying the environment, geology, and cosmic evolution is beyond his comprehension, his approach to Native cultures had the pretense of being more scientific, documenting linguistic and social taxonomies and searching for rational explanations for Indigenous origins and behaviors. Despite these differences in Bratley's approach to the study of the environment and to humans, it is clear that his scholarly readings directly influenced his documentary practices, as seen in his sketch drawings of the Grand Canyon and in his many landscape photographs (figure 2.14).

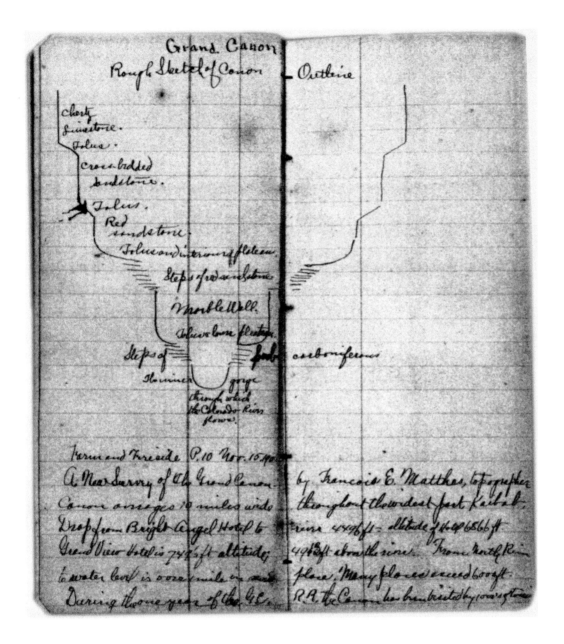

FIGURE 2.14. During his visit to the Grand Canyon, Bratley drew this geological sketch. Arizona, 1900–1901. (Children of Dr. Forrest G. Bratley)

Bratley left unremarked the interconnection among land, culture, and representation. And yet, through geology and cartography, ethnography and history, art and photography, the American West was colonized and conquered. Bratley's images of place and people were thus deeply intertwined—they all helped advance control and dominance over America's Western frontier, a "free land" of which the Indian was a natural part.[80]

Corners and Fairs

The large collection of Native American objects Bratley amassed during the late nineteenth and early twentieth centuries was situated within the context of anthropology's disciplinary formation and the growth of museums as well as a larger history of the public's curiosity about the Indian's past, present, and future. The image of pre-contact Native Americans that early twentieth-century ethnographers presented to the public was inspired in part by wistfulness for the pure and noble savage.

This penchant for what can be called imperialist nostalgia—a longing by colonizers for that which they destroyed—was heightened by emerging anxieties over urban industrial capitalism, which was radically altering American society.[81] The increasing labor demands for building standardized railroads and sustaining industrial factories were supplied by an influx of ethnically diverse immigrants who needed to be incorporated into American society. These new social realities generated a profound cultural shift that "encouraged the objectification of products and people alike."[82] The alienating effects of modernization and immigration left many Americans feeling unhinged and in search of authenticity. Many Americans found this authenticity in the perceived simplicity and natural purity that Native cultures represented.

Bratley was clearly caught up in what the art historian Elizabeth Hutchinson has called the "Indian craze," which lasted from 1890 to 1915.[83] Hutchinson describes this period as one of deep fascination with Indian arts, spurred on by Anglo-American artists, critics, collectors, and businesses seeking to profit from selling Indian crafts. In 1901, Indian education converged with this fad when Estelle Reel—a powerful administrator who dramatically shaped Indian policy in her role of superintendent of Indian schools between 1898 and 1910—introduced a program for students to make traditional handicrafts as part of the Indian school curricula.[84]

Although it might seem contradictory for Indian schools at this time to encourage traditional practices, the program fundamentally aspired to assimilationist goals.[85] The incorporation of Native practices into the education system removed their original meaning and replaced it with a new commercial one. In a similar vein, many Indian schools incorporated traditional dances into performances of plays about Hiawatha and Pocahontas. Produced for public consumption, both plays and craft objects were presented as "authentic" while being completely divorced from "traditional" beliefs and practices.[86]

These practices were in part intended to remind citizens of all the hard work federal schools were doing on behalf of the larger American society.[87] In addition to their use as positive propaganda for the Indian school system, the crafts Native children produced were sold to department stores, which were tapping into the burgeoning Indian craze. Thus, training students to produce saleable crafts would encourage Indians to develop a work ethic and provide a means of self-support.[88]

Such a work program, officials hoped, responded to what Commissioner of Indian Affairs Thomas J. Morgan had once identified as a central task of the government: to turn Indians away from "indolence and indifference" and in its place inculcate "habits of industry and love of learning."[89] But whether the program was successful or not—it formally ended in 1910 when Reel retired, though many schools continued to encourage Native crafts as a step toward wage labor—a clear practical effect of these efforts was an entirely new commodity for wide public consumption: Indian arts and crafts.[90]

FIGURE 2.15. Photographed by Bratley, Gold's Curiosity Shop on the plaza in Santa Fe was one of numerous shops in the American Southwest that sold Native American artifacts and crafts to tourists at the turn of the twentieth century. New Mexico, 1901–1902. (DMNS BR 61-140)

The desire to access an authentic past represented by Native people not only pushed consumers to department stores in urban centers but also fueled ethnographic tourism and curio collecting, particularly along the Northwest Coast and in the American Southwest (figures 2.15 and 2.16). Collectors arose from diverse backgrounds, including middle-class missionaries, merchants, and Indian schoolteachers, as well as wealthy urbanites, hoping for a glimpse of "real" Native people. Between 1880 and 1930, amateur collecting skyrocketed. Individuals acquired vast quantities of Native American art and artifacts. The line between scholarly and amateur collecting was often blurry, with both anthropologists and amateur collectors striving to systematically document and categorize Native material culture and associated practices.[91] Bratley fell somewhere within this gray zone.

During this period, an array of Native American traditional art forms were featured in public lectures, exhibits, books, and hundreds of popular magazine articles. This movement came most intimately to its followers' homes in the form of "Indian corners," which were "dense, dazzling domestic displays" of Indian objects.[92] Hutchinson describes these corners as constructed by rich and poor alike, some of large collections and some small but all placed in an organized jumble and set against simple furnishings.[93] The Indian corner was an iteration of the Victorian domestic space known as a "cozy corner" and followed on the heels of the Japanese craze, which started in the 1870s.[94] Inspired by the sympathetic writings of Helen Hunt Jackson, who advocated for the fair treatment of Native

Americans, and the adventures of the first ethnographer Frank H. Cushing, during the 1890s the exoticism of Indian cultures increasingly attracted many American urbanites.[95] The widespread consumption of Indian artifacts was encouraged by a new class of savvy collectors and dealers, such as Joseph "Udo" Keppler.[96]

A self-portrait of Bratley and his young family on the Rosebud Reservation captures perfectly the prototypical Indian corner (figure 2.17). Although constructed on a modest scale—no doubt reflecting Bratley's modest means at the time—his corner neatly parallels that of the Chicago industrialist Edward Everett Burbank, as depicted in a painted portrait from 1897 by his uncle, Elbridge Ayer Burbank.[97] In both scenes, a rocking chair is framed by a bookshelf, which is surrounded by Indian artifacts carefully placed to seem casual. Like Udo Keppler's own home, captured in a 1903 magazine article, Bratley's corner features a few animal trophies—a deer head and a fur on the floor.[98] Like both Burbank and Keppler—and most Indian corners—Bratley's corner includes several images of Indians. Hutchinson notes that these images were included to create a "simulated presence" of the maker of the things displayed.[99]

Bratley's contemporaries in Indian country—such as Charles Hume and his amateur photographer wife, Annette Ross Hume, who lived in Oklahoma among the Kiowa, Comanche, and Wichita—also kept a version of the Indian corner, although scholars have not always identified it as such.[100] Like the Humes, the Bratleys' corner includes a portrait of a US president, a visual nod to the government's role in overseeing Indian culture. Later, once the Bratleys had retired from their work among Native Americans, their home display grew even more elaborate (figure 2.18).

FIGURE 2.16. Bratley captured this scene of tourists at Hopi roaming around, with Hopis perched along the pueblo walls watching the scene below. (DMNS BR61-128)

FIGURE 2.17. Jesse, Della, and Homer Bratley pose in their home's "Indian corner" while living at Lower Cut Meat Creek Day School. Rosebud Reservation, 1895–1899. (DMNS BR61-346)

For many, the Indian craze was fed by anti-modernist sentiments and a cultural retreat from the "overcivilized urban industrial American and a turn to ostensibly preindustrial cultures perceived as more physical, authentic, and direct."[101] But this description seems a poor fit for the Bratley family. They were not removed from pre-industrial cultures but embedded among them. And given their employment, they welcomed the coming modern age.

It seems more likely that the Bratleys embraced the Indian craze because they could embody it so fully. They had a kind of access to the authentic artifacts that urbanites could only dream of. In a peculiar way, at a far remove in their rural home, the Bratleys could be

seriously urbane and chic—the search for authenticity found nowhere closer than the heart of Indian country. In addition, it is noteworthy that the Indian corner juxtaposed the uncultivated Indian with the orderly Victorian home, the "wild forest and the comfortable study."[102]

Perhaps the Bratleys created their corner as a place where they could organize, control, and make sense of these two spheres—the savage and the civilized—which the Bratleys knew not in an abstract way like most urban Americans but intimately every time they walked out their front door.

▼ ▽ ▼

BRATLEY'S COLLECTION IN CONTEXT

In response to non-Indians' insatiable appetite for the exotic and the authentic, Native people and objects were transported from the walls of the museum onto the grand stage provided by Wild West shows, international fairs, and trade expos.[103] As part of this emerging genre of entertainment, fairs offered a stage on which the "drama of civilization" could be performed.[104]

Starting in 1851, when the first world's fair was held in London to display the "Works of Industry of All Nations," governments and local boosters held a plethora of fairs to celebrate Western industrialism and imperialism.[105] Trumpeting the successes of European and American civilization over the primitive, these celebrations of progress came to the United States in 1876 with the Centennial International Exhibition held in Philadelphia.[106] Held in honor of the nation's centennial, the Philadelphia exposition marked "a century of progress" and focused primarily on the display of Indian life, including descriptions of missionary work and educational efforts among Indigenous people, as well as displaying "traditional" cultural objects.[107]

As exotic "Others" and the focus of America's civilizing project, Native people remained central figures in the fairs held across the United States at the end of the 1800s.[108] Resembling in many ways the exhibition halls of America's growing number of natural history museums, fair exhibits were intended to distinguish the "civilized" visitor from the "uncivilized" objects and performers on display.

Working closely with federal administrators, professional anthropologists played an important role in organizing fair exhibitions. Exhibitions throughout the nineteenth and early twentieth centuries referenced a core set of beliefs about Native Americans, including the notion that Indians were fundamentally different from Whites and that assimilation into the dominant Euro-American society was inevitable. Furthermore, both anthropologists and visitors to these fairs shared a persistent ambivalence toward Indigenous people: a paradoxical mix of contempt and admiration that fueled scientific endeavors and popular interest in natural history museums, fairs, and Wild West shows.[109]

Within the fair's context, anthropology's position as a "scientific" discipline conveyed elite ideas regarding race and social progress to a broader audience.[110] Unlike Wild West shows, which glorified the Indian Wars through elaborate battle reenactments, anthropological exhibitions presented Native people as subjects of study rather than as entertainers. Drawing on evolutionary theory and the comparative method, anthropology exhibits at world's fairs sought to make Native people knowable to the public.[111] The public platform afforded to anthropology by fair expositions supported American expansionism and superiority while strengthening the legitimacy of anthropological methods and interpretations.

In 1893, Bratley and his siblings attended one of the largest displays of Native American culture of this period, held at the Chicago World's Columbian Exposition, which marked the 400th anniversary of Christopher Columbus's passage to North America. Although many exotic cultures were represented at the Chicago fair, American Indian life was displayed in dozens of locations, including an American Indian Village and a simulated cliff dwelling to display Pueblo architecture from the Southwest.[112] Thousands of artifacts were presented in densely packed display cases along with descriptive labels, murals, and small-scale models.[113] These exhibits might have inspired Bratley; in 1904, he sent a letter to the BAE offering to sell sixty-five objects to the institution for display at the St. Louis Exposition that summer.[114] Picture cards and photography books of Native Americans

FIGURE 2.19. Bratley, along with three siblings, attended the World's Columbian Exposition in Chicago in the summer of 1893. The fact that Bratley kept this token from the exposition suggests the significance of the event to him. (Children of Dr. Forest G. Bratley)

were also widely circulated in Chicago, which might have been another source of inspiration for Bratley's pursuits.[115] Bratley kept a token from the event with his collection that is still held by his descendants today—an indication of the fair's importance to Bratley (figure 2.19).

The federal government sponsored two exhibitions on Native life at the Chicago fair, one of which was organized by the Harvard Peabody Museum and closely followed the evolutionary approach that dominated anthropological thinking of the age. The Peabody's exhibition focused on the chronological development of Native people and demonstrated daily life prior to Columbus's arrival. Thomas J. Morgan, the commissioner of Indian affairs between 1889 and 1893, who sought to demonstrate the potential of the government's assimilation program, organized the other exhibition. The creation of two unique displays, one emphasizing the exotic and the other fixated on progress, marked an important change from previous fair exhibitions in which the BIA and the Smithsonian worked closely together to create a single exhibition.[116]

The BIA's contribution to the Chicago fair included a full-scale replica of a government boarding school for Indian children. The school's dormitories, workshops, and classrooms were inhabited by Native boys and girls who had been nominated by their teachers and selected from government and religious schools across the country (figure 2.20).[117] While on display, Native pupils and White teachers conducted their daily routine, including exercises in grammar, math, rhetoric, history, penmanship, and civics (figure 2.21). More dynamic displays of vocational training in domestic arts—such as cooking and housekeeping, along with technical demonstrations of farming and carpentry—supplemented these programs.[118]

The classroom exhibits were juxtaposed with displays of traditional Native craftsmanship in the American Indian Village, which surrounded the school. Strategically placed displays of adult Natives producing traditional crafts were meant to contrast the "old" and the "new" Indian—the savage and the civilized. Within the anthropology building, architectural models, photographs, and artifacts were displayed alongside living Native people hired to work as guides in the model villages and to demonstrate traditional crafts.[119] In attempting to educate the public on Native culture, these exhibits depicted living peoples as static relics—a depiction that did not accurately reflect their contemporary struggles or practices.[120] Although cloaked in scientific taxonomies and evolutionary theory, anthropology exhibitions—just like Wild West shows—were in many ways pure fantasy, presenting a romanticized image of Native people. Yet these displays glorified traditional culture and afforded Native people an opportunity to practice in public the very customs the Indian School system sought to erase (figure 2.22).

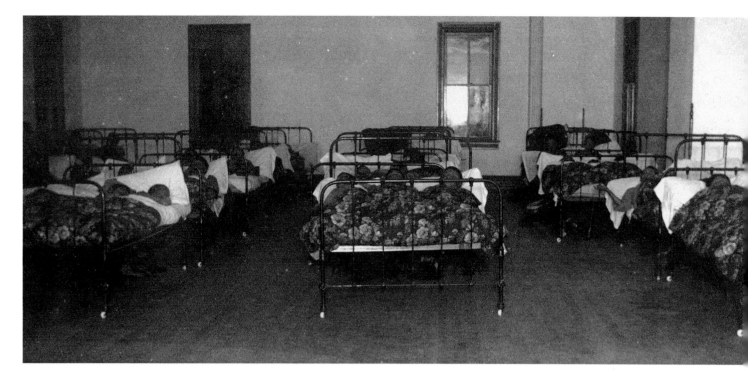

Attending the 1893 fair just before his first Indian school teaching assignment thus likely planted a seed of fascination that would flower over the course of Bratley's life. The week-long excursion to Chicago would have afforded Bratley a glimpse inside the exotic difference of Native American cultures as well as the government's work to eradicate these very differences. Accompanied to the Columbian Exposition by his siblings, Bratley recalled in his later years that this "was all new to us, but it was worthwhile to see the people from all countries in their peculiar costumes, together with their exhibits."[121] Bratley's comment reflects his early interest in Native culture and hints that his experiences at the 1893 fair likely shaped his approach to Indian education and collecting.

The comparative framework the BIA employed at the world's fair resembles the curriculum used in the Indian schools, which Bratley would have taught. For example, teachers structured history lessons around contrasting contemporary practices with the arts, industries, and stories of the ancestral Native groups among whom the school was situated. Superintendent Estelle Reel clearly outlined this course of study and its goal in 1901: "Examine their methods of agriculture, and compare them with those of today, showing them how many more advantages they will have than their ancestors . . . distinguish between those arts of the old Indians that are useful and those that are not and encourage them to preserve and carry on the latter."[122] Both history lessons in the school and the BIA fair displays compared Native lifeways to denigrate the past and embrace the future.

Morgan clearly articulated this tactic's intended effect. While planning the BIA's Indian school exhibit, he accurately predicted: "though the old may attract popular attention by its picturesqueness, the new will impress the thoughtful with the hopefulness of the outlook and the wisdom, as well as fairness, of extending to the weaker the helpful hand of

FIGURE 2.20. Children, three to a bed in neat rows in a sterile, spotless room, at the Cantonment Boarding School was the kind of image BIA authorities sought to highlight at world's fairs and expositions. Cheyenne and Arapaho Reservation, 1899–1900. (DMNS BR61-373)

Primer.   May 22, '99.

a nut   a fan

a pail   a cup

a top   a cat

Hattie With Horns,
Age 8.   Sioux.
In school 4 years.

FIGURE 2.21. Hattie with Horns's primer work provides another example of the curricula Bratley taught—in this case combining art and English vocabulary. Cheyenne and Arapaho Reservation, 1899. (DMNS Archives)

the stronger race."[123] Morgan's predecessor, Daniel M. Browning, echoed this expectation, proclaiming that the BIA's 1893 exhibit concretely showed the Indian's "readiness and ability for the new conditions of civilized life and American citizenship upon which he is entering."[124] In his photographs, Bratley consistently captured this contrast of traditions receding and modernity arriving.

These perspectives also reveal the paternalistic chauvinism underlying BIA programs, which Bratley himself seems to have accepted during his time as an Indian schoolteacher. Federal administrators believed that the superiority of American civilization made the success of the Indian education system inevitable. Officials viewed the comparative approach

employed by the BIA at the Chicago World's Fair as such a success that it became the backbone of the bureau's exhibition strategy at subsequent expositions.

The BIA's exhibition at the St. Louis World's Fair in 1904 embodied the importance of the comparative approach officials used to promote the Indian education system. Similar to the Chicago exhibition, administrators erected a full-scale model of a government Indian school on the St. Louis fairgrounds and populated it with Indian pupils as well as "old" Indians. Bratley himself often took images that captured multiple generations, commenting on the changes they represented. As he wrote on the back of one photo: "I am sending this so you may see that the squaw's style of headdress has changed to the present day big visor like across [the] front of [the] head.[125] In 1911, they wore it in a high knot on the top of the head and trimmed bangs similar to the way they wore it sixty years ago—see fifth Annual Report of the Bureau of Ethnology, page 485" (figure 2.22).

Unlike previous exhibitions, however, traditional Native craftsman were not confined to the Indian villages that surrounded the school.[126] Instead, Native artisans dressed in traditional costume occupied booths *within* the school building itself (figure 2.23). This new layout allowed viewers to directly compare savagery and civilization, thereby highlighting the transformational effects of Indian education. The displays' designers' intended uplifting message seems to have been largely accepted by the crowds of people who flocked to

FIGURE 2.22. Bratley printed this image—a group of Seminole men and women on Miami River—and wrote on the back a comment about changing traditions. Florida, 1911. (DMNS BR61-339)

FIGURE 2.23. This image of a Lakota Sioux man wearing traditional clothing and standing next to a horse would have represented the passing of Indian traditions in Bratley's mind. By the late 1800s, such men were both resented and romanticized for their adherence to old ways. Rosebud Reservation, 1895–1899. (DMNS BR61-294)

the Indian school displays. "I always have been told that the Indians were lazy and worthless," one visitor to the Indian school exhibit at the 1904 St. Louis World's Fair wrote, "but those boys at the manual training and blacksmithing classes are as good workers as I ever saw."[127] Through education, Native people could stand as exemplars of—at long last, not impediments to—Western progress.

This, then, is one potential reading of why Bratley, an Indian schoolteacher, would collect traditional crafts and arts: as artifacts—things *past*—they signify the advance of Indians who no longer need them. The history of the fairs and Bratley's interest in them could help explain how his collection was not a paradox—a teacher whose work was to assimilate but who spent his free time collecting traditional objects—but parts of a whole, a man who saw the passing of one way of life as evidence of his work to help usher in a new era.

Although both the Chicago and St. Louis exhibitions drew on the comparative approach and evolutionary frameworks of the period, by the early twentieth century there was a growing pessimism among many federal administrators regarding the ability of Native people to assimilate fully into American society. This shift in popular sentiment was reflected in the design of world's fair exhibitions. By the St. Louis fair in 1904, the emphasis on the future of Indians had given way to an increasing belief that Native Americans were the last of their race.[128] This growing tension between an optimistic view of the assimilation program and the belief that Native people were limited by their inherent backwardness came to be a defining feature of both official conversations about Indian policy and popular thought.

In 1933, thirty years retired from the Indian Service, Bratley returned to Chicago for his last world's fair, this time accompanied by his wife, Della, and daughter, Hazel. During this fair, the Bratleys happened upon an exhibit of a Lakota Sioux village, jarringly set before a full-scale reproduction of a Mayan temple.[129] Although the camp had been deserted for the day, Bratley found an elderly man who had stayed behind and inquired in his best Lakota, as he later wrote, "Wasoso Wakpala Wyaway Tipi?" He had asked if there were any people from Lower Cut Meat Creek Camp, where Bratley had been employed from 1895 until 1899. Bratley discovered that one of his former students, Elk Teeth, was indeed there. After waiting a long time for Elk Teeth to return from visiting the fair's exhibits, Bratley finally encountered his former student dressed in a large war bonnet. Immediately recognizing each other, Elk Teeth called out Bratley's Lakota nickname "Siokmi" and rushed to greet his former teacher, throwing his arms around him and embracing him.

In his autobiography, Bratley described his surprise and joy at seeing Elk Teeth. It was a fitting location for a reunion at the close of Bratley's life—a venue that epitomized the clash between tradition and modernity, survival and conversion. Bratley wrote that Elk Teeth "had not seen me for thirty-four years, still he remembered me." He added, "I would not have missed seeing him for a good deal."[130]

Notes

1. McCowan 1899:385.

2. Bratley n.d.a:101

3. Bratley n.d.a:101.

4. Collins 2000.

5. Szasz 2007.

6. Calloway 2010.

7. Oberly 1885:LXXVIII.

8. Rockwell 2010:59.

9. Oberly 1885:LXXX–LXXXIII.

10. Hamilton 1827:146.

11. For many years after this administrative transfer, the BIA was known as the Indian bureau, Indian office, Indian department, and Indian Service.

12. http://www.bia.gov/WhatWeDo/ServiceOverview/IndianEducation/, accessed October 30, 2015.

13. Szasz and Ryan 1978:290.

14. Prucha 1986:482.

15. Prucha 1986:503.

16. Reel 1898:334.

17. Szasz and Ryan 1978:293.

18. Oberly 1885.

19. In Hutchinson 2009:55.

20. In Hutchinson 2009:56.

21. Prucha 1984:720.

22. Jones 1913:13.

23. DeJong 2007:256.

24. Szasz and Ryan 1978:291.

25. Reel 1901:5.

26. Jones 1899:561.

27. Jones 1900:635.

28. Heater 2004:113.

29. Cooper 2015:13.

30. Cooper 2015:14.

31. Adams 1977; Seniors 2008.

32. Cooper 2015:73; Trennert 1989:596.

33. Fear-Segal 2007.

34. Cooper 2015:83–84.

35. Blalock-Moore 2012; Huff 1997:5.

36. Cooper 2015:2.

37. Jones 1898:4.

38. Jones 1898:5.

39. Reel 1903:385.

40. Reel 1898:339.

41. Bratley n.d.a:101.

42. S'Klallam advisers told us that Siwash was a common term during the late 1800s but a derogatory one used against them, similar to the term *squaw*.

43. Bratley n.d.a:101.

44. Bratley n.d.a:101.

45. Bennett 2013; Berlo 1992; Hinsley 1981; Patterson 2003.

46. Quote from McGee 1897:373; see Powell 1987.

47. Theodossopoulos 2013:338.

48. Berlo 1992:3; Clifford 1987; Gruber 1970; Stocking 1985.

49. King 1986:70.

50. Hoxie 1984:16.

51. Boas 1974; Cole 1999; Darnell 2000; Jacknis 2002.

52. Clifford 1988:25.

53. Hoxie 1984:17; Morgan 1901.

54. Hoxie 1984:18–19.

55. Bratley 1902b.

56. Bratley n.d.b.

57. N.A. n.d.

58. N.A. n.d.

59. Bratley 1893–1897:83.

60. See Williams 2003:139.

61. Mithlo 2014; Smith 2016.

62. Bratley 1897–1901:176–177.

63. Bratley n.d.c:13.

64. Bratley n.d.c:12.

65. Bratley n.d.c.

66. Bratley 1961:2.

67. Murdock 1939.

68. Bratley 1961:1.

69. Bratley 1961.

70. Hoyt 1902.

71. Bratley 1938.

72. Bratley 1898a, 1898b.

73. Rahder 2004:xi.

74. Donaldson 1890; Mindeleff 1891; Riggs and Powell 1890.

75. Beadle 1897; Bratley n.d.b:21; Royce and Thomas 1895.

76. Bratley 1902b.

77. Bratley 1901.

78. Matthes 1905; Powell 1882; Warren and Brewer 1890.

79. Bratley n.d.b:8–9.

80. Bernadin et al. 2003:4–5; Turner 1893.

81. Rosaldo 1989.

82. Deloria 1998:99.

83. Hutchinson 2009.

84. Lomawaima 1996.

85. Slivka 2011.

86. Gram 2016:266.

87. Gram 2016:255.

88. Hutchinson 2009:8, 51.

89. Hutchinson 2009:56.

90. Bsumek 2008:194–196; Hutchinson 2009:88.

91. Berlo 1992:7; Conn 2004; Heckwelder 1819.

92. Hutchinson 2009:3.

93. Hutchinson 2009:11.

94. Hutchinson 2009:18, 25.

95. Hutchinson 2009:19.

96. Hutchinson 2009:20–22.

97. Hutchinson 2009:28.

98. Hutchinson 2009:12–13.

99. Hutchinson 2009:14–15.

100. Southwell and Lovett 2010:224.

101. Hutchinson 2009:4.

102. Hutchinson 2009:16.

103. Grossman 1994; Katzive 1981; Russell 1970; Slotkin 1992; Warren 2007.

104. http://centerofthewest.org/learn/western-essays/wild-west-shows/, accessed February 18, 2016.

105. Auerbach 1999; Badger 1979; Brown 2001; Hoffenberg 2001; Kargon et al. 2015; Kosmider 2001; Parezo and Fowler 2007:5.

106. http://www.csufresno.edu/library/subjectresources/specialcollections/worldfairs/index.html#intro, accessed April 1, 2016.

107. Hoxie 1984:86.

108. Parezo and Fowler 2007:4–7.

109. Hoxie 1984:112–113.

110. Rydell 1984:157.

111. Moses 1996:130.

112. Breckenridge 1989; Hinsley and Wilcox 2016:22–40; Maurer 2000:22.

113. Nash and Feinman 2003.

114. Bratley 1904.

115. Edwards 2008:54.

116. Hoxie 1984:88–89.

117. Trennert 1987:207.

118. Parezo and Fowler 2007:144–149.

119. Maurer 2000:23.

120. Maurer 2000:24.

121. Bratley n.d.a:90.

122. Reel 1901:143–144.

123. Morgan 1891:79–80.

124. Browning 1893:20.

125. This photograph (DMNS BR61-339) is found in the Denver Museum Archives.

126. Trennert 1987:213.

127. Affairs 1904:56; see also Parezo and Fowler 2007:161.

128. Hoxie 1984: 94.

129. Ganz 2008:115; http://www .idaillinois.org/cdm/ref/col lection/lakecou02z/id/3064, accessed July 28, 2017.

130. Bratley n.d.a:91.

3

THE PIONEERING LIFE OF JESSE H. BRATLEY

We primeval forests felling,
We the rivers stemming, vexing we and piercing deep the mines
within
We the surface broad surveying, we the virgin soil upheaving
Pioneers! O pioneers!
—Walt Whitman, 1855[1]

As the eighteenth century turned to the nineteenth, America was humming with restless energy. With the memory of the revolution still palpable, citizens of the freshly formed United States of America were looking for an identity that would firmly distinguish them from their former colonial master, Great Britain, and from the various European nations from which they had embarked. For the new republicans, the answer to this dilemma entailed in part a return to a simpler way of life and the conquest of wilderness.[2] The siren call of progress seemed to whisper in the winds that whipped across the open grasslands west of the Mississippi. In search of their new country's new beginning, Americans abandoned the comforts of their cities that hugged the Atlantic Ocean and surged westward.

A homesteader, farmer, accountant, salesman, postman, Indian school teacher, and amateur anthropologist, Jesse H. Bratley's life is intimately intertwined with the uniquely American quest to settle and civilize its Western frontier. Bratley's extraordinary life begins with his parents who were pioneers in their own right. Jesse's father, Joseph Bratley, was born in Lincolnshire, England, in 1838. He immigrated to Savannah, Georgia, in 1853—where his father was already living—with his mother and two brothers. After Joseph's father died unexpectedly, he survived as a teenager selling cups of coffee, then farmed in New York, then took up a milling apprenticeship in Wisconsin, then served in the Union Army. In the summer of 1865, the army discharged Joseph. He bought a 22-acre plot of land nestled in the rolling hills of southwestern Wisconsin.[3] There Joseph met Mary Emma Hastings, descended from a line of Prussian immigrants, and married her.[4] On May 17, 1867, Jesse Hastings Bratley was born.

Yet life in Wisconsin did not hold enough promise. In 1870, the family piled into a covered wagon; took their $400 in cash, six chickens, three pigs, and one cow; and set off for Kansas. After two arduous months, covering more than 600 miles, the

FIGURE 3.1. Bratley briefly returned to farming after retiring from the Indian Service. Here Homer Bratley de-tassels corn—employed to hybridize different varieties—in a field in Wichita. Kansas, 1903–1905. (DMNS BR61-351)

family eventually ended up on the Western frontier in the fledgling hamlet of Wichita, which then consisted of 123 men and 1 woman.[5] There, among the bluestem grass, the family established a farm by purchasing a plot of land, designated Section 36, from the Kansas government.

The Bratleys' time at this first home was short-lived and full of heartache. Not six months after they purchased the 160-acre plot, the US Congress passed a law that annulled the Bratleys' purchase from the state and transferred ownership of the land to the federal school system. Congressional surveyors appraised the Bratleys' land at seven times the dollar value they had originally paid. Although brief, this event came to define Jesse's childhood. Over the next twenty years, Jesse saw his parents fret, skimp, save, and slog through grueling hours of labor to pay the $1,184 they owed the government.[6] For eight years, the Bratleys lived in Wichita, but then they moved back out to Section 36. The Bratley homestead consisted of a cottonwood shanty accompanied by two lean-tos. Although humble, the house was made cheery by the pages of the *Wichita Weekly Eagle*, which Mrs. Bratley perennially plastered onto the rough walls. During Jesse's seminal years on the homestead, the family primarily raised corn, potatoes, cabbage, fruit, and livestock for consumption and sale (figure 3.1).

Life was testing for the Bratley family. Weighing on them was a shared set of persistent threats, including poverty, bad harvests, inclement weather, fires, and Indian attacks. During his first twelve years in Kansas, Jesse noted the "almost continuous string of covered wagons, going west, and carrying people seeking homesteads," and the just as persistent trail of dejected wagons returning east with signs painted on their covers saying "Busted" or "Going Back to the Wife's Folks."[7] Yet moments of youthful reprieve punctuated the hardship of everyday life on the frontier. A combination of hard work and unbridled freedom defined Jesse's youth on the Section 36 homestead; he spent much of his day tending crops, fishing, trapping rabbits, and tramping across the prairie. It was not until Jesse was fourteen years old that he realized for the first time that "we were poor people and mighty hard up."[8]

Much to his chagrin, Bratley's energizing work on the homestead was curtailed by three months of school each year, which were held during the fall and winter. Although he eventually taught at both public and Indian day schools, his early experiences in the classroom were far from pleasant. During his brief stints at the Leesummit and Highland schools, Bratley developed a strong distaste for arithmetic and especially grammar—an academic failing he attributed to his first teacher, Miss Ella Bowman, who was not "worth a continental [a dollar coin] as a teacher."[9] Bratley often grumbled that he had such a dislike for grammar that he did not begin to conquer the subject until he was assigned to teach it to S'Klallam Indians in Washington State at age twenty-six.

▼ ▽ ▼

In 1885, the Bratley family purchased another homestead, 180 miles west near Dodge City. The following year, at age nineteen, Jesse moved out to the Dodge City homestead with his mother and youngest brother, Hugh, to farm full-time. In addition to planting corn and breaking sod on the homestead, Jesse also took up work hauling rocks for three dollars a load from the Sawlog Creek quarry into Dodge City. During one of these trips to the quarry, Jesse was caught in a severe hailstorm from which he developed inflammatory rheumatism in his lower limbs. Jesse was bedridden for months. Although his condition eventually improved, Jesse was crippled by pain in his feet and ankles for the rest of his life. Described by Jesse as his "handicap," this injury disqualified him from achieving his dream of becoming a farmer.

Forced to wear a steel brace to support his impaired foot and unable to sustain the physically demanding labor of farm work, Bratley searched for an alternate career. He found his opportunity at the Southwestern Business College in Wichita, securing a fifty dollar loan from a family acquaintance, William H. Ranson, who owned a small real estate and

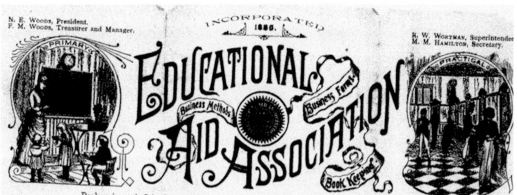

Dealers in such School Supplies as the People's Needs Demand, and Actual Utility Justifies.
214-220 CLARK STREET.

DICTATED.

Chicago, July 12ᵗ, 1890.

TO WHOM IT MAY CONCERN:-

This is t ccertify, that the bearer, Prof. J.H.Bratley, is our authorized solicitor and salesman and hold ourselves responsible for the faithful fulfillment of his contracts.

Any favors shown him will be appreciated by his many educational admirers.

Respectfully,

Edl. Aid Assn.

R.W. Wortman Sup't.

FIGURE 3.2. Bratley's contract with the Education Aid Association, around 1890, attests to his struggle to find steady employment. (Children of Dr. Forrest G. Bratley)

loan office in Wichita. The next nine months were mentally and physically exhausting, as Bratley studied tirelessly to master advanced arithmetic while working nights as a janitor to pay for his apartment. By June 1889, Jesse had completed his coursework and received a diploma in accounting.

But no accounting jobs presented themselves when Bratley finished his degree. Defeated and insolvent, Bratley returned to blue-collar labor, reluctantly taking up work as a section hand on the railway. He later wrote, "No one will ever know the pain, agony, and humiliation that I passed through and endured. Besides the 10 hours on the railroad I had to spend about one hour sweeping the hall and stairway to pay for my room and rent."[10] Bratley soon left the hard life of paddying on the railroad and established a business as an

THE
PIONEERING
LIFE OF
JESSE H.
BRATLEY

71

independent accountant. Jesse's business processing taxes for his neighbors in Wichita flourished, and he was able to repay most of the interest on his college loan. After thirteen hectic months, Jesse headed back to the family's homestead outside Dodge City.

Upon returning home, Bratley began his career as a teacher—an ironic turn given his youthful distaste for formal education. Although he needed to take the grammar certification test several times to pass, Bratley managed to successfully teach at various public schools over the next three years. To make ends meet, Bratley took up summer employment with the Learning to Do by Doing Chart Company, touring Kansas, Montana, Colorado, and New Mexico selling arithmetic charts (figure 3.2). Bratley's traveling adventures were a revelatory experience, affording him the opportunity to explore parts of the country he had never seen before.[11]

Bratley proved to be a capable salesman. He earned more money in one summer peddling charts than he had made in his previous twenty-three years of life. Bratley paid off all his loans and used his newfound prosperity to buy material comforts—such as formal clothes—he did not have as a child. As Bratley moved from county to county selling charts to public schoolteachers, he also sent extra earnings back to his family. Using these savings, along with the earnings of his sister Leoni, who was also a teacher, the Bratley family finally paid off their Section 36 homestead debt.

In 1893, amid a severe economic depression sweeping the United States, Bratley fortuitously saw an announcement in the *Eagle* advertising teaching opportunities at federally funded Indian schools. Although he barely passed the civil service exam's grammar sec-

FIGURE 3.3. In 1893, Bratley used this American flag during his run for the Cherokee Strip, Oklahoma. (Children of Dr. Forrest G. Bratley)

tion, Bratley received his teaching certification and patiently waited for his appointment from the BIA. Five months later, Bratley was still unemployed and at a crossroad. With hard times at hand and few better jobs available, he resolved to try his luck obtaining a piece of prairie land in an area called the Cherokee Strip in Oklahoma.

Originally allotted to the Cherokee Nation in the early 1800s, the strip was ceded to the United States in 1891. Two years later, the government opened the 6.5 million acres of prime grassland to Euro-American settlement. Despite Bratley's physical limitations, he dreamed of owning and farming one of the 160-acre homestead plots up for grabs in the valley. On the day of the land run, Bratley recalled that tens of thousands of families, destitute from the economic slump of the 1890s, "joined in the mad rush for a home and flooded over the prairie in a thundering cloud of dust, like the greatest cavalry charge in history. Injury and death was the only reward for some in the violent chase."[12]

Unfortunately for young Bratley, his hopes of a claim were expeditiously dashed; he was outmaneuvered by "Sooners," men who had gone out against the law and claimed plots before the opening (figure 3.3). Although disappointed, Bratley later came to terms with his lost chance. "Today it looks to me that I was very unwise to have made such plans, not only on account of the lack of money, but with my handicap," he mused. "I would never have been able to follow a plough."[13]

Port Gamble Day School, 1893–1895

A few days after Bratley's unsuccessful run for the Cherokee Strip, he received a letter from the US Department of the Interior stating that he had been selected as a teacher at the Port Gamble Day School in Puyallup, Washington. It was on the shores of Port Gamble Bay where Bratley first learned to live among and teach American Indian children and developed, he later self-deprecatingly noted, "a very prolific pair of side burns," which would distinguish him for most of his adult life (figure 3.4).[14]

After submitting his acceptance to the BIA in September 1893, Bratley used all of his savings to purchase a railroad ticket from Wichita, Kansas, to Puyallup, Washington, where he was to meet with Edwin Eells, the region's US Indian agent. Seven days of train travel later, Bratley arrived. Eells promptly sent him to Port Gamble, a small village about 32 miles northwest of Seattle, Washington, across the Puget Sound. The village's primary industry was milling lumber, which was shipped twice daily on three- to five-mast ocean-going schooners.[15] Inhabited primarily by millworkers and their families, the town of Port Gamble consisted of two sawmills, a post office, bakery, general store, and two churches (figure 3.5). Across the bay from the town, on a 5-acre plot called Point Julia or more commonly the "Spit," lay the Port Gamble Indian village and school. The village was composed of two rows of houses, which were surrounded by unbroken miles of Douglas firs and cedars. So far removed from the open plains and farmland of Kansas, Bratley described Port Gamble as "altogether a different world."[16]

By the time of Bratley's arrival, the S'Klallam had been undergoing decades of tectonic change. In the 1850s, White settlement in Washington Territory skyrocketed as homesteaders sought out gold and then old-growth forests to harvest.[17] Lumber companies began to restrict access to the peninsula's dense forests—which had previously been used as a sustainable source of materials for S'Klallam canoes and homes (figure 3.6). The mills incorporated tribal people into America's modern capitalist system by providing an income for tribal members (primarily men). The money earned was used to purchase Euro-American-style clothing and machine-made goods. To concentrate Native peoples and extinguish their land title, in 1855 the US government signed the Treaty of Point No Point with the S'Klallam, Chimakum, and Skokomish, which allowed the tribes to retain traditional fishing territories but ceded approximately 750,000 acres of land.[18] The treaty also stipulated the construction of agricultural and industrial schools.

FIGURE 3.5. The ships taking on lumber in Port Gamble would have been a daily scene for Bratley while he lived among the S'Klallam. Washington, 1893–1895. (DMNS BR61-498)

In 1865, a boarding school was opened on the Skokomish Reservation and was placed under the direction of a Catholic priest.[19] From its inception, the school suffered from poor attendance and incompetent teachers.[20] It was not until 1885 that the school became regularly attended, with an estimated student body of about fifty-five students.[21] Around 1890, several day schools were constructed to serve the dispersed S'Klallam tribal members living in the area, including a school on the Spit, which the Catholic Church directed, and a day school at Jamestown, approximately 40 miles from Point Julia (figure 3.7).[22]

S'Klallam families traditionally lived in plank houses, with men splitting their time among seasonal fishing, hunting, and woodworking, while women cared for families, gathered wild foods, and produced a range of household goods, such as mats, baskets, and blankets.[23] Although S'Klallam families did live in permanent homes, they inhabited these structures for only six months annually, spending the remainder of the year in temporary camps along travel routes and in seasonal settlements along Hood Canal, where families fished for salmon, picked berries, and performed ceremonial activities.[24] At the time of Bratley's arrival, 325 S'Klallam residents occupied small, scattered villages between Port Gamble and Clallam Bay, with about 75 individuals living in the Point Julia village. In 1893, each day, between 20 and 25 children were reported to be in attendance at Port Gamble Day School.[25]

Bratley was instructed to live among the S'Klallam villagers on the Spit rather than in the predominantly White town at Port Gamble to avoid having to journey each day across the bay's turbulent waters. Recounting his journey across the bay to his new home, Bratley vividly described the Port Gamble Indian community: "As we approached the Spit,

FIGURE 3.6. The Port Gamble sawmills had already set in motion a series of profound socio-economic changes among the S'Klallam by the time Bratley arrived there. Washington, 1893–1895. (DMNS BR61-497)

I could see the old black huts, heaps of clams, cockle and muscle [*sic*] shells that had been accumulating for many years where the Indians had eaten these shell fish. The walls of the huts both inside and out were black and dingy from age and the smoke from the fires on their dirt floors. Their lean and hungry looking dogs and half-naked children gave me a picture of the like of which I had never seen before and I just wonder[ed] if I could work with this people under these conditions."[26] Bratley's description suggests that despite his youthful curiosity, he found the task of raising the S'Klallam out of poverty and savagery a daunting, if not impossible, feat. Left to his own devices and thrown into close contact with the very people he had feared as a child, Bratley's foreboding as he journeyed across the bay was palpable.

Bratley's first year in Puget Sound was trying. For five weeks, Bratley subsisted on sandwiches and slept on a bench in the schoolhouse until he finished building his cabin, a 12 × 14 foot shanty. By the time Bratley had finished his cottage, he had but thirteen cents in the bank and a bill of twenty-seven dollars at the general store. Reflecting on his dire straits, Bratley wrote in his journal on November 3, 1893, that he hoped "to never see such times again."[27] The drastic change in scenery and climate made his adjustment to life among the S'Klallam more difficult. He later remembered, "Instead of the dry prairies that I was used to, in the Puget Sound country we had great forests and arms of salt water all around with snow-capped mountains in the background. Out there, we had rain instead of droughts. We traveled in canoes or boats, while in Kansas we traveled in a lumber wagon drawn by horses. We dug clam[s] like we dug potatoes in the east."[28]

FIGURE 3.7. This image captures Bratley's lived experience of place while among the S'Klallam—with Port Gamble on the left and the Spit on the right. S'Klallam Reservation, 1893–1895. (DMNS BR61-500)

While in Puget Sound, Bratley lived an unpretentious and simple life, during which he recalled doing his "own cooking, always having a pot of cut oats (rolled oats were not made then) for breakfast. I did not drink tea or coffee. I bought my bread at the sawmill store. With so much fish, my meat bill was not large. Butter was twenty-five cents for a pound."[29] A local resident named Skookum John rented out the schoolhouse where Bratley taught; it consisted of a large single room furnished with plain wooden benches, a teacher's desk and chair, and "a long shelf on the north wall filled with all kinds of school textbooks."[30]

Bratley corrected the loneliness and alienation he experienced during his first year in Port Gamble by marrying his longtime love, Della Ranson (figure 3.8). The daughter of William H. Ranson—Bratley's business college creditor—and Mary Elizabeth Groves, Della was born in Jacksonville, Illinois, in 1869 and was raised in Wichita. According to Jesse, the greatest achievement in his young life was meeting and eventually marrying Della. A case study in true romance, Jesse and Della's meeting is a tale of happenstance and love at first sight. One day sometime in 1880—when he was thirteen years old and she was eleven—Jesse was sent by his mother to deliver a message to Mr. Ranson. Upon arriving at the Ranson home, Jesse was struck by "two of the cutest little girls I had ever seen," Della and her sister.[31] It was on that day that Jesse resolved to make Della his wife. Over the next thirteen years, Jesse waited patiently for the opportunity to marry Della, persisting through unemployment and debt, Della's engagement to another gentleman from Wichita, and Mrs. Ranson's refusal to allow Della to accompany Jesse during his first year among the "wild" Indians.

During his summer vacation, Bratley returned home to Wichita and married Della on September 24, 1894.[32] Departing for Washington on October 3, the newlyweds spent their honeymoon traveling by rail through Las Vegas, Barstow, and Sacramento.[33] Upon Della's arrival, Bratley immediately set about building an additional lean-to on his humble cabin for a bedroom. Although feeling "guilty for taking my wife from a big two-story farmhouse with many rooms all well-furnished," Bratley later described 1894 as a "very happy year."[34]

In addition to starting a family, Bratley's years on the Spit were formative in other ways. It was during his many free hours in this isolated territory that Bratley finally learned "to distinguish a verb from a noun, which was something [I] could not do after studying Harvey Grammar in the district school."[35] Spending his time in the mornings and evenings

THE PIONEERING LIFE OF JESSE H. BRATLEY

reviewing Reed and Kellogg's *Word Lesson*, which he used to teach his students English grammar, Bratley was finally able to achieve a high rating on the teacher's examination. In addition to these educational experiences, Bratley gained a deep appreciation for work as an Indian schoolteacher—a passion that would define the next decade of his professional and personal life.

Inspired by the prospect of continuing in the Indian school system, Jesse and Della joined the first summer institute for BIA employees in 1894. Attended by government employees as well as missionaries and philanthropists interested in Indian school work, summer institutes offered an opportunity for teachers to commiserate and share their experiences in the field.[36] The success of the first BIA institute held in Seattle inspired

FIGURE 3.8. By all accounts, Della and Jesse had a good marriage, providing each other with companionship on isolated Indian reservations and sharing in the work of teaching Native children. Rosebud Reservation, 1895–1899. (DMNS BR61-152)

FIGURE 3.9. Regular conferences among Indian Service teachers, like this one on the Pine Ridge Reservation, provided the Bratleys with a sense of community despite their isolation. South Dakota, 1895–1899. (DMNS BR61-317)

the Department of the Interior to officially sponsor and expand those meetings, which convened annually in cities across the country. During the conferences, participants presented papers covering such challenges as sanitation, employment of Indians within the school system, morality, amusement, the physical health of pupils, suppression of Indian language during school hours, courses of study, and methods of discipline.[37]

These institutes, of which the Bratleys were perennial participants, played a pivotal role in the development of Indian school curricula on a national level (figure 3.9). Although regulated and supported by the federal government, the actual content and daily operation of Indian schools were highly variable and constantly evolving. These institutes were important staging grounds for the synthesis of disparate pedagogical practices and the creation of a more comprehensive educational system that integrated academic, industrial, and domestic training. In addition to these policy-driven benefits, the summer meetings unintentionally generated a broad body of knowledge about the various tribal communities in which teachers were employed. As Superintendent of Indian Schools William N. Hailmann wrote in his 1896 report, teachers "are learning to appreciate the fact that behind the individual Indians with whom they had to do [sic], lie their tribal surroundings, the history of these tribes, and their association with other tribes, and the entire ethnological development of the Indian race."[38] Superintendent Hailmann's statement suggests that participants in the Indian Service summer institutes acted as ersatz ethnographers, recording the beliefs and practices of Native people. Given the context of his employment, it is not surprising that Bratley began his vast collection of Indian artifacts while employed at the Port Gamble Day School.

On May 11, 1895, Della took the examination for matron in the BIA, becoming eligible for a faculty appointment alongside Jesse (figure 3.10). A matron was to be "responsible

FIGURE 3.10. Della Bratley's matron examination
scores reveal the skills
she was expected to
have as an employee of
the Indian Service. Date
unknown. (Children of
Dr. Forest G. Bratley)

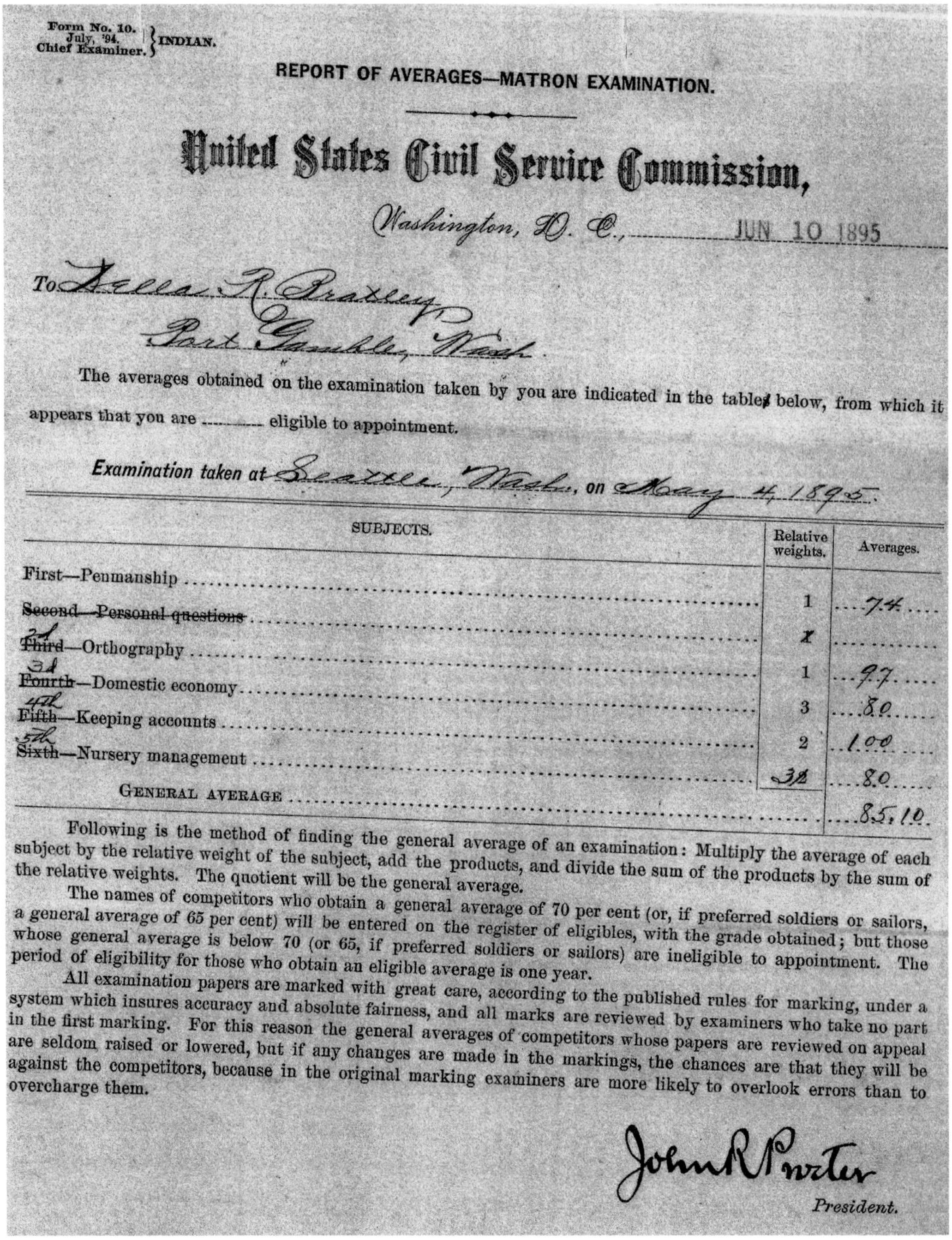

for the management of all the domestic affairs of the school."[39] Della's application was far more than a case of potential nepotism. In the 1890s, government officials intended the Indian school to be a kind of surrogate home—the teachers to be simulated parents.[40] Staffing a school with a husband and wife team ensured that the students experienced a model of American domesticity, a couple whose affection would replace that of their biological family and thus further entice students away from their former homes.[41] By 1893, more than half of all boarding school superintendents had a wife employed at the same school.[42]

Form No. 10.
July, '94.
Chief Examiner. } INDIAN.

REPORT OF AVERAGES—MATRON EXAMINATION.

United States Civil Service Commission,

Washington, D. C., JUN 10 1895

To *Della R. Bratley*
Port Gamble, Wash.

The averages obtained on the examination taken by you are indicated in the table below, from which it appears that you are _____ eligible to appointment.

Examination taken at *Seattle, Wash.* on *May 4, 1895.*

SUBJECTS.	Relative weights.	Averages.
First—Penmanship	1	74
Second—Personal questions	1	
Third—Orthography	1	97
Fourth—Domestic economy	3	80
Fifth—Keeping accounts	2	100
Sixth—Nursery management	30	80
GENERAL AVERAGE		85.10

Following is the method of finding the general average of an examination: Multiply the average of each subject by the relative weight of the subject, add the products, and divide the sum of the products by the sum of the relative weights. The quotient will be the general average.

The names of competitors who obtain a general average of 70 per cent (or, if preferred soldiers or sailors, a general average of 65 per cent) will be entered on the register of eligibles, with the grade obtained; but those whose general average is below 70 (or 65, if preferred soldiers or sailors) are ineligible to appointment. The period of eligibility for those who obtain an eligible average is one year.

All examination papers are marked with great care, according to the published rules for marking, under a system which insures accuracy and absolute fairness, and all marks are reviewed by examiners who take no part in the first marking. For this reason the general averages of competitors whose papers are reviewed on appeal are seldom raised or lowered, but if any changes are made in the markings, the chances are that they will be against the competitors, because in the original marking examiners are more likely to overlook errors than to overcharge them.

John R Procter

President.

A few weeks after Della's appointment, the Bratleys requested to be transferred to a school in Oklahoma or Kansas, where they could be employed as teacher and matron. In his letter to Superintendent Hailmann, Bratley stated that the principal reason for requesting a transfer was that "our parents live in Kansas and are growing old and . . . we would like to be near enough to them that we might reach them if anything serious happens, which we would hardly be able to do at this distance."[43] At the end of the school year, the Bratleys' request was granted. The couple was transferred to South Dakota.

Upon leaving Port Gamble, Bratley recounted a feeling of pride at all he had accomplished. "I left feeling well-pleased with the progress I had made with the little Siwash children," he wrote. "When I left this class, they had finished the chart, primer, first and second readers and could do number work to correspond. They had learned to write their names and their lessons."[44] Bratley's achievements among the S'Klallam were endorsed in a report to the commissioner of Indian affairs in 1895. It declared that the "Port Gamble Day School, taught by J. H. Bratley, is successful from every standpoint."[45]

Lower Cut Meat Creek Day School, 1895–1899

Twelve hours after receiving their transfer notification to the Lower Cut Meat Creek Day School on the Rosebud Reservation in South Dakota, the Bratleys had their two trunks and three bags packed. Hiring two local S'Klallam men to transport them by canoe, the Bratleys crossed Port Gamble Bay for the last time, boarded a steamboat, and then took a train headed west at 10:00 p.m. that same day. A full week later, the couple reached the Rosebud Agency. When the Bratleys arrived at Rosebud in August 1895, approximately 4,316 Lakota Sioux residents lived in small, scattered encampments across the reservation.[46]

The Rosebud Reservation was the result of centuries of conflict, as a Sioux group known as the Teton, or Lakota, had sought to weather Euro-American colonialism and the transformations it had wrought.[47] In 1868, the Teton, along with representatives from other Sioux branches, signed the Fort Laramie Treaty, which established the Great Sioux Reservation in the western half of South Dakota and stipulated the construction of an Indian agency and the issuing of allotments to individual families in exchange for thirty years of annuities.[48]

Despite the peace agreement signed at Fort Laramie, conflict among Sioux militants—such as Red Cloud, Crazy Horse, and Sitting Bull—persisted as Sioux lands were systematically reduced to accommodate Euro-American settler and mining interests (figures 3.11 and 3.12).[49] After the Battle of the Little Big Horn and Colonel Custer's infamous defeat, Congress enacted a policy of extermination—sending soldiers to occupy the Black Hills, confiscating most of the Sioux's sacred territory, and passing the Black Hills Act in 1877.[50] By 1889, Congress and the BIA had forced the Sioux to surrender 9 million acres—breaking up the Great Sioux Reservation into five smaller reserves. One of these,

FIGURE 3.11. Bratley paid Chief Red Cloud one dollar to pose for this photograph and noted that the Lakota Sioux medicine men refused to have their picture taken without compensation. Rosebud Reservation, 1895–1899. (DMNS BR61-258)

the Rosebud Reservation, became predominately the home of the Sicangu Oyate, also known as the Upper Brulé Sioux Nation or Sicangu Lakota (figure 3.13).[51]

Formal education among the Lakota Sioux began in 1868 with the signing of the Fort Laramie Treaty, which stipulated that the government provide a schoolhouse and teacher for every thirty school-age child on the Great Sioux Reservation.[52] In 1871, the Episcopal

Missionary Society established the first school designated specifically to serve the Brulé and Oglala Sioux along the Missouri River. Four years later, administrators moved the school 200 miles west along the White River and reopened it as a day school.[53] Attendance at the day school varied greatly as families continued to move across the Great Plains (figure 3.14).

In 1882, Major James G. Wright was appointed agent of the Rosebud Reservation. Wright, a member of the Episcopal Church and known among the Lakota Sioux as

FIGURE 3.12. Bratley took this portrait of Short Woman, the sister of Sitting Bull, the famous warrior who fought against American colonialism. It is striking that she is dressed in traditional clothing, including a netted caplet, yoke-breast plate, and ear ornaments. Rosebud Reservation, 1897. (DMNS BR61-271)

FIGURE 3.13. Bratley took this photo of the Rosebud Agency along the Rosebud River during a visit there later in his life. Rosebud Reservation, 1939. (DMNS BR61-483B)

Kicking Bear for once beating and imprisoning an innocent Indian petitioner, discovered that day school education had largely been neglected because of poor attendance, limited resources, and widespread cynicism among reservation officials regarding the day school system's efficacy.[54] Wright funneled a significant proportion of the agency's resources into education.[55] The number of schools on the reservation steadily increased, to twenty-one day schools and two boarding schools operated by Episcopal and Catholic missionaries. In 1895, the total enrollment at these schools was 946 pupils.[56] To accommodate the growing number of Indian students, an additional eighteen teachers were hired, including Jesse H. Bratley, who was assigned to the Lower Cut Meat Creek Day School (figure 3.15).

When Jesse and Della reached the reservation, however, the Lower Cut School was under construction, so administrators temporarily assigned them to a joint position at the Whirlwind Soldier's Camp School. Traveling by covered wagon over 60 miles of rough open prairie, it took two days for the couple to reach their new school. Set in a valley adjacent to the dry Oak Creek, Bratley's initial impression of the camp and school was unenthusiastic at best: "I tell you, it did not look very home-like, set out there one hundred miles from the railroad. Sixty miles from the agency and we would have been satisfied to get our mail once in every ten or twenty days. No white faces nearer than thirty miles away. Water for drinking and cooking had to be carried one mile. When I would reach the schoolhouse, I had to skim the flies and grasshopper from the water."[57] Bratley's comments reveal the isolated nature of life on the Rosebud Reservation and suggest that after two years among the Native people of Port Gamble, his sensibilities had changed little.

Fortunately, the Bratleys' time at Whirlwind Soldier's Camp was cut short. Several weeks after arriving, John Dunbar, a representative of the Rosebud Agency, reached the school. Bratley recalled that Dunbar "came out to get us and [said] that we must be packed and loaded, ready to start for the agency by sunrise in the morning."[58] Filled with fear and

FIGURE 3.14. The fact that Bratley could take a picture of a woman traveling with a child on a horse-drawn travois at the turn of the twentieth century suggests the continuing mobility of the Lakota Sioux into the reservation period. Rosebud Reservation, 1885–1899. (DMNS BR61-254)

uncertainty at the hurried command, the Bratleys quickly packed their belongings and departed at first light. Unaware of the rationale behind their rushed flight from Whirlwind Soldier's Camp, the Bratleys' questions were soon answered.

Upon arriving at Syple Issue House—a hotel on the way to Rosebud—Bratley received a letter from his mother, which contained a simple statement of concern: "Jesse, we are scared that the Indian Agent is not telling you what is happening at Rosebud Agency."[59] Stitched to the top of the letter was a newspaper clipping from the *Daily Eagle*, which reported that "the Brulé Sioux Indians have gone on the war path under the leadership of Chief Hollow-Horn Bear and have given the employees twenty-one days to leave the reservation, or they will have to suffer the consequences."[60] The following morning the Bratleys were escorted to the stockade in Rosebud for their own safety, where they learned that Hollow-Horn Bear had been successfully captured (figure 3.16).

Although overt military violence between the US Army and Native communities had largely concluded by the 1890s, the Bratleys' early experience on the Rosebud Reservation is indicative of the simmering discontent that still pervaded frontier settlements. The son of Brulé Chief Iron Shell, Hollow-Horn Bear, or Matȟóhéȟloǧeča, was an iconic figure.[61] Eventually immortalized by having his picture—in full headdress—placed on the five dollar silver certificate and later on a fourteen cent postage stamp, Hollow-Horn Bear was described by a contemporary as "one of the handsomest men in his race. His profile . . . reminds one of Alexander the Great, so strong and chaste is its outline . . . a good type of intellectual and progressive man."[62]

Hollow-Horn Bear began his political career as a teenager, participating in raids against White settlers, miners, and Union Pacific Railroad workers in Wyoming and the Dakotas in the late 1860s.[63] After the conclusion of the Black Hills War in 1877, Hollow-Horn Bear remained on the Rosebud reserve.[64] In 1889, the Sioux signed a treaty with a federally

FIGURE 3.15. Bratley took this photo of his students in front of the Lower Cut Meat Creek Day School. BACK ROW, SEATED (LEFT TO RIGHT): Kittie Turning-Eagle, Emma Elk Looks Back, Maggie Otterman, Rosa Elk Teeth. BACK ROW, STANDING: Nellie Foot, Policeman Underwater, Frank Sleeping Bear. SECOND ROW FROM THE REAR, SEATED: Gracie Good Bird and Bessie Elk Looks Back. SECOND ROW, STANDING: Stella Good Bird, Lee Wood, Tommy Otterman, Tommy Wood. THIRD ROW, KNEELING EXCEPT LAST BOY: Eddie Foot, Nat Elk Teeth, Silas Plenty Holes, Samuel Yellow Robe, Claudie Blue Horse, Freddie Sitting Bear. FRONT ROW, SITTING: George Kills Plenty, Allen Otterman, Willie Good Bird, John Underwater, Charles Black Calf, Charles New, Lucy Kills Plenty, Nancy Pony, Hattie With Horns, Minnie Underwater. Rosebud Reservation, 1898. (DMNS BR61-282)

appointed commission led by General George Crook, a military officer whom the Sioux knew and respected as an adversary from the Indian Wars of the previous decades. The treaty transferred a significant portion of the Great Sioux Reservation to the federal government, opening up land for homesteaders. A warrior and politician, Hollow-Horn Bear vehemently opposed the Sioux land cession, believing that the treaty meant tribal disintegration and the loss of political power.[65]

The 1895 uprising, to which the Bratleys were bystanders, was a product of the lingering discontent many Lakota Sioux residents felt toward the treaty and the tribal members who supported it. These intra-tribal animosities were exacerbated by economic stress resulting from devastating droughts, the withdrawal of beef rations, and the federal government's failure to pay the annuities pledged in the Treaty of Fort Laramie.[66] Although Hollow-Horn Bear's resistance was short-lived—once captured he was promptly jailed and later became a police chief for the Rosebud Agency—the dissatisfaction that had sparked the 1895 uprising lingered throughout the Bratleys' time among the Lakota Sioux.

Following the capture of Hollow-Horn Bear, for their safety the Bratleys spent two weeks confined to the stockade until the resistance movement was fully subdued. With order sufficiently restored, the Bratleys established themselves at the Lower Cut Meat Creek Day School—buying a cow, a team of horses, a couple of pigs, and some chickens. Similar to other day schools on the Rosebud Reservation, the Bratleys' living and working quarters were all under one roof, in a one-story T-shaped building. Years later, Bratley vividly described the family's Rosebud residence (figure 3.17):

Beginning at the west end was our bedroom, living room, dining room and kitchen— all in a row from west to east. The sewing room was entered from our dining room. It had a door to the anteroom. The sewing room was some thirty feet square with shelves along the south wall for storing shoes, socks, clothing and bolts of yard goods. The room was well-lighted by windows on the east and west sides. In the room were a cutting table, three sewing machines, a number of chairs and a cook stove. The stove was used to cook the noon lunch for the children and to heat the sewing room when the weather was cold.[67]

FIGURE 3.16. Hollow-Horn Bear was the Sioux chief who in 1895 ordered all the White settlers living on the reservation to leave within twenty-one days. Rosebud Reservation, 1895–1899. (DMNS BR61-268)

FIGURE 3.17. The teacher's cottage and sewing room at the Lower Cut Meat Creek Day School was where the Bratleys lived and taught. Rosebud Reservation, 1895–1899. (Children of Dr. Forrest G. Bratley)

The fact that Bratley was able to provide such an in-depth account of his home nearly forty years later in his autobiography speaks to the positive impression the Rosebud facilities made on him, particularly compared to the two-room shanty the couple had braved in Puget Sound.

With the exception of occasional flashes of conflict, the Bratleys spent five rather peaceful years at Rosebud. During this time, their first two children, Homer and Hazel, were born (figure 3.18). Although isolated from much of Anglo society, Bratley led a remarkably normal life for someone of his station—regularly attending church services at the local Episcopal mission, gardening, and playing the violin. Bratley spent much of his free time at Rosebud reading newspapers, including the *Omaha Bee* and the *Kansas City Star*; professional publications such as *Teachers Quarterly* and *History and Pedagogy*; and scholarly books such as *Prehistoric World* and *Geology Elements*.[68] Bratley and Della quickly integrated into the local community of schoolteachers at Rosebud and the neighboring Pine Ridge Reservation. Over the course of their five years at the Lower Cut Meat Creek School, Jesse and Della attended local teachers' meetings in Valentine, Nebraska, and weekend camping excursions with their colleagues.[69]

Similar to his experiences in Puget Sound, many of the Native residents of the Lower Cut Meat Creek Camp welcomed Bratley. He often attended community activities, such as parades and sporting events. Many day school teachers became important cultural brokers, helping to heal sick people, provide advice on settling estates and securing government benefits, or attending local events.[70] Bratley seems to have embraced these opportunities.[71] In his personal journal, Bratley excitedly recounts his participation in local activities, regularly attending the feasts and dances that occurred every Friday night during the winter season. He describes these occasions as "wild affairs" in which "the men dancers were dressed in buckskin breech cloths, jingling bells, paint and feathers only. Some five or more men would sit around an Indian drum in one corner of the room and beat it."[72]

In an interview with us, Leland Little Dog reflected on his ancestors' largely positive relationship with Bratley: "I think if Bratley would have exhibited, or would have consciously been no good, I think the Indians would have picked it up and said all White people are like that. But this guy put up a good first impression, a lot of his own interpersonal skills, his sincerity. I don't know what it was."[73] Little Dog's comments suggest that despite facing hostility from some tribal members, Bratley was in many ways likely considered a valued member of the Lower Cut Meat Creek community.

FIGURE 3.18. Hazel Bratley—Della and Jesse's second child—would later sell her portion of the Bratley collection in the hope of honoring her father. Cheyenne and Arapaho Reservation, 1900–1901. (DMNS BR61-020)

During his tenure at Rosebud, Bratley took up photography in earnest. Bratley's newfound passion for photography may have been inspired in part by the work of John Alvin Anderson, a Swedish immigrant and pioneer photographer who worked among the Rosebud Sioux for nearly forty-five years. Anderson's photographs document a transitional period on the reservation, capturing everyday life, historical events, and portraits of prominent leaders such as Hollow-Horn Bear, High Horse, Fool Bull, and He-Dog.[74] A year after Bratley arrived on the reservation Anderson published his first book, *Among the Sioux*, which showcased thirty-four photographs depicting Lakota Sioux customs and home life.[75]

Although Bratley never explicitly mentions Anderson in his writings, as one of the few Euro-Americans on the reservation and sharing a common interest in documenting Native culture, Bratley and Anderson were most likely aware of one another, if not in direct communication. There are also several notable overlaps in imagery between Anderson's and Bratley's photographs from Rosebud, which suggests that the two men were acquainted. For instance, both Bratley's and Anderson's collections contain images of the beef ration distribution at the Rosebud Agency, women preparing rawhide, and a giveaway (figures 3.19 and 3.20).[76] Perhaps drawing inspiration from Anderson's earlier photography and artifact collections, Bratley quickly developed an extensive and distinctive collection of his own, contributing to the documentary record of this important period in Lakota Sioux history.

FIGURE 3.19. Two women paint geometric designs with bone brushes on a staked bison hide. One large hide will make two parfleches, which were used to carry household items and foodstuffs on horseback. Rosebud Reservation, 1895–1899. (DMNS BR61-187)

FIGURE 3.20. On the Rosebud Reservation, Bratley collected this parfleche, decorated with geometric designs in blue, pink, and green. (DMNS AC.5804)

Cantonment Boarding School, 1899–1900

FIGURE 3.21. The Cantonment Boarding School, viewed here from across the Canadian River, was the third Indian school at which the Bratleys taught. Cheyenne and Arapaho Reservation, 1899–1900. (DMNS BR61-382)

At the end of the school year in 1899, the BIA transferred the growing Bratley family to Oklahoma (figure 3.21). After six years teaching Indian children, Bratley was promoted to the position of superintendent at the Cantonment Boarding School, where his salary was increased from $600 to $1,000 a year.[77] The Cantonment Boarding School was located on a reservation in northwestern Oklahoma, which members of the historically allied but culturally distinct Southern Cheyenne and Arapaho tribes occupied.[78]

Like the S'Klallam and Lakota Sioux, in Oklahoma Bratley encountered a community that American colonialism had fundamentally reshaped.[79] By the early 1800s, the Arapaho and Cheyenne had established a formal alliance, sharing a wintertime campground in the Arapaho's traditional territory in Colorado and separating during the spring and summer months onto the Great Plains.[80] In the mid-1800s, the Cheyenne-Arapaho alliance engaged in persistent and violent conflict with neighboring Lakota Sioux communities over the dwindling bison supply as well as with the growing number of Euro-American emigrants colonizing the northern and central Plains.

In 1851, the Arapaho and Cheyenne signed the Treaty of Fort Laramie, agreeing to curtail attacks on US citizens in exchange for control over vast tracts of Wyoming, Nebraska, Colorado, and Kansas.[81] Yet raiding and violence continued. On November 29, 1864, rising anti-Indian sentiment exploded. Colonel John Chivington led US Army troops in a surprise attack on a large group of peaceful Cheyenne and Arapaho settled along Sand Creek in eastern Colorado. The massacre culminated in the slaughter of more than 150 people, primarily helpless women, children, and the elderly.[82] Within a year of the Sand Creek Massacre, the Southern Cheyenne and Arapaho signed the Treaty of the Little Arkansas, declaring peace with the United States and agreeing to settle in south-central Kansas and Oklahoma Territory.[83]

In 1869, a presidential Executive Order established the Cheyenne-Arapaho Agency and Reservation.[84] Originally encompassing 4 million acres, the Cheyenne-Arapaho reserve was dramatically reduced in 1891. The transition from a mobile lifestyle to sedentary confinement on reservations was hard, as encampments of extended families were broken up and pressured to adopt foreign social, economic, and political practices. Cheyenne elder Chester Whiteman recounted one such story. He told us that the "Indians would come over here [to the Concho Agency] to get their payment for whatever lease or something, but they didn't know how to handle money. They would get paid in coin. Some place along that river [the Canadian River] probably you could go take a metal detector and go find a bunch of coins, because they didn't know the value of it. They'd just bury it."[85] Whiteman's story reveals how radically different the Euro-American cultural system was—requiring tribal people to adopt new forms of currency, labor, and standards of wealth and prosperity.

Formal education began on the reservation with the signing of an 1867 treaty, which required that the government provide schools and teachers to the community.[86] In 1871, the son-in-law of the Cheyenne-Arapaho Indian agent, Brinton Darlington, opened the first day school, which soon came under the direction of the Quaker Church.[87] By December 1875, this day school had evolved into a full manual training and boarding school with 112 enrolled scholars, primarily Arapaho, structured around a basic curriculum composed of academics, religion, and training in domestic or industrial trades.[88] Government reports from the 1870s suggest that the Cheyenne and Arapaho often rebelled against White efforts to convert and educate them.[89]

Antagonism toward government-mandated education seems to have been particularly strong among the Cheyenne, whom Superintendent Enoch Hoag declared "were not yet whipped."[90] Although in 1879 Cheyenne and Arapaho chiefs willingly sent 25 children to Carlisle—likely as a way to try to build strategic alliances with the US government and ensure that some tribal members were familiar with American English and culture—more often parents fought sending their children to boarding schools.[91] To fill the schools, the government withheld rations and threatened military action.[92]

In the late 1870s, two events dramatically weakened Cheyenne opposition to education: the decimation of the buffalo herds—forcing dependence on government rations—and a pronounced increase in federal funding for Indian education.[93] The impact of these events on attitudes toward education is reflected in the increasing number of Cheyenne children enrolled in the Darlington Agency boarding school, which nearly doubled, from 33 in 1876 to 61 in 1878.[94] Following the arrival of over 200 Northern Cheyenne to the reservation in 1878, another boarding school was built several miles north of the agency in current-day Concho, Oklahoma. In addition to educating and converting Cheyenne and Arapaho children, these schools served to discourage the children's parents from rebelling against the government.

In a letter to Commissioner of Indian Affairs Ezra Hayt in 1878, Agent John D. Miles articulated the utility of Native children as deterrents to rebellion: "I would respectfully represent that there is no other means so effectual in holding restless Indians in check as to have their children in school."[95] While some tribal members, such as Chief Little Raven of the Arapaho, saw education as a way to keep his people alive after the demise of the buffalo, others followed the Cheyenne leader Little Chief in refusing to let their children attend the agency schools. This tension between acceptance and rejection was a defining feature of Indian education on the Cheyenne and Arapaho Reservation for the next several decades.

When Bratley arrived on the reservation in 1899, the reservation population consisted of 2,037 Cheyenne and 981 Arapaho who primarily depended on government-issued rations for survival, with only about 15 percent of the adult population actively cultivating their own land.[96] The small number of Cheyenne and Arapaho tribal members to take up agriculture and their continued dependency on rations at the turn of the century point to the general failure of the Indian education system, which was intended to alleviate the federal government of its financial responsibility to its Indian wards by teaching them Euro-American values and industries.

Bratley assumed control of the Cantonment Boarding School on July 1, 1899. Under Bratley's supervision was a team of ten employees: Katherine Earlocker, grade school teacher; Grace Wright, kindergarten teacher, F. M. Setzer, industrial teacher; Paul Good Bear, assistant industrial teacher; Willie Meek, farmer; Delia Briscoe, matron; Fannie Harris, assistant matron; Artie Bailey, laundress; Mittie Taylor, cook; and Della Bratley, seamstress.[97] Bratley described his employees as all having "done good work in their schoolrooms" but mentioned that one in particular was "especially slow to do any work asked of her outside of the schoolroom."[98]

Although it was in better condition than many other schools in the area, Bratley filled his annual report to the commissioner of Indian affairs with appeals for additional funding and suggestions for improvement. In addition to requesting a separate cottage for the superintendent, Bratley's report notes the need for auxiliary school buildings, which would provide a much-needed sick room, workshop, and storeroom. Bratley also hoped to build basement cellars for use as play and dressing rooms and to acquire a wood saw so the boys would no longer have to saw the dense, locally available blackjack wood by hand for the twenty-one stoves that heated the school during the winter months.[99]

Along with the need for more facilities, Bratley also noted the lack of proper clothing for the pupils, stating "we had not enough clothing for the boys, received but 49 work suits during the school year. Some of the boys have not received a suit since the school was first begun at this place."[100] Although the federal government had steadily increased spending on Indian schools since the mid-1800s, the schools under Bratley's charge remained seriously underfunded and poorly equipped.

In contrast to his time at Rosebud, Bratley collected comparatively few objects while living on the Cheyenne and Arapaho Reservation. Bratley's account books from 1900 indicate that he purchased approximately twenty objects while on the reservation, including a

breast plate, gambling games, war bonnet, deer hoof rattle, bone spoon, hand axe, winter count, pipe stem, and several eagle feathers.[101] While at Rosebud, Bratley seems largely to have bartered for curios; at Cantonment, Bratley's records indicate that he acquired almost all of his objects through purchase. Notably, Bratley mentions several individuals by name from whom he purchased objects, including an eagle feather from Little Raven—an Arapaho chief—for 40 cents and a war bonnet from Real Bull for $7.50 (figure 3.22).

The fact that Bratley had to purchase rather than barter suggests that in Oklahoma he might have had fewer opportunities for friendly intercourse. Alternatively, Bratley's purchases may indicate that the Cheyenne and Arapaho were more desperate for money—or that they were simply savvy businesspeople.

Many of the materials Bratley purchased seem to have been sold or misplaced over time, as the collection at the Denver Museum currently contains only five objects specifically identified as either Cheyenne or Arapaho: three pairs of moccasins, a beaded headband, and a child's doll. At least one of the objects, a gambling game, mentioned in Bratley's accounts remained in the possession of his family. Several of the Cheyenne and Arapaho descendants we met with recognized the game. They described it as a women's game during which the players placed the pieces in a basket and tossed them into the air (figure 3.23).[102]

The reasons Bratley acquired so few objects while at Cantonment are likely varied but may reflect the contentious atmosphere surrounding his position as superintendent. Although Bratley's object collection from his year at Cantonment is quite small, his passion for photography during this time seems to have continued unabated; he took over 200 photographs while on the Cheyenne and Arapaho Reservation. Bratley focused these images on a familiar set of themes, including landscapes, posed images of men and women dressed in regalia, and scenes from everyday life.

FIGURE 3.23. Bratley purchased this gambling game made from carved fruit pits on October 6, 1899, for fifty cents. Tribal member Marie Whiteman explained that Cheyenne and Arapaho women played the game using a basket to toss the pieces into the air. (Children of Dr. Forrest G. Bratley)

Havasupai Day School, 1900–1901

In the summer of 1900, the government transferred the Bratleys to Supai, Arizona, to join the staff of the Havasupai Day School. Known as the Havasu'Baaja, meaning "the people by the blue-green water," the Havasupai occupied a large territory on the Coconino Plateau before the 1800s, ranging from the south banks of the Colorado River in the Grand Canyon south to the San Francisco Peaks near present-day Flagstaff, Arizona.[103]

The Havasupai's traditional economy was defined by a seasonal dichotomy between summer cultivation of corn, beans, and squash in Cataract Canyon and winter hunting-gathering on the plateau. During the late nineteenth century, White mining prospectors and cattle ranchers began to encroach upon the Havasupai's traditional territory. In response, President Rutherford B. Hayes issued an Executive Order in 1880 to reserve 38,400 acres of farmland along Havasu Creek for the community.[104] By the mid-twentieth century, White settlement and increased competition for land from the neighboring

Walapai and Navajo (Diné) further diminished Havasupai landholdings, dramatically reducing the reservation to a meager 518 acres.[105]

During Bratley's time among the Havasupai, the tribe was composed of approximately 200 or 300 people.[106] Established in 1895 by the BIA, the Havasupai Agency and day school was huddled at the bottom of a 3,000-foot canyon along the Colorado River (figure 3.24).[107] In 1900, the day school had 60 enrolled pupils and was under the jurisdiction of Henry P. Ewing, an industrial teacher who had been federally appointed to administer affairs among both the Walapai and Havasupai tribes (figure 3.25).[108] Superintendent Ewing's official report from this time paints a dire picture of the education system: "Of the progress made in the educational department of the school, I regret to say that I cannot speak so highly as of the Walapai schools. Few of the pupils, even those who have been in school [for] four years, are as far advanced as Walapai pupils of the same age who have been in school but one session. It seems advisable that under the present conditions and circumstances more attention should be given to industrial training among this tribe, and the pupils of suitable age and advancement could be put at school in the Truxton Canyon Boarding School."[109]

Ewing's report suggests that the day school system, which allowed students to remain among their traditional community, was a failure and that more intensive measures of acculturation were necessary to transform the pupils. The apparently poor state of affairs at the Havasupai school was reiterated in Bratley's official letter of transfer from Cantonment. In the letter, Ewing stated that the Havasupai Day School was in desperate need of "an energetic, intelligent, and perfectly reliable person" to replace the current teachers, Horace and Tama Wilson.[110] Although the exact reasons behind the Wilsons' departure are murky, Superintendent Ewing made an explicit request to "not let them send another Wilson here"—suggesting that the couple was removed for indolence and incompetence and perhaps far worse.[111]

To facilitate the transition away from reservations, the commissioner of Indian affairs sought to consolidate the reservations' administrative bureaucracy by combining the position and duties of the Indian agent with that of the school superintendent. Between 1893, when Bratley entered the BIA, and 1902, the total number of Indian agencies decreased from fifty-eight to forty-nine.[112] The Havasupai and Walapai school system was one of the agencies reorganized in 1901; it was aggregated under the jurisdiction of the superintendent of the Truxton Canyon Boarding School, about 100 miles northwest of Flagstaff, Arizona. During this time, administrators expanded the Havasupai Reservation day school and re-classed it as a boarding school, housing seventy-five pupils (figure 3.26).

Bratley's brief autobiographical statements regarding his time at Havasupai do not hint at how this transformation affected him personally. The fact that the official report to the commissioner of Indian affairs during the year of Bratley's employment there fails to mention the Havasupai school further obscures our understanding of the reservation's atmosphere at his time. What we can glean from these events is that while Bratley was in

FIGURE 3.24. Bratley was fascinated with living at the bottom of the Grand Canyon and spent his free time exploring it. This image captures a trip to Mooney Falls, which required Jesse—and perhaps Della; a woman is on the ladder in the middle of the photo—to go down a 100-foot ladder. Arizona, 1900–1901. (DMNS BR61-037)

FIGURE 3.25. It appears that Bratley took regular photos of his students, and arriving at the bottom of the Grand Canyon was no different. Here, he cleaned up his Havasupai Day School students and lined them up in front of the school building. Like his photos among the Lakota Sioux (e.g., BR61-282), he included in the photo the reservation police officer named Lenoman, who would have helped forcibly ensure school attendance. Havasupai Reservation, 1900–1901. (DMNS BR61-048)

Arizona, the Havasupai's traditional subsistence practices and the structure of community life were undergoing a series of radical transformations.

The children at Havasupai Day School followed a daily routine similar to those adhered to at the other Indian schools at which Bratley worked, including academic and industrial instruction, structured play time, and the sharing of a noonday meal (figure 3.27). Bratley left few notes or stories about his time at the bottom of the Grand Canyon. We do not know much about his living conditions or his feelings about the community.

However, amid his work of teaching, he continued photographing and collecting (figure 3.28). From these images, we can see that he explored the surrounding area. He watched men farm and undertake traditional crafts. He collected more than thirty exquisite baskets, as well as cradleboards, bows and arrows, and other tools. Some of his images show a more playful side of Bratley's life, as suggested by the photo of six children crammed on the back of a tiny burro (figure 3.29).

In short, Bratley continued to amass evidence of a tribe's cultural life, which he was helping to supplant as a teacher (figure 3.30).

Polacca Day School, 1902

In May 1901, Jesse and Della resigned from the BIA. The Bratleys' departure was not so much a result of dissatisfaction with the work itself as of the growing financial strain of raising two young children—Homer and Hazel—on a government salary (figure 3.31).[113] Yet after returning to the family homestead in Wichita for several months, Jesse

FIGURE 3.29. Homer and
Hazel Bratley found ready
playmates while living in
the Grand Canyon. Hava-
supai Reservation, 1900–
1901. (DMNS BR61-017)

landscape on Bratley's employment decisions, his great interest in Indian traditions and
relics also seems to have inspired his choice to return to the BIA. On February 18, 1902,
the BIA reinstated Bratley and sent him back to northern Arizona, as he requested, to the
Hopi Reservation.

By 1902, the reported population of Hopi was 1,845; its residents lived in villages distributed across three mesas. Hopis had lived in the region for untold generations, developing a
complex agricultural system focused on corn, beans, and squash.[116] Underlying their farming life was an intricate ceremonial system organized by each traditional village, clans, and
medicine societies and structured around honoring supernatural powers to obtain rain,
good harvests, peace, and health.[117] Even after Spanish conquistadors arrived in the US
Southwest in 1540, the Hopi remained relatively isolated (figure 3.32).[118]

Following the end of the US-Mexican War in 1848, American excursions into Hopi
country steadily rose. The US government established a Hopi Indian Agency in 1870 at the
village of Oraibi on Third Mesa. After the completion of the Atlantic and Pacific Railroad in
1881, settlement in the region—particularly by Mormons—abruptly swelled, precipitating

THE
PIONEERING
LIFE OF
JESSE H.
BRATLEY

101

FIGURE 3.30. During an educational slide show presentation of his artifacts, Bratley provided the following description of these objects and their respective uses: "This and this are *kathoks*, or what we would call burden baskets, they will hold about two bushels of shelled corn. These are *yakas* or baby cradles. These are *esewas* or water bottles made of willow wickerwork coated on the outside with pinon gum. Here is one before it is coated. Set them down or push them around as careless as you please[;] the mouth will not remain turned down. They hold from a half to four gallons. A wisp of grass or small boughs is used for stoppers when traveling. These are *hydruas*[,] they are beauties, they are treasure caskets. These are *coooos*, they are the most common basket made by this people, however, these largest ones represent nearly a month's work each. They are used by the Indians for dishes, pans, pots and the like. They mix their dough; roast their corn by putting live coals on the shelled corn or seeds whichever the case may be and vigorously shaking and whirling all by holding the basket in both hands during the operation. They put their stewed peach sauce in them. These baskets becoming water tight after very little use for they are nearly so when first made. When mush is served it is placed in the *coooo* and the family being seated around it, all on the ground, then each using the index and second finger of one hand as a spoon, with a downward stroke on the side of the mush heap a small amount is scraped off and carried to the mouth. With this mescal fiber stub brush they brush out their hair over a *coooo* catching all the livestock. This is a spur made of a forked stick and two buckskin strings. It looks very much like a bean snapper. This and this are skin scrapers or combs; they are made from a piece of bone about 6 inches long, one end is tapered to a point, the other end has a hole by which it is attached by string to the clothing or around the neck. It is used to scratch the head or any part of their bodies as the occasion demands. This is a mountain sheep horn spoon, holding a quart or more." Date unknown. (DMNS BR61-054)

Is Leaving Supai.
[...]u[...] Trail

the creation of a reservation. The next year, President Chester A. Arthur's Executive Order established the Hopi Reservation, encompassing 3,863 square miles.[119] In 1883, the Hopi and Navajo Agencies were formally joined under the supervision of Charles E. Burton.

At the turn of the century, the government operated five schools on the Hopi Reservation: the Hopi Boarding School, Western Navajo Boarding School, Oraibi Day School, Polacca Day School, and Second Mesa Day School (figure 3.33). In 1902, 420 pupils attended these various schools—a 182 percent net increase in attendance from 1899 when Burton first took charge of the joint Navajo-Hopi Agency.[120] Bratley's sudden appointment at the Polacca Day School several months into the school year was a result of the unexpected death of the schoolteacher's wife, Louise Barnes, in January 1902.[121] Her husband, Richard Barnes, subsequently transferred to Fort Shaw, Montana. Following Barnes's departure, administrators placed the Polacca Day School under the temporary direction of the two field matrons, Ms. Ritter and Ms. Abbott, until the Bratleys' arrival in early March.[122] In addition to their instructor duties, the Bratleys also served as postmaster and postmistress.[123]

FIGURE 3.31. This image captures Bratley's family traveling out of the Grand Canyon by burro, apparently leaving the Havasupai and making their way home to Kansas. Arizona, 1901. (DMNS BR61-013)

THE
PIONEERING
LIFE OF
JESSE H.
BRATLEY

FIGURE 3.32. Catholic missions had been built on the Hopi Mesas for centuries. Hopi Reservation, 1902. (DMNS BR61-131)

FIGURE 3.33. Polacca Day School pupils line up and show off their Euro-American-style clothing while remaining in bare feet. Hopi Reservation, 1902. (DMNS BR61-431)

The Polacca Day School was located at the base of First Mesa. When the Bratleys took charge of the school, there were thirty-eight students enrolled, with an average daily attendance of thirty-seven students.[124] Each of the three villages atop First Mesa had an appointed chief who conducted monthly visits to the Polacca Day School, sharing a meal with the children and observing the teacher's behavior. In addition to Jesse and Della, two Hopi assistants were employed at the school to aid in preparing the noonday meal as well as sewing and washing clothing. Receiving a salary of twenty dollars per month—ten dollars less than a White cook or laundress—these assistants not only facilitated school operations but served as important cultural mediators between the Hopi children and their instructors.[125]

Although Bratley was employed on the Hopi Reservation for only six months, a significant portion of his object and photograph collections was acquired there. While at Hopi, Bratley collected more than 250 objects and took almost 150 photographs. Although

THE
PIONEERING
LIFE OF
JESSE H.
BRATLEY

104

Bratley collected some sacred materials and took a handful of photos of ceremonies, he seems to have been primarily interested in documenting the quotidian aspects of Hopi life, amassing a large number of ceramics, basketry, dolls, and stone tools (figures 3.34 and 3.35).

This focus on commonplace objects and events is a defining characteristic of Bratley's collecting aesthetic, distinguishing him from the growing number of anthropologists and tourists flocking to the American Southwest in the early 1900s. The uniqueness of Bratley's collecting style was articulated by Hopi tribal member Lee Wayne Lomayestewa, who told us that "a lot of the researchers came out just looking for stuff to buy and a lot of them went for the ceremonial stuff . . . the museums went for altar pieces, katsinas, the

FIGURE 3.34. Bratley collected this polychrome ceramic canteen decorated with a katsina figure. Hopi Reservation, 1902. (DMNS AC.5848)

FIGURE 3.35. During an educational slide show presentation, Bratley used this image of a Hopi potter named Mrs. Chua (Rattlesnake) making clay coils and explained the production process for Hopi ceramics: "On this pottery plate she has her mud dough. Each time she takes off a piece as large as a biscuit and after working it in her hands she rolls it out into a string or rope between her hands as you see. This string of mud will just go around the vessel upon which she is working. She presses it firmly to the last tier and then with a piece of gourd shell which she dips into a bowl of water she smoothes [*sic*] the ring of mud on both the outside and the inside, and so on until the piece is finished. These four large pieces have just been finished and after they have dried a week or more she will polish the surface with a smooth rock dipped into water. Then after drying again for several days she will mark these pieces with various designs. These two small pieces are marked and ready to burn." Hopi Reservation, 1902. (DMNS BR61-221)

masks, and stuff like that. With his [Bratley's] collection, I think he was mostly interested in the dolls, the everyday stuff, not really sacred items."[126]

Although distinct in some ways from his peers, Bratley's collecting efforts at Hopi shared several similarities with other amateurs and professionals. For example, interviews with Hopi tribal members suggest that he posed subjects in some of his photographs, a practice common among photographers from this period (figures 3.36 and 3.37).[127]

Bratley was an avid reader, and early twentieth-century ethnographers also shaped his collecting practices. The influence of ethnographic texts on Bratley's collecting is exemplified by the fact that he took a significant number of notes on the Snake Dance during his reading of Thomas Donaldson's manuscript on the Hopi as well as diligently documenting the ceremony through several photographs.[128] Similarly, after reading and taking notes on the katsina dance described in the *15th Annual Report of the Bureau of Ethnology*, Bratley took photographs of the dance as Hopis performed it at the First Mesa village of Tewa.[129] While most Hopis we interviewed agree that Bratley likely took some photographs and objects without permission, many found his collections to be a useful reference. "We didn't preserve much when we were growing up, when things were happening," Lyman Polacca, an eighty-one-year-old Hopi elder, explained. "It's [museum collections] more

FIGURE 3.36. Bratley took this likely posed photo of Ruth Honavi (LEFT) and her friend Mabel (RIGHT) grinding corn on mealing stones. Along an evolutionary continuum, Bratley would have seen the Hopi as more advanced because of their agricultural traditions. Hopi Reservation, 1902. (DMNS BR61-220)

or less like a reference for us, when you look back. This is what they eat; this is the people who did this."[130]

In addition to photographing and collecting ethnographic objects, Bratley and his family spent their free time at Polacca hiking around the mesas—taking in the magnificent views and visiting historic sites. Bratley took a particular interest in archaeological sites, such as

Walnut Canyon and the ancient villages of Sikyátki and Awat'ovi (figure 3.38). Sikyátki is a pueblo on the eastern side of First Mesa that ancestral Hopi people resided in between AD 1300 and 1700.[131] Awat'ovi is located on nearby Antelope Mesa, occupied between AD 1150 and 1700; after a violent conflagration, surviving Hopis moved to the other mesas.[132] Years later, in 1932, inspired by a burned and deserted mansion the family passed by during a road trip from Yellowstone National Park to Miami, Bratley reminisced:

> It brought me back twenty years ago when my wife and I were teaching among the Hopi Pueblo Indians in northeastern Arizona and when we used to go out and look upon the ruins of Sikyátki and Awatovi, two ancient ruined cities all in ruins and of whom our Indians knew nothing. Fragments of pottery was [sic] everywhere around both ruins while at the latter ruin we found acres and acres of bones, where was their city of the dead ages ago. I am fearfully impelled as I look upon these relics of ages to ask: Is this the necessary fate of all peoples, of all civilization? Must all grow old, become effete and wither and die like an individual, while genius, learning, and progress take their flight to other lands? And must we, too, cover our lands with connecting lines of wire and rail, and build cities and temples, only that thousands of years hence other people may dig among our ruins and wonderingly inquire of us and our works. Who were these people and what was their fate?[133]

Bratley's journal entry offers insight into how he conceptualized the archaeological sites he visited. First, it seems he was unable to draw out Hopis to share their traditional stories about these special places, though highly contested in the case of Awat'ovi.[134] Furthermore, in conjuring parallels between Hopi ruins and American civilization, Bratley suggests that there is an overarching trajectory all societies share; they rise, they fall. His musings on social evolution also seem to reflect popular discourses in anthropology during the early 1900s, which placed societies on a linear trajectory in which

THE
PIONEERING
LIFE OF
JESSE H.
BRATLEY

108

FIGURE 3.38. Della Bratley stood by the doorway of a cliff dwelling in Walnut Canyon, an archaeological site, for a snapshot. In his personal journal, Bratley wrote: "The walls of Walnut Canon were deeply eroded in horizontal lines, forming recesses, roofed and floored by hard strata. In these niches are found the cliff dwellings, the front having been walled up with stone and mud. Charred corn cobs may be found where burned the cliff-dweller's last fire, centuries ago." Jesse's photographs and notebooks from his time in the Southwest exhibit a serious interest in archaeology. Arizona, 1901. (DMNS BR61-230)

FIGURE 3.39. Hopis herded sheep and goats, which likely would have helped Bratley see the tribe as industrious. Hopi Reservation, 1902. (DMNS BR61-124)

groups progressed from hunting-gathering through pastoralism and agriculture into modern industrialism (figure 3.39).

Kansas and Florida, 1903–1948

At the close of Polacca's school year, Bratley officially retired from the BIA. The greater opportunities for education available for the Bratley children back in Kansas prompted this decision. The Indian Service, in fact, had long discouraged couples from having children, in part because it did not allow White children to attend Indian day schools (a policy that changed in 1907), even as the service could not provide White children with any educational alternatives on reservations (figure 3.40).[135] More significant, even if White children could attend, Indian schools were not meant to provide anything more than a rudimentary education and were therefore perceived as too inferior for White children.[136]

In 1903, Bratley resumed his former life as a farmer, purchasing a 40-acre homestead near Wichita (figure 3.41). The Bratleys' last two children, Cyril and Forrest, were born. Unfortunately, Bratley's dreams of farming were again dashed in 1907, when the Arkansas River flooded, destroying the family's crops and livestock. Financially ruined and in search of a new life for his family, Bratley courted another change. After happening upon a newspaper clipping during jury duty, Bratley became enamored with Miami, Florida— entranced by the idea of fresh oranges and the temperate climate.

Upon setting foot in Florida in 1908, Bratley was so impressed that he immediately filed a homestead entry on a section of land near Redland, 30 miles south of Miami. Briefly returning to Wichita in 1909, Bratley quickly sold the ruined farmland and moved his family to Florida (figure 3.42). Yet even this new home did not present all the opportunities Bratley sought for his family. Bratley's own struggles with education had confirmed the importance of obtaining proper schooling for his children. He proclaimed that "the difficulty I encountered in taking examinations for the BIA, public school teaching jobs, and for the postal service . . . demonstrated the advances of a higher education. I promised myself that if possible, each of my children should receive a college education and degree."[137]

After two years, the Bratleys sold their rural home and accompanying lemon grove and moved to an estate along the Miami River. Because of Bratley's insistence on higher education for his children, all of them graduated from college and enjoyed successful white-collar careers: Homer became an etymologist at the University of Florida, Hazel became a teacher, Cyril became a professor of plant pathology, and Forrest became a pathologist in Jackson, Mississippi.

During the next several years, Bratley held various positions for the US Postal Service, working as clerk in the Miami post office and later as a rural letter carrier. He occasionally continued his collecting efforts, gathering a few items from the local Seminole community (figure 3.43). After two successive auto accidents on his postal route in 1923 and 1924, Bratley left the service and joined a real estate firm, selling property in the Miami area. Finally, in 1932, Bratley's long and miscellaneous career drew to a close. After retiring, Jesse and Della spent the rest of their days touring the country.

FIGURE 3.40. In this image, a small group of students receives instruction at the Cantonment Boarding School. The child to the front right center appears to be the Bratleys' son, Homer. He, too, is in uniform, which would suggest that the Bratleys understandably violated the BIA rule against including White children at Indian schools. Cheyenne and Arapaho Reservation, 1899–1900. (DMNS BR61-371)

THE
PIONEERING
LIFE OF
JESSE H.
BRATLEY

112

Following an unsuccessful operation for stomach cancer, in the summer of 1948, Jesse H. Bratley passed away. He was eighty-one years old. Although Bratley's life ended, his legacy would persist in the artifacts he collected, the photographs he took, and the stories his life encompassed.

FIGURE 3.43. Bratley collected this Seminole doll in Miami, Florida, which illustrates his continuing fascination with Native Americana even after his days as an Indian schoolteacher. Date unknown. (Children of Dr. Forrest G. Bratley)

Notes

1. Whitman 1900:183–186.
2. Turner 1893.
3. http://www.wisconsinhistory.org/Content.aspx?dsNav=N:4294963828-4294963788&dsRecordDetails=R:BA5410, accessed June 4, 2016.
4. Bratley n.d.a:2.
5. http://wichitachamber.org/experience_wichita-moving_here-history_of_wichita.php, accessed March 20, 2016.
6. Bratley n.d.a.:7.
7. Bratley n.d.a.:41.
8. Bratley n.d.a.:51.
9. Bratley n.d.a.:48.
10. Bratley n.d.a.:75.
11. Bratley n.d.a.:79.
12. Bratley n.d.a.:93.
13. Bratley n.d.a:94.
14. Bratley n.d.a.:100.
15. Bratley n.d.a.:96.
16. Bratley n.d.a.:96.
17. Purser 2012; Suttles 1990; Suttles and Lane 1990.
18. Lane and Lane 1977:1.
19. Rudy 1891.
20. Knox 1867.
21. Rudy 1891.
22. Eells 1894; Purser 2012:186.
23. Suttles 1990:457–459; Suttles and Lane 1990:489.
24. Beckwith 2015.
25. Eells 1893.
26. Bratley n.d.a:96–97.
27. Bratley 1893–1897:35.
28. Bratley n.d.a:100–101.
29. Bratley n.d.a.:99.
30. Bratley n.d.a.:97.
31. Bratley n.d.a.:52.
32. Bratley 1893–1897.
33. Bratley 1893–1897.
34. Bratley n.d.a.:102.
35. Bratley n.d.a.:100.
36. Browning 1895a:21.
37. Reel 1898.
38. Hailmann 1896:356.
39. Cahill 2011:56.
40. Cahill 2011:54.
41. Andrews 2002:413; Cahill 2011:55.
42. Cahill 2011:85.
43. Browning 1895b.
44. Bratley n.d.a.:103.
45. Browning 1895b.
46. Wright 1895:294.
47. DeMallie 2001a; Fenelon 2014:17; Ostler 2004; Wissler 1912.
48. DeMallie 2001b:796.
49. Ostler 2004.
50. Edwards 2012; Gonzalez and Cook-Lynn 1999.
51. Fenelon 2014:20.
52. Oberly 1885.
53. Ekquist 1999.
54. Foley 2002:18–20; Wright 1883.
55. Wright 1883.
56. Wright 1895:297.
57. Bratley n.d.a.:104.
58. Bratley n.d.a:104.
59. Bratley n.d.a.:104.
60. Bratley n.d.a.:104.
61. Waggoner 2013:489–490.
62. Hill 1912:10.
63. Dodge and Rogers 2000:62.
64. Hodge 1907:557.
65. Greene 1970:50.
66. Greene 1970:71.
67. Bratley n.d.a:105.
68. Bratley 1893–1897, 1897–1901.
69. Bratley 1893–1897.
70. Andrews 2002:429.
71. Cahill 2011:147.
72. Bratley n.d.a:109.
73. Little Dog 2016.
74. Jacobson 2009.
75. Jacobson 2009.
76. Dyck 1971.
77. Gonzalez 2016; Jones 1900c:706; McChesney 1900.
78. Mann 1997.
79. Dyck 1971; Fowler 2001:840; Kroeber 1902:5–7; Mooney 1907:72–74; Shakespeare 1971.
80. Coues 1897:384.
81. Mann 1997.
82. Scott 2009; Hoig 1974.
83. Cooley 1866:2; Dole 1861:17; Fowler 2001:842; Taylor 1868.
84. Parker 1869.
85. Whiteman 2016a.
86. McKellips 1992:12.
87. Walker 1871.
88. Miles 1878a.
89. Mann 1997.
90. Hoag 1875.
91. Berthrong 1992:82; Fowler 1982:73; Szasz 2006.
92. Moore 1996:273.
93. Mann 1997.
94. Miles 1878a.
95. Miles 1878a.
96. Stouch 1900:326.
97. Jones 1900c:706.
98. Bratley 1900:329.
99. Bratley 1900:330.
100. Bratley 1900:330.
101. Bratley 1897–1901.
102. Whiteman 2016b.
103. Atencio 1996:5; Schwartz 1983:13.
104. Atencio 1996:5; Dobyns and Euler 1971; Hirst 1985.
105. Dobyns and Euler 1971.
106. Bratley n.d.b.:110.
107. Schwartz 1983.
108. Jones 1900b.
109. Ewing 1900b:203.
110. Ewing 1900a.
111. Ewing 1900a.

112. Jones 1901:11.
113. Ewing 1901.
114. Bratley 1902b.
115. Frehill 1996.
116. Brew 1979:514; Kennard 1979:554.
117. Frigout 1979:564.
118. Dockstader 1979:524.
119. Jones 1902a:594.
120. Burton 1902:152.
121. Burton 1902:152.
122. Burton 1902:152.
123. Bratley n.d.a.:110.
124. Jones 1902b.
125. Bratley 1902d.
126. Lomayestewa 2016.
127. Lomayestewa 2016; Polacca 2016.
128. Bratley n.d.b.:21; Donaldson 1890.
129. Bratley n.d.b.:11; Fewkes 1880.
130. Polacca 2016.
131. https://www.britannica.com/place/sikyatki, accessed May 22, 2016.
132. Brooks 2016.
133. Bratley 1932.
134. Brooks 2016.
135. Cahill 2011:93–96.
136. Cahill 2011:97.
137. Bratley n.d.a.:113.

4

THE CIVILIZING MACHINE

Now the war against savagism would be waged in gentler fashion. The next Indian war would be ideological and psychological, and it would be waged against children.

—David Adams[1]

In 1893, when Bratley joined the Indian Service, the United States was suffering from what was euphemistically known at the time as the "Indian problem."[2] The problem was fairly straightforward: contrary to the hopes and predications of many government officials and citizens, Native Americans were not only still surviving but were continuing to inhabit large territories and practice traditional cultures. Persistence made Native people a liability, from the perspective of US federal policy. Surviving Native Americans stood in the way of a growing population of Euro-American settlers in search of land and the new economic opportunities that life on the frontier promised.

To solve the dilemma Indians posed, the US government developed a civilizing machine. Three interlocking cogs powered this machine: a martial force capable of ensuring compliance through real or threatened violence; a corps of civil employees who would educate Indian children in how to dress, speak, and work like "good Americans"; and an eager army of missionaries who would convert Native philistines into moral Christians. Once set in motion, the government intended the civilizing machine to transform the remaining Indigenous population of the United States into obedient and industrious citizens. As a member of the corps of Indian educators, Bratley intimately intertwined himself into the civilizing process.

The civilizing mission was rooted in a hope that Indians were capable of being assimilated once they were properly exposed to the superior influences of Anglo-American society—especially its beating heart, the Christian nuclear household (figure 4.1). To achieve this ideal, the federal government needed to transform family relations within Native homes as well as the social, economic, and political environment that surrounded them.[3] In the view of most government officials, the tribal community itself was the biggest barrier to its own advancement.[4]

In the late 1800s, the federal government took a two-pronged approach to removing this barrier: allotment and education. As the historian Paul Stuart has documented, after 1865 "Congress

and the Indian Office established a reservation system for American Indians and subsequently created a mechanism for destroying it. Education and the allotment of Indian lands, they thought, would end the reservation system and assure the civilization of the Indians."[5]

First, they sought to dissolve traditional forms of leadership and social organization through the allotment of reservation lands to individuals.[6] In addition to breaking down communal social and economic systems, the federal government sought to sever the ties between individuals and their tribal units by removing Indian children from the corroding influences of Native society. Government administrators and teachers sincerely believed that with education would come, as the commissioner of Indian affairs wrote in 1900, "morality, cleanliness, self-respect, industry, and, above all, Christianized humanity, the foundation stone of the world's progress and wellbeing."[7]

Work Conquers All

The boarding school became one of the primary means to achieve these ends, an institution perfected by the Civil War veteran Richard Henry Pratt. In 1875, authorities charged Pratt with reforming seventy-two resistance leaders of the Kiowa, Comanche, Caddo,

FIGURE 4.1. A Havasupai man named Prince Wado poses with a woman, presumably his wife, and two children. Many of Bratley's images depict the nuclear family—the ideal family model in the Protestant Anglo-American mode. Havasupai Reservation, 1900–1901. (DMNS BR61-068)

Cheyenne, and Arapaho Tribes the US Army had captured and exiled to Fort Marion in St. Augustine, Florida. There Pratt experimented with various techniques that would later become part of the Indian school system—including cutting the prisoners' hair, dressing them in army uniforms, imposing forced physical labor, and providing instruction in reading and writing English.[8]

The driving force behind Pratt's civilizing experiment was their physical transformation from hostile savages to friendly citizens, a goal that was realized for some prisoners such as Howling Wolf. Marveling over the change in Howling Wolf's appearance, Pratt latter wrote, "We saw a dapper gentleman, with hand satchel, derby hat and cane pass up the sea wall into the fort with a quick step, and I went to the fort to see who it was, and found that Howling Wolf had returned unannounced, his eyes greatly benefited, and in addition, in his dress, manner, and conduct, he had imbibed a large stock of Boston qualities."[9] For Pratt, Howling Wolf's new style of dress and speech demonstrated the transformative effects of exposure to proper Anglo-American society.

With the sponsorship of White philanthropists, twenty-two of those imprisoned at Fort Marion—most of them young bachelors—sought further schooling at the Hampton Institute in Virginia, the Episcopalian "School for the Prophets" in New York, and as private students of Amy Caruthers, a former instructor at the fort in Tarrytown, Pennsylvania. Other former prisoners showed their support for Pratt's vision by assisting him in reconstructing the Carlisle barracks, and some even volunteered to send their children to Carlisle.[10] The vast majority of these prisoners, however, returned to their tribal communities on the Plains following their release in 1878.[11] While some of these former prisoners faced difficulty finding employment, others found a means of applying their newly acquired education by working in agency schools and clinics.[12]

Although achieving some success in transforming his prisoners, Pratt's experiment in education ultimately led him to the conclusion that his adult prisoners learned too slowly. Therefore, the best means of civilizing Indians was through the education of their children.[13] To achieve this vision, in 1879, Pratt converted an old military barracks in Carlisle, Pennsylvania, into the Carlisle Indian School—an early example of the physical transformation of barracks into schools.[14]

At Carlisle, Pratt created a military-style system of discipline. He issued uniforms, organized students into companies, and conducted drills.[15] Pratt's avid promotion of technical training also became a central tenet of the Indian education system. Although Jesse H. Bratley likely never knew Pratt, the legacy of Pratt's movement lived on in Bratley's approach to teaching: the uniforms, orderly presentation of students, regimented schedules, and technical training (figure 4.2).

School administrators embraced Pratt's assimilationist goals, believing that their work was a humane way of cleansing Indians of their culture while allowing them to join the American way of life.[16] As Pratt famously wrote in 1892, the aim was to "kill the Indian in him, and save the man."[17] Congressional acts passed in 1891 and 1893 expanded Pratt's

FIGURE 4.2 (above). The crisp uniforms and ordered lines of students outside the Cantonment Boarding School emphasize the military logic imposed in Indian boarding schools. Cheyenne and Arapaho Reservation, 1899–1900. (DMNS BR61-378)

FIGURE 4.3 (left). The issuing of rations was a central part of the US government's efforts to control Native Americans. Rosebud Reservation, 1898. (DMNS BR61-446)

approach to Indian education, which authorized the US commissioner of Indian affairs to "withhold rations, clothing, and other annuities from Indian parents or guardians who refuse or neglect to send and keep their children of proper school age in school" (figure 4.3).[18] Although these injunctions were often sufficient to produce compliance from Native families, the government occasionally used imprisonment and martial force to coerce families into acquiescence.[19]

In contrast to boarding schools, day schools allowed children to return home to their families each night. The structure of the day school created a more fluid dynamic between teachers and the surrounding community. In this system, teachers were often participants in the same "barbarous" activities their presence was intended to discourage and replace.

Bratley's experiences epitomize the close relationship that could develop between teachers and tribal communities. In many of the reservations he worked on, Bratley seems to have developed close ties with tribal members, attending communal clambakes among the S'Klallam and collective giveaways at Rosebud (figure 4.4). In addition to attending

FIGURE 4.4. Bratley captured an image of Lakota Sioux men giving away horses. Generosity is one of the basic moral values of Lakota Sioux society, and giveaways were used as public demonstrations of generosity and provided a means of honoring an individual's accomplishments. Rosebud Reservation, 1895–1899. (DMNS BR61-249)

FIGURE 4.5. According to Lee Wayne Lomayestewa, a Hopi tribal member, the Hopi band traveled across the United States playing marching music in parades from the 1930s through the 1950s. This image of the band outside the Bratleys' Miami home suggests that some Hopis made lasting friendships with Jesse. Florida, 1936. (DMNS BR61-426)

communal events, Bratley seems to have developed real friendships with community members, as exemplified by his heartfelt encounter with his former student Elk Teeth at the Chicago World's Fair and with Hopi musicians who once visited him in Miami (figure 4.5).

Although Indian day schools were situated close to or within Native communities, they were also totalizing institutions that "served as the educational outposts of civilization."[20] In addition to transforming Indian boys and girls into embryonic citizens, officials believed that day schools were strategically placed to alter Native home life. In his 1898 report, Commissioner of Indian Affairs William A. Jones noted the particular contribution of day schools, stating that "these schools bring a portion of the 'white mans' civilization to the home of the Indian. His children are in daily contact with the old

Within the image: No. 119. Sewing Girls, Lower Cut Meat School, Rosebud Agency, S.D. Sioux. '98

traditions and the new ideas of the school."[21] The child thus became the means of civilizing the Indian home. Stationed in distant outposts, day schoolteachers like Jesse and Della served as exemplars of civilized living: married, industrious, and faithful.[22]

Della Bratley accompanied her husband so he could pursue a career in the Indian Service, but she became a part of the school system herself, filling the role of field matron. First created in 1890, the duties of the matron were to "improve and elevate the home life of Indians, instructing the women in cooking, dress-making, etc., also instructing and assisting in the care of the sick."[23] In the government's carefully crafted civilizing program, the White man's home was "a radiating center of enlightenment and refinement," which provided a model Indian women could emulate.[24]

As field matron at Lower Cut Meat Creek Day School, Della Bratley was burdened with the task of teaching Sioux girls and women the new ways of eating, sleeping, dressing, working, and sanitation that accompanied the transition from tipi to cabin (figure 4.6).

FIGURE 4.6. This portrait of Lakota Sioux girls at the Lower Cut Meat Creek Day School reveals the total physical transformation of Indian school students. SEATED: Gracie Good Bird, Emma Elk Looks Back, Bessie Elk Looks Back. STANDING: Maggie Otterman, Rosa Elk Teeth, Nellie Foot, Kittie Turning Eagle. Rosebud Reservation, 1895–1899. (DMNS BR61-283)

THE CIVILIZING MACHINE

121

FIGURE 4.7. Bratley titled this image *Before Entering School*, likely capturing in his mind the need to transform the students on the left in traditional outfits to be more similar to those students on the right in Western clothing. LEFT TO RIGHT: Cora Search the Enemy Out, Alice Good Kill, Lucy Kills Plenty, John Underwater, Willie Good Bird, Paul Grey Eagle Tail, Allen Otterman. Rosebud Reservation, 1897. (DMNS BR61-286)

The success of such efforts was uneven. As Luther Standing Bear, a Carlisle graduate, acidly observed about a new teacher at Cut Meat Creek sometime in the 1880s, "While this young woman was smart enough in books, she knew very little else."[25]

At both day and boarding schools, Indian students underwent a full physical and cultural transformation that was to rid them of the malady of savagery.[26] This conversion commenced with the physical transformation of the pupil's appearance, which teachers such as Bratley helped administer (figure 4.7).

Part of this transformation involved the regular bathing of all schoolchildren. At the Lower Cut Meat Creek Day School, this ritual occurred every Monday morning, during which time the girls were sent to the sewing room with Della and the boys to the carpentry shop with Jesse. As Jesse recalled, "With three tubs in each place, and with the help of the older pupils, we soon put the younger children through and on up until all had their bath."[27] During one bath, Bratley came face to face with the legacy of the wounds that remained from the Indian Wars—specifically, the Massacre at Wounded Knee, during which upward of 300 Native Americans were slaughtered (figure 4.8). Bratley wrote:

One time, when I was bathing the boys in the shop I noticed a very white spot on the right thigh of Sammy Plenty-Holes, a six-year-old boy. I asked him what caused the white spot. He said, "I was shot." The bullet passed through his leg where the two white spots indicated. I inquired of the mother, Mrs. Plenty-Holes, how it all happened. She said she was with Sammy, who was nearly one year old, in the Wounded Knee Battle. A terrific blizzard was coming on as the battle took place. The dead and wounded were covered with the drifting snow and laid there three days before rescue parties reached them. Mrs. Howling-Elk, who received thirteen bullet holes, and her wounded baby, laid three days in the snow drifts and both survived. Sammy's mother's name was changed to Plenty-Holes on account of the thirteen wounds.[28]

Bratley's account speaks to the inherent corporality of the colonial project in North America: whether through the tearing of flesh with bullets on the battlefield or the cleansing of savage bodies in the school bathing house, the conquest of the American frontier was intimately intertwined with the subjugation of Native bodies.

In addition to bathing, teachers forced all pupils to undergo an additional set of corporal transformations at the beginning of each school year (figure 4.9). This annual ritual involved cutting the boys' hair, removing their Indian camp clothes, and dressing them in school uniforms. For new students, their transformation was complete once they were issued an Anglicized first name (figure 4.10).[29] In addition, students were to take new last names, typically retaining their father's Indian name as their surname.[30] Even this change was not always welcome. As a former missionary turned teacher, Corabelle Fellows, recalled her experience on the Cut Meat Reservation in the mid-1880s: "I nearly precipitated civil war when I attempted to call each child in the family by the father's name. The men stormed the schoolroom, wagging their heads fiercely and vociferously repeating, 'Hecca tu sni!' ('This is all a mistake!')."[31]

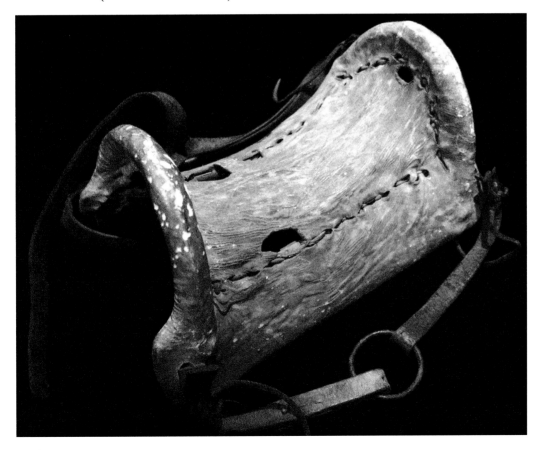

FIGURE 4.8. Bratley collected this elk horn saddle. A written note underneath claims that Chief Big Foot used the saddle during the Massacre at Wounded Knee in 1890. (Children of Dr. Forrest G. Bratley)

FIGURE 4.9. Students present themselves in front of the Lower Cut Meat Creek Day School. STANDING (LEFT TO RIGHT): Eddie Foot, Policeman Lee Wood, Tommy Otterman, Emma Elk Looks Back, Cora Search the Enemy Out, Gracie Good Bird, Frank Sleeping Bear, Bessie Elk Looks Back, Maggie Otterman, Kittie Turning Eagle, Nellie Foot, Lucy Kills Plenty, Tommy One Wood, Minnie Underwater, Stella Good Bird, Hattie With Horns. KNEELING: Sammy Slow Fly, George Kills Plenty, Levi Elk Looks Back, Charles Black Calf, Freddie Sitting Bear. FRONT ROW: Nat Elk Teeth, Jesse Foot, Allen Otterman, Samuel Yellow Robe, John Underwater, Chas New, Harry With Horns, Thomas New, Jossie Elk Teeth, Standing Little Tail. Rosebud Reservation, 1899. (DMNS BR61-281)

Despite institutional efforts to create new Anglo-American identities for Native children, these new names were largely superficial markers that many children left behind in the class-room at the end of the day.[32] Once at home, children were not known by their Anglicized name—a practice that continues among Native people today.

The total physical transformation Native students under-went is captured in a statement by Rita Black, a Cheyenne elder, in discussing her father's, Dana Black Kettle's, return to the reservation from Carlisle in the 1920s. Laughing, Black told us Cheyenne tribal members "thought that he was a White boy when he got back. He had no braids and a real light complexion."[33]

The community's reaction to Dana Black Kettle's return was precisely the response the program of Indian education aimed to evoke. Stripping students of all outward signs of "Indianness" was the first step toward eradicating all other elements of tribal culture. As many scholars have noted, in contexts of asymmetrical power, clothing and hairstyle are not simply benign forms of self-expression; rather, the body acts as a key site for the daily exercise of social control (figure 4.11).[34]

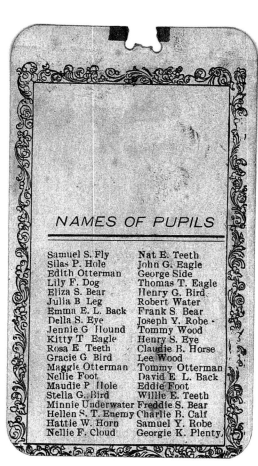
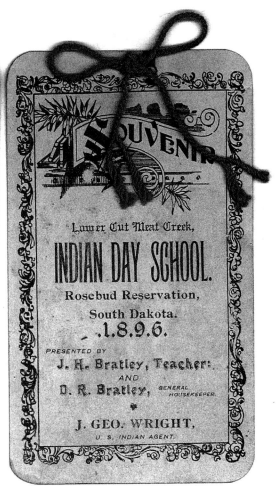

NAMES OF PUPILS

Samuel S. Fly	Nat E. Teeth
Silas P. Hole	John G. Eagle
Edith Otterman	George Side
Lily F. Dog	Thomas T. Eagle
Eliza S. Bear	Henry G. Bird
Julia B Leg	Robert Water
Emma E. L. Back	Frank S. Bear
Della S. Eye	Joseph Y. Robe
Jennie G Hound	Tommy Wood
Kitty T Eagle	Henry S. Eye
Rosa E Teeth	Claudie R. Horse
Gracie G Bird	Lee Wood
Maggie Otterman	Tommy Otterman
Nellie Foot	David E L. Back
Maudie P Hole	Eddie Foot
Stella G. Bird	Willie E. Teeth
Minnie Underwater	Freddie S. Bear
Hellen S. T. Enemy	Charlie B. Calf
Hattie W. Horn	Samuel Y. Robe
Nellie F. Cloud	Georgie K. Plenty.

SOUVENIR

Lower Cut Meat Creek,

INDIAN DAY SCHOOL.

Rosebud Reservation,

South Dakota.

.1.8.9.6.

PRESENTED BY

J. H. Bratley, Teacher:

AND

D. R. Bratley, GENERAL HOUSEKEEPER.

J. GEO. WRIGHT,

U. S. INDIAN AGENT.

Although often cloaked in moralizing language, these bodily transformations were fundamentally about manufacturing "civilized and obedient souls in civilized and obedient bodies."[35] As historian William E. Farr has suggested with photographs of schoolchildren elsewhere, Bratley's images likewise "clearly demonstrate that white modernity arrived via a succession of small and seemingly insignificant things. . . . boots for moccasins, cotton for hide, sewing machines in place of needles and thread."[36]

The physical transformation of Native children into civilized citizens is embodied by a hair-cutting episode that occurred during Bratley's tenure at Polacca. During the winter of 1902, an official order was issued to cut the hair of all Indians on the reservation. It was argued that as an overt symbol of barbarism, long hair was "the last tie that binds them [Indians] to their old customs of savagery, and the sooner it is cut, Gordian like, the better it will be for them."[37] Bratley himself echoed the important role of hair cutting in the civilizing process, stating:

It does make me—yes, I'll use the term—"hot" to have squaw men, editors, and other so-called Indian sympathizers make such a howl about the hair cutting. They do not know anything about it, but if they had gone as an employee to an Indian school to some of the wily Plains tribes and remained five or more years, then I dare say that every one of them would say with us that "had every male Indian below the old grandfather been required to

FIGURE 4.10. A printed list of pupils at the Lower Cut Meat Creek Day School in 1896 documents the students' mix of Anglicized and Indigenous names. (DMNS Archives)

FIGURE 4.11. The image of a Lakota Sioux man wearing a Euro-American suit with his wife and two children dressed in traditional clothing suggests how different members of a single family might choose to adopt or reject Western norms. It also illustrates how an individual's willingness to embrace Western norms likely reveals deeper expressions of self-identity. Rosebud Reservation, 1895–1899. (DMNS BR61-307)

cut and to keep his hair short for the last five years, then the civilizing of the Indian would at least have been ten years further along than it is today."[38]

Bratley's statement articulates the perceived connection between physical conformity to Anglo standards of appearance and a deeper internal transformation. It was well understood among federal administrators that long hair was not simply an aesthetic practice but, as Bratley wrote in the official report on the Polacca Day School he submitted to the commissioner of Indian affairs in 1902, was "a part of their [Native peoples'] very being and religion" (figures 4.12 and 4.13).[39]

Divested of all outward indicators of "Indianness," students then underwent a rigorous program of intellectual re-programing and technical training.[40] Each day, teachers instructed students in reading, writing, music, drawing, history, and arithmetic to develop "the child's aesthetic sense."[41] Even play and sports were tools for indoctrination of Western ideals of personal character.[42] Coupled with proper instruction in the Protestant work ethic, these acts of transformation created a new identity for each pupil—an identity that subscribed to dominant American norms of appearance and manner.

Bratley rigorously followed the civilizing mission and liberal arts curriculum mandated by the Indian Service. He collected and saved some of these lessons, including art projects, mathematical ledgers with simple addition, and writing samples from his students at the Lower Cut Meat Creek Day School.[43]

The scope of the transformation Native people were undergoing during the nineteenth century—and the school as a site for "cultural production," where Native children had to actively construct new meanings for their lives—is captured in one such writing assignment composed by a young Lakota Sioux girl named Emma Elk Looks Back in 1899 (figure 4.14).[44] In perfect cursive, Emma describes her family's home, detailing all the modern trappings of their cabin, including stove, red curtains, and bedding. While Emma's description resembles the cabin of a typical White homesteader from the period, it stands in stark contrast to the traditional trappings that would have made up Lakota Sioux tipis.

FIGURE 4.12. As gentle, life-giving creatures, Hopi culture likens women to butterflies, a belief that was reflected in the butterfly whorl hairstyle worn by women who had completed the puberty ceremony and were eligible for marriage. A U-shaped wooden frame maintains the "butterfly" shape. (DMNS AC.5959A)

▼ ▽ ▼

Many of the community members we interviewed discussed the trauma associated with these physical and cultural transformations. In reminiscing about her mother's, Clare

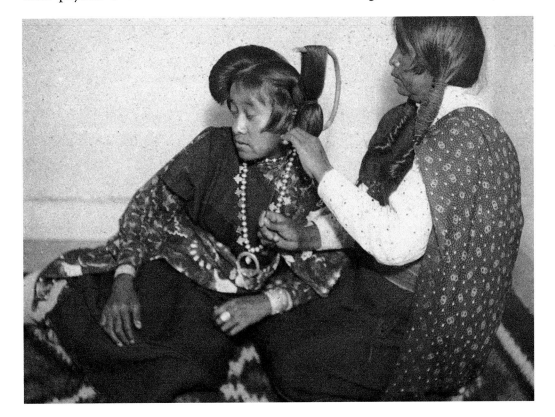

FIGURE 4.13. Bratley captured this scene, likely posed, of Ruth Honavi having her hair dressed in the traditional butterfly style. Hopi Reservation, 1902. (DMNS BR61-233).

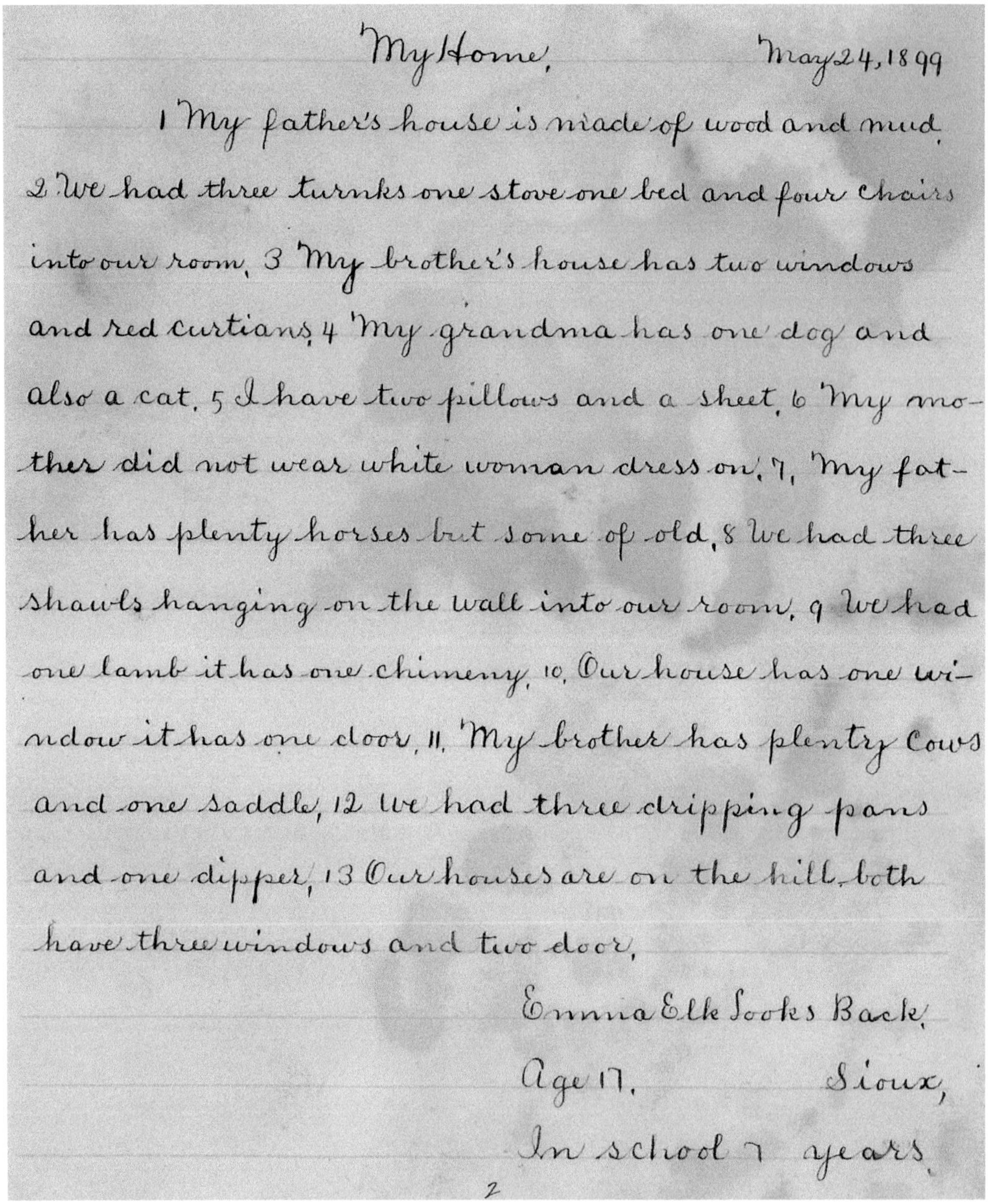

My Home,   *May 24, 1899*

1 My father's house is made of wood and mud. 2 We had three turnks one stove one bed and four chairs into our room. 3 My brother's house has two windows and red curtians 4 My grandma has one dog and also a cat. 5 I have two pillows and a sheet. 6 My mother did not wear white woman dress on. 7, My father has plenty horses but some of old, 8 We had three shawls hanging on the wall into our room. 9 We had one lamb it has one chimeny. 10, Our house has one window it has one door, 11, My brother has plenty cows and one saddle, 12 We had three dripping pans and one dipper, 13 Our houses are on the hill, both have three windows and two door,

                          Emma Elk Looks Back,
          Age 17.   Sioux,
               In school 7 years,

                    2

FIGURE 4.14. Emma Elk Looks Back describes her house and family in the "My Home" writing lesson she completed at the Lower Cut Meat Creek Day School in 1899. It is striking that the essay focuses on the home—the true target of the civilizing machine—and that Elk Looks Back notes that "my mother did not wear white woman dress on." The comment likely revealed to Bratley the failure of Elk Looks Back's home to fully conform to White Victorian standards of domesticity. (DMNS Archives)

Whitehat's, days at Cantonment Boarding School, Patricia Gonzalez said, "I guess the transition was really hard for her because everything she talked about Cantonment was negative. She talked about having her mouth washed out with soap when they talked their language—the Arapaho language."[45]

As early as 1886, Commissioner of Indian Affairs John Atkins proudly proclaimed that there is "not an Indian pupil whose tuition and maintenance is paid for by the United States Government who is permitted to study any other than our own vernacular—the language of the greatest, most powerful, and enterprising nationalities under the sun."[46] In 1890, a new BIA regulation gave Atkins's declaration legal heft, requiring that "pupils be compelled to converse with each other in English, and should be properly rebuked or

punished for persistent violation of this rule."[47] Although not everyone agreed with this diktat even at the time of its issuance, administrators eventually softened on the level to which tribal dialects should be permitted in school while continuing to foreground the English language's essential civilizing role.[48]

Throughout his teaching career, Bratley experienced many difficulties in communicating with his pupils and fulfilling the government mandate to exclusively speak and teach English in the classroom. Bratley's first challenge in teaching English occurred during his early years among the S'Klallam (figure 4.15). This was a decisive moment in Bratley's life as an educator. He later vividly recounted his struggles to accomplish this goal:

> I then got out the chart. It had a picture of a big cat on the first page with the word "cat" printed in big black letters. I tried to get them to say cat, but I did not succeed. They did not understand English. They did not know what I said or wanted. I tried this two times a day for a couple of days. I became so disgusted and sick of teaching Indians that I wrote home for $165 to buy a steamboat ticket to Seattle, then a railroad ticket back to the old farm in sunny Kansas. It took five weeks for the money to reach me. During the night after I had mailed the letter home, the idea came to me if I got Anna [an elderly S'Klallam woman he had commissioned to bring truant children to the school] to teach me the Indian words to use, I could get the children to speak. So the next morning, I found Anna very pleased to do this and she said, "You say *meskia chahko wauwau* cat, then they will say cat." I wrote this out and studied it. Then we went out and brought the children in and lined them up by the

FIGURE 4.15. This image of Bratley and his students on the Spit is one of the few he took while in Port Gamble. Although the quality of the image is no doubt without meaning, it is hard not to read the burned print as a metaphor for Bratley's struggles among the S'Klallam. (Children of Dr. Forrest G. Bratley)

chart and I repeated what the squaw had told me and the little boy next to the chart, whom I had named Cyrus, looked at me in such a manner as to say, "the teacher has gone crazy." That is just the way I felt. I repeated "*Mesika* (you) *chahke* (come) *wauwau* (speak or say) cat." Cyrus spoke right up, saying "cat." I cannot describe my elation for I realized at once that I could teach these Indians. Only I must get Anna to teach me the Indian equivalent. This she very willingly did. I got along well by this system.[49]

Bratley's interaction with Anna is notable in several ways. To teach Bratley how to communicate with his Native pupils, Anna chose to use Chinook Jargon as opposed to the S'Klallam language—a linguistic difference Bratley likely failed to recognize. Many considered S'Klallam—along with other Northwest Coast languages—too complex for non-Native speakers to learn.[50] As a result, Chinook Jargon developed as a polyglot trade language. As a simplistic language with a small vocabulary, Chinook Jargon offered an efficient mode of communication among Bratley, Anna, the students, and the larger S'Klallam community.[51]

The encounter between Anna and Bratley is also notable for Anna's willingness to assist Bratley in educating S'Klallam youth. As an elder, Anna would have held high status in the community; her actions would have been seen as setting an example for other residents. Reflecting on this encounter, S'Klallam tribal member Kelly Sullivan told us, "One thing I noticed just from the little bit of reading is that Anna is advocating, like she can see that maybe there is some value in getting them to learn some English."[52] Sullivan's statement suggests that while many parents opposed the Indian education system, some tribal members may have viewed learning English as a beneficial skill—a sentiment that would have been particularly true for many of the Port Gamble residents who regularly worked in the White town and sawmill across the bay.

Yet even Indian Service leaders recognized the devastating psychological impact of suppressing tribal languages. As Superintendent of Indian Schools William N. Hailmann wrote in 1896: "To throw contempt upon the child's vernacular, in which he has heretofore given expression to thoughts and feelings dear to him, and by means of which he is held in ties of sympathy and love with his kindred[,] is so manifestly unreasonable and so pernicious in its perverting and destructive influence upon the child's heart-life that it is a wonder that it ever should have been attempted by the philanthropic fervor of workers in Indian schools."[53]

The lasting impact of these policies for Native people is revealed in the frequent reticence of many tribal members to teach their children Native languages. Although it seems that not all tribal schools tightly enforced compulsory English, even the rhetoric of tribal languages as inferior discouraged parents who had attended a BIA school from passing on a Native tongue to their children.[54]

The sentiment that tribal languages were a part of the past and were not needed to be successful in America was articulated by Arapaho elder Fred Mosquida when discussing his mother, Armin Jean Howling Buffalo, who had attended Concho Boarding School during the 1920s. "Our mother, when we were growing up, she would basically tell us we didn't need to learn it [Arapaho]," Mosquida said. "I guess it still stuck in her mind about how when she was at the boarding school she was restricted from speaking it."[55] Cheyenne elder Gordon Yellowman recalled a similar experience; he recounted that his parents had consciously decided to not speak the Cheyenne language in the house and had pushed him and his siblings to attend public school and learn English.[56]

Mosquida's and Yellowman's comments suggest that many Native people during the twentieth century internalized the rhetoric of the civilizing paradigm. It was so successful that many Native American languages are today on the brink of extinction.

In addition to regular lessons in English and the liberal arts, the Indian school curriculum was structured around industrial training, particularly in those "mechanical arts and pursuits supposed to be most closely related to their chances of earning a livelihood in later years."[57] Accordingly, teachers instructed Indian girls in domestic arts while boys were given manual training in carpentry, metalworking, and agricultural industries. Such training, however, was geared less toward vocational achievements and more toward inculcating gender and social roles.[58]

Bratley captured the transformational impact of vocational education in his photographs of students at the Lower Cut Meat Creek Day School. In one image, Della Bratley watches patiently as four Lakota Sioux girls practice their sewing and ironing (figure 4.16). Sewing and mending were part of a larger program of study that included lessons in the care of bedrooms, preparation of food, laundering, dairying, and care of the sick.[59]

The training Native girls received was modeled on a Victorian standard of middle-class White domesticity, which presumed "that the pupil will not go out to work but will return home after finishing the day or reservation boarding school course."[60] Underlying this model of domesticity was a belief that manual labor in domestic arts would create subservient and productive citizens (figure 4.17).[61] "Knowledge of sewing means a support for many," as Superintendent of Indian Schools Estelle Reel wrote in her 1901 annual report to Congress. "Skill in the art of using the needle is important to every women and girl as an aid to domestic neatness and economy and as a help to profitable occupation."[62] By teaching young girls how to sew, cook, and clean, Della Bratley reinforced the basic Victorian vision of women as efficient homemakers.

At many of Bratley's schools, he also instructed students in agriculture and livestock rearing. For example, at Cantonment, Bratley taught boys how to cultivate oats, onions, peanuts, potatoes, and alfalfa (figure 4.18).[63] In addition to these crops, under Bratley's supervision students planted a large number of fruit trees (apple, peach, plum, cherry, and nectarine) as well as 150 grapevines and 50 blackberry bushes.[64] While attempts at large-

FIGURE 4.16. Lakota girls learned how to make clothes under the watchful eye of Della Bratley in the Lower Cut Meat Creek Day School's sewing room. FROM LEFT TO RIGHT: Gracie Good-Bird, Della Bratley, Emma Elk Looks Back, Nellie Foot, and Bessie Elk Looks Back. Rosebud Reservation, 1895–1899. (DMNS BR61-284)

scale agriculture on the southern and northern Plains often failed, small garden plots, like the one created by Bratley, were frequently successful.

These plots were typically located near narrow, well-watered bottomlands. Consisting largely of hardy root crops like potatoes and onions, gardens like those at Cantonment fared better than agriculture plots filled with industrial products such as wheat and corn. Furthermore, in contrast to the expensive water projects necessary to support irrigation agriculture, school gardens required minimal capital, and students had enough time during the day to tend to their plots.[65] The cultivation of garden plots was a fundamental component of the education system, providing students with technical training in Western industries while alleviating some of the financial burden of feeding pupils.[66]

Over time, industrial training, then commonly referred to as the "art of living," became more important than the kind of book learning that might lead to white-collar professions. In 1900, Superintendent Reel—Bratley's boss—stressed the role of labor and, by association, training in manual industries in producing a sustainable social structure for tribes. "Labor is the basis of all lasting civilization and the most potent influence for good in the world," Reel wrote. "Whenever any race, of its own volition, begins to labor its future is assured."[67]

Ideology lay at the heart of the federal government's emphasis on technical training. While for Native girls, education in domestic arts was intended to inculcate Victorian ideals of femininity and modesty, for Native boys, education in farming and metalworking was used to instill a particular notion of manhood. During the late nineteenth and early

twentieth centuries, American manhood was defined as a combination of masculinity, exemplified by bodily strength and fitness, and manliness demonstrated through displays of morality and courage.[68]

In addition to academic and technical training, White notions of manhood were introduced to Native boys through athletic competitions, particularly football. Uniting formal efforts to train Native boys in industrial arts and athletics was a belief in the power of physical labor to transform the mind and soul. The football field was an arena in which Native boys could publicly demonstrate these accepted notions of manhood. As suggested by historian Matthew Bentley, on the pitch, Native boys displayed that they "held power over their innate Indian and savage nature" and in doing so, "the players demonstrated their civilization and subsequent manliness."[69]

Although Richard Henry Pratt was initially reticent to allow his students to play football, he soon came to see these athletic contests as a valuable propaganda opportunity. According to Pratt, by winning games against Anglo-Saxon athletes from elite schools like Harvard and Yale, Carlisle athletes would accomplish several goals. Through displays of strength, intelligence, and sportsmanship, Carlisle players would provide a counterpoint to the popular Wild West shows that emphasized the barbarity of Native people through violent reenactments of the Indian Wars. Instead of treacherous savages, football matches would promote an image of Native people as brainy, self-disciplined, courteous athletes who could beat the White man at his own game. In addition to providing an alternative image of Native men, the growing popularity of football offered a strategic opportunity to win the support of a wider public for the government's assimilationist agenda.[70]

The impact of football on Native communities is captured in a story shared by Cheyenne tribal member Marie Whiteman about meeting Jim Thorpe, a Sac and Fox tribal member who was a standout football player and two-time All-American at Carlisle:

> We were at Anadarko [Oklahoma] and he was Indian of the Year that year. And, he was sitting there and of course we didn't know him right off, we had just walked in for the afternoon performance and I was going to dance. And he first said, "Hello girls," and we said "Hello there," and then went on and they introduced him. And, I said to my cousin I'm going to introduce myself to him because my dad went to school with him and knew him. So, I went over and introduced myself to him and he said, "Oh, White Bird's daughter!" And, he went on and was saying what good friends they were.[71]

While Pratt may have viewed football as transforming Native men into American gentlemen, Whiteman's story suggests that for some Native people, football served a different purpose. Team sports like football provided an opportunity for Native boys to work together toward a common self-defined goal: victory over non-Native athletes. In doing so, these competitions created a sense of solidarity and a shared identity among athletes from diverse backgrounds and tribal nations, a process reflected in Thorpe's description of White Bird as a "good friend." Furthermore, athletes like Thorpe provided a positive role model for Native students, demonstrating how to achieve success within a new system while maintaining one's cultural values and identity.

In addition to teaching local residents Euro-American forms of irrigation and agriculture, Bratley proudly recalled his effort to introduce the icehouse to the Lakota Sioux (figure 4.19):

> I went to work with the Indian boys, a scraper, and with my team, we made a dirt dam across the creek. We cleared the three acres in the bend [and] were ready for the winter snows, which always came in the cold Dakotas. When the snow melted up-creek, it filled

our pond to the brim. We had another late cold spell that first winter which froze all the water in the pond. This gave me another idea, which was to build an icehouse and fill it with ice, so as to have ice during the hot summer days. The boys and I went to work and dug into the Badland bank just back of the shops. This faced the north. The Indian Agent supplied enough lumber to line the walls and for the roof. We put dirt on the board roof to insulate the top. The ice was too thick to saw. We had to cut it out in big chunks with axes. It did not pack well in the icehouse. However, we put up more than enough to last us all summer. The next season and each winter thereafter, we watched the ice and when it became eight inches thick, we sawed the ice into squares that we would lay up nicely in the icehouse. We had ice continuously to the end of the four years we were at this school. Our milk house was in front of the ice house and we set our milk and butter in the drain from the ice. The ice was something that no other of the twenty schools had.[72]

Although the community eventually adopted many of these foreign practices, including Euro-American-style irrigation, this transition was not always immediate. Bratley noted that Lakota Sioux children initially refused to eat the tomatoes, milk, and ice cream they produced each year, preferring to eat more traditional crops, such as raw pumpkins and watermelons (figure 4.20).[73]

Such efforts toward transformation in the schools were set within the Indian Service's larger effort to transform entire communities (figure 4.21). The Indian Service also under-

FIGURE 4.19. Bratley and the schoolboys built a pond to provide water for irrigating the school's garden. In winter, students cut ice from the pond and stored it in a house built into the north wall of the badlands. The icehouse kept milk, butter, and ice cream cool throughout the school year. Rosebud Reservation, 1895–1899. (DMNS BR61-327)

FIGURE 4.20. In this image, schoolboys drive a horse-drawn cart and carry watermelons grown in the Lower Cut Meat Creek Day School garden. Rosebud Reservation, 1895–1899. (DMNS BR61-180)

FIGURE 4.21. Planners outfitted Indian schools with industrial equipment for students to learn new trades. A group of boys playing in front of the carpenter and blacksmith shops at Lower Cut Meat Creek Day School—pretending to ride bicycles by using the wheels of the teacher's spring wagon—suggests the students' fascination with the new technology rising in industrial America. Rosebud Reservation, 1895–1899. (DMNS BR61-269)

took projects that focused on building new houses, educating adults, distributing food and clothes, and introducing new tools and machinery. As Superintendent Reel wrote in 1909, all these undertakings together "are educational factors to be given their full weight in preparing the Indians to take a place in the civilized body."[74]

Beginning in the early 1900s, the BIA introduced training in "Native industries"—arts and crafts—as an important subject to be taught to Indian children. In addition to fostering a sense of pride, administrators intended the program to offer students some hope of future income. Even dropouts might be provided some means of self-support, since making arts and crafts for sale did not require a degree.

Indian schools consistently failed to advance students through the educational system. For example, over several decades, the Hampton Institute served 1,388 students from 65

No. 154.

enjamine Brave and Children. — Sioux.

FIGURE 4.22. Benjamin Brave attended the Hampton Institute, a technical school for Native Americans and African Americans in Virginia. Attired in "civilized" dress, Brave and his children's clothing shows the transformative effects of the Indian education system. Rosebud Reservation, 1895–1899. (DMNS BR61-301)

tribes—but only 160 graduated (figure 4.22).[75] Even those few who matriculated through the Indian school system found it difficult to find work because of the isolated nature of many reservations and systematic discrimination against Indians in cities.[76]

To address the problem of employment, the Indian Service began to hire Native people to staff its programs, including schools. The proportion of Indian employees working for the Indian Service gradually increased, from 15 percent in 1888 to 45 percent in 1899 (figure 4.23).[77] Bratley himself recognized the difficulties faced by many educated Native Americans. "What is the Reservation Indian to do when he gets his higher education?" he once mused. "Loaf?"[78] While serving as the superintendent of Cantonment, Bratley supervised several Native employees (figure 4.24). It was through paid labor that Indian

FIGURE 4.23. Bratley's
image of an Indian policeman likely had several
resonances for him. Native
Americans who took on
this role were themselves
examples of the civilizing
machine's effects—and
they were central in
helping teachers maintain
control and ensure atten-
dance. Rosebud Reserva-
tion, 1895–1899. (DMNS
BR61-471)

men and women would learn, as Superintendent Reel wrote, to "understand that *labor omnia vincit*; and the result of his toil will make him independent and happy."[79]

Labor omnia vincit: Work conquers all.

Inserting former Native students back into Indian schools not only validated the education system's existence but also benefited those Native people employed.[80] Similar to their former instructors such as Bratley, who primarily came from poor working-class backgrounds, employment in the BIA offered Native people a steady paycheck and benefits. When faced with the choice of moving to urban centers and enduring the prejudices inherent in private-sector work, the Indian school system offered educated Native Americans a middle ground.[81] By entering the BIA as teachers, laundresses, or cooks, former Native students could remain with their families and communities while earning enough money to survive, if not prosper.[82] Although some Native employees would come to speak out against the BIA's mission of assimilation, others came to enjoy the work (figure 4.25).[83]

As employees within the Indian school system, Native workers were also likely able to help Native children negotiate the alienating and often harsh realities of school life. For example, Oglala teacher Clarence Three Stars employed a pedagogical technique that combined traditional teaching methods, references to the local physical environment, and bilingual instruction to teach Native students on the Pine Ridge Reservation. Three Star's exercises began with him drawing a stick figure of an English word, typically representing an action from everyday life on the reservation (e.g., hunting or housework). Students were then asked to draw a story using their new vocabulary—a practice that drew directly on the Oglala tradition of representing stories pictorially on tipis, hides, and ledgers.[84]

FIGURE 4.24. In his role supervising at the Cantonment Boarding School, Bratley oversaw the work of six Native Americans employed in the Indian Service. BACK ROW STANDING, LEFT TO RIGHT: Ms. Earlocker (teacher), Ms. Crisoe (matron), Paul Good Bear (Cheyenne, disciplinarian), Willie Meek (Arapaho, assistant farmer), Leah Meek (Arapaho, assistant matron). FRONT ROW SEATED, LEFT TO RIGHT: Margaret Spooner (Washita, boys' matron), Edna Eagle Feather (Osage, teacher and pianist), Jesse H. Bratley (superintendent), Ms. White (cook), Ms. Odell (Idaho, seamstress), Mrs. Bailey (laundry). Cheyenne and Arapaho Reservation, 1899–1900. (DMNS BR61-328)

FIGURE 4.25. Recess at the Lower Cut Meat Creek Day School—the boys likely in a piggy-back race, the girls playing a game holding hands in a circle—suggests that there were moments of fun and joy for Bratley and his students. Rosebud Reservation, 1895–1899. (DMNS BR61-478)

Similarly, Luther Standing Bear, a Carlisle graduate who started teaching on the Rosebud Reservation in 1884, recounted not only his enjoyment of teaching but also his ability to help students because he spoke their language: "At that time, teaching amounted to very little. It really did not require a well-educated person to teach on the reservation. The main thing was to teach the children to write their names in English, then came learning the alphabet and how to count. I liked this work very well, and the children were doing splendidly. I would have the children read a line of English, and if they did not understand all they had read, I would explain it to them in Sioux."[85]

Arapaho elder Patricia Gonzalez also once articulated this role of Native instructors as cultural mediators. "Some of the Natives who were more receptive to the change would help, would be den mothers," Gonzalez told us during an interview. "I guess they decided that if they had some Native people, the kids would be a little different."[86]

▼ ▽ ▼

America's imagined identity as a Christian civilization fundamentally structured the federal government's approach to Indian education. Christian lobbyists particularly shaped the assimilationist solution to the "Indian problem" that emerged during the nineteenth century.[87] Self-proclaimed "Friends of the Indians," reformers were driven by a shared moral code that emphasized individual salvation and a duty to seek out opportunities to share the good word through acts of Christian love.[88] "Savage though he may be," one Presbyterian minister proclaimed about the Indian, "he can be redeemed, and in this redemption can be raised to the highest manhood."[89] The proselytizing ethos, which undergirded Christian religion in America, fueled efforts to accelerate the social development of non-Western people through religious instruction.[90]

The efforts of Protestant missionaries became formally tied to federal Indian policy under President Ulysses S. Grant's peace policy. With the guidance of a coalition of Episcopal and Quaker reformers, Grant authorized the creation of the Bureau of Indian Commissioners (BIC) and appointed William Walsh to lead it.[91] In 1869, Walsh proposed several important reforms that would remake Native communities, such as the cessation of treaty making, the dispossession of Indian lands, and the education of Native people in agriculture and other "pursuits of civilization" through the assistance of Christian churches and school.[92]

Accompanying these coercive measures to assimilate Native people was a series of reforms, including efforts to ensure that the supplies given to Natives were of high quality and reasonably priced and that BIA employees were "competent, upright, faithful, moral, and religious."[93] Guiding the BIC's policies between 1869 and 1874 was the belief that non-Indians—specifically, wealthy, educated, Christian philanthropists—best understood the interests of Native communities.[94] This paternalistic vision became a central tenet of federal Indian policy for the next several decades.

An evangelical ethic informed the BIC's driving philosophy that encouraged the laity to pursue social justice and spiritual welfare on behalf of the less fortunate.[95] As suggested by anthropologist Harvey Markowitz, late nineteenth-century American Protestants combined Calvinism, Puritanism, and Enlightenment principles to advocate for a "Christian civilization" that embraced an "optimistic understanding of salvation, stressing the importance of individual volition and cooperation."[96]

The moral code that emerged among early nineteenth-century American Protestants stressed an individual's duty to find ways of carrying out acts of Christian love. These acts of love took on many forms, including prison reform, prohibitions on alcohol and gambling, and the active propagation of the faith at home and abroad.[97] For non-Western people, Protestant missionaries believed they could dramatically accelerate their social development through various modes of intervention. Specifically, advancement along social evolution's path required the abandonment of non-Christian beliefs and practices and education in Protestant Christian principles and values.

This evangelism informed Grant's decision to distribute the seventy-one Indian reservations among the mainstream Christian denominations.[98] Although the US government helped establish some seminaries for overt religious training, maintaining on-reservation schools, particularly boarding schools, became one of the primary means through which Christian reformers fulfilled their duty to convert and uplift their Native wards.[99] While Catholic missionaries played an important role in the new colonizing effort, Protestantism dominated the civil branch of the Indian Service.[100] Informed by a pan-Protestant ethic, day school curriculums stressed Bible reading, individual salvation, and personal morality.[101]

This emphasis on individualism mapped neatly onto the secular values of broader American society, including personal industriousness and private property. In addition to teaching Christian values in the schools, instructors supplemented day school education with a weekly regime of Sabbath school and preaching services, conducted primarily by Catholic, Presbyterian, and Episcopalian ministers.

Raised by industrious Protestant homesteaders, Bratley embodied the Protestant ideals and capitalistic work ethic the Indian Service hoped to instill in Native American children. Bratley's autobiography is filled with small anecdotes that convey his commitment to imparting Christian values on his pupils. For example, during his time among the S'Klallam, Bratley compelled his students to attend Easter service, bought the community a Christmas tree and presents, and even bribed his students with one cent prizes for learning the Lord's Prayer.[102] Bratley's actions and statements suggest that he dutifully accepted the BIA's uplifting mission of progress through Christianization.

Some of the objects Bratley collected while on the Rosebud Reservation also capture the profound impact of missionary efforts. For example, he collected a Bible cover adorned with quillwork and a small leather bag decorated with a beaded image of the community church (figure 4.26). These objects are notable for the way traditional crafts were adapted to depict Christian institutions and decorate newly introduced religious objects.

FIGURE 4.26. Bratley collected this hide pouch with a beaded image of a church on the Rosebud Reservation. (DMNS AC.5608)

In many ways, this juxtaposition points to the unique avenues by which tribal cultural institutions combined with Christian practices to create new identities, aesthetics, and habits. Some Rosebud tribal members, who see Lakota Sioux traditional beliefs as compatible with Christianity, expressed this sentiment to us. "I've always grown up learning to respect both ways," Travis High Pipe said during an interview, "and I think a lot of elderly were like that because when you look at the similarities, we all worship the same creator."[103] High Pipe's comments in part reflect the common practice among missionaries of using Lakota theological vocabulary for their instructions and homilies, a practice that created parallels between traditional Lakota thought and Christian doctrine.

For example, Catholic missionaries working on the Rosebud Reservation used the Lakota term *wanikiye wakan* (sacred giver of life) to convey beliefs and practices related to the Christian concept of God and the word *hanbleceya* (vision quest) to describe Catholic retreats.[104] By blurring some of the fundamental differences between Christian and Lakota belief systems, missionaries unintentionally facilitated the creation of an indigenized interpretation of church doctrine and led many Lakota people to view Christian rituals as a source of strength in the midst of traumatic change.[105]

While some Lakota Sioux refused to accept Christian doctrines, others accepted conversion and began the process—either consciously or unconsciously—of altering Christian practices to conform to Indigenous notions of spirituality. For example, Lakota converts used the Catholic Congress's annual celebration held in early July as an opportunity to reunite with friends and family—a practice previously associated with the summer Sun Dance. As with the Sun Dance ring, the congress enclosure was circular and divided into two parts with a flagpole in the center. Although clergy perceived the American flag flying from this central pole as a sign of Christian civilization, for many Lakota people this pole likely represented the point of convergence for the six sacred directions.[106]

Reflecting on the reasons behind why some Lakota Sioux chose to join Protestant or Catholic churches, Leland Little Dog stated, "My grandmother was a big convert, Episcopalian. Yeah, I think it was really important because they represented peace of spirit, whatever comfort the Church could give them" (figure 4.27).[107] Little Dog's comments suggest that for tribal members living in the early twentieth century, the church provided a source of stability and spiritual guidance during a time in which their entire religious, social, and economic structure was being reconfigured.

While schools and churches served as sites of conversion, they also became increasingly important community centers for Native people. For example, at the turn of the century, Mennonite and Baptist missionaries provided a reliable source of supplies to Hopi tribal members during a time when government-issued rations and commodities were unreliable. Recounting stories told to him by his grandmother, Hopi tribal member Leigh J. Kuwanwisiwma reflected on the particularly important role of churches in the lives of Hopi women. "My grandmother remembers how when she was [a] little kid back in the late 1880s, early 1890s, how her mom and them would line up there [at the Hopi

FIGURE 4.27. Solomon Elk, an Episcopal convert—he wears a large cross and holds a Bible upright on his lap—and his wife dressed in Euro-American-style clothing pose outside their sod home. For Bratley, the Elk family would likely have embodied the civilizing mission's success. Rosebud Reservation, 1895–1899. (DMNS BR61-267)

Mission] for a delivery day with wagons full of food like flour, staples like coffee and sugar," Kuwanwisiwma said. "For the woman folks the big enticement was sewing classes. They would get programs out there and get all the quilting materials."[108]

In this sense, churches acted as communal gathering places, where women could socialize with their peers while learning valuable domestic skills. Although these classes were intended to entice Hopi women to join the church, it seems that for many Native women the religious aspects of these events were relatively inconsequential. Both Little Dog's and Kuwanwisiwma's comments suggest that the relationship between Christian institutions and tribal people was far from straightforward.

As with many of the civilizing machine's offerings, Native community members could manipulate the benefits of these institutions to their own advantages. Some they accepted. Others they actively resisted.

Resistance

Indian schools waged a psychological and cultural war on Native Americans in an effort to mold them into "Americans." The fallout of this intellectual warfare for many Native children was confusion, alienation, trauma, and resentment.[109] Although the government's policies transformed generations of Native people, collectively, they were not passive victims.[110] Rather, Native students and their parents were active participants—they had choices on how to react, however constrained they were—in defining the educational experience through acceptance, accommodation, selective participation, rule breaking, and sometimes violent acts of resistance (figures 4.28 and 4.29).

Throughout his tenure in the Indian Service, Bratley directly experienced rebelliousness, both subtle and overt, against the civilizing mission he was employed to fulfill. Bratley's

first encounter with Indigenous defiance occurred at the Port Gamble Day School. During Bratley's time in Washington, the S'Klallam community was weathering a series of assaults on their cultural survival from religious institutions, milling interests, and the federally appointed Indian agents. In response to these changes, many S'Klallam negatively perceived and actively confronted the Indian education system.

This dissension arrived in various ways, beginning with the refusal to send children to school—a common tactic Native parents employed across the United States.[111] In his 1893 report, the superintendent of Indian schools recounted one such instance of opposition to education in Lemhi, Idaho: "A boy was in school. His mother came and took him away; she lived half a mile off; the agent ordered the boy back, but the chief, his father, would not bring him back. The agent withheld the chief's rations, but his colleague chief (the younger) divided his own rations with the old chief. The old man was made a hero, and it broke the agent's power."[112] This account suggests that Indian agents' harsh tactics could backfire, strengthening traditional communal ties instead of weakening them.[113] This act of defiance in Idaho and similar ones reveal slippages between official policy and the lived reality of the Indian school experience, in which administrators and teachers, who were supposed to have ultimate authority over their wards, could not fully control the actions of students or parents.

On his first day at Port Gamble, Bratley was only able to find three students, and even those children were distressed to attend. In a journal entry from that day, Bratley sketchily describes the tense scene as he attempted to bring the children into the schoolhouse: "First morning only three scholars which I had to carry in, afraid of me—they were five years old each—and such a noise with my watch and some spools and heaps of talk and coaxing I got them quieted."[114]

FIGURE 4.28. Despite discouragement of traditional clothing—especially for children—this image shows how Lakota Sioux children and adults selectively withstood such prohibitions. Bratley took this photograph of the children before they entered school. LEFT TO RIGHT: Thomas New, Harry With Horns, Standing Little Tail, Alice Slow Fly, Jesse Foot. Rosebud Reservation, 1899. (DMNS BR61-285)

THE
CIVILIZING
MACHINE

145

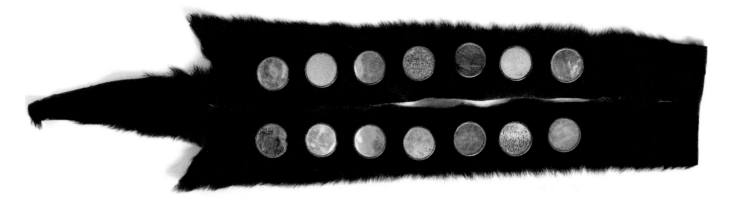

FIGURE 4.29. Bratley collected this otter neck piece (also known as a cape) with mirrors, similar to the ones worn by several Lakota Sioux in photographs Bratley took (e.g., Jesse Foot in DMNS BR61-285). (DMNS AC.5772)

Bratley's initial attempts at compelling S'Klallam youth to enter the schoolhouse met strong opposition. In his autobiography, Bratley commented that students "would not willingly come so we carried or dragged them into the school house. One boy ran away so I found I had to nail the windows down and lock the door."[115] Bratley's account reveals the S'Klallam children's reticence to attend school and the often extreme physical measures teachers employed to force Native children into school.

Bratley's experience in Washington was not unique. Contemporary tribal members shared with us similar instances of S'Klallam opposition to education. For example, tribal elder Ted George recounted that his grandfather Eddie George, who was born in 1863, "didn't want his kids to be taken away from him, so he went up on Hood canal," located 30 miles east of Port Gamble.[116] Eventually, Indian agents caught up with George and forced him to send his children to boarding school—threatening jail time if he refused. This was not an empty threat. After Congress made Indian education mandatory in 1891, the police regularly imprisoned Native American parents.[117]

The tensions between Native community members and teachers often erupted into physical violence (figure 4.30). In 1898, a young female student named Kittie at the Lower Cut Meat Creek Day School was allowed to take a four-month leave of absence from school to watch her father's—Chief Turning Eagle's—cows while he was away attending the Trans-Mississippi and International Exposition in Omaha, Nebraska.[118] After she reluctantly returned to school, Della Bratley found that Kittie's hair was full of nits. For the next several days, Kittie was required to return to the sewing room where Mrs. Bratley would proceed to examine her hair, only to find that the nits remained. Unless Kittie rid herself of the nits, her hair would have to be shorn off.

On the fourth day, Kittie was once again ordered to the sewing room for inspection. While there, a group of Lakota Sioux warriors began to gather on the back of the large hill adjacent to the school building. Noticing this through the classroom window, Bratley innocently believed the group had come to "pow-wow," he later wrote, or to add a newborn's name to the ration list. Bratley had no idea what was to come. He continued teaching. In the middle of Bratley's lecture, Chief Turning Eagle—dressed in war bonnet, paint, and feathers—burst into the schoolroom. War club upraised, Turning Eagle leaped toward

Bratley, who was holding his three-year-old son, Homer, at the time (figure 4.31). Even years later, Bratley firmly believed Turning Eagle would have "driven the club into my skull had it not been for two things. First, he was afraid he would strike Na ta ska (Homer), and, second, his daughter, Kittie, sprang from her seat halfway back toward the rear of the room, with outstretched arms and rushed forward, begging her father not to strike me."[119]

There is some debate among contemporary descendants of the Lower Cut Meat Creek Camp about how to interpret Bratley's harrowing tale. While many descendants conceded that there must have been some truth in Bratley's account, they question the motives behind Turning Eagle's actions. Pondering over the incident, Leland Little Dog—a descendent of Bratley's pupil Annie Broken Leg—mused, "I think they were just messing with him in some ways, but, then, on the other hand, it seems like a lot of drama to teach him a lesson."[120] Little Dog's comments suggest that Turning Eagle's attack was never meant to harm Bratley. Perhaps instead it was an act of resistance intended to demonstrate the chief's fearlessness against American authority and hence his power over Bratley.

Other descendants of the students who attended Lower Cut Meat Creek Day School suggest that Turning Eagle's violent reaction to Bratley's threat to cut Kittie's hair was rooted in deeply held cultural beliefs regarding hair. Hair is an important part of Lakota Sioux identity and is believed to be infused with an individual's *ni* (spirit). Hair cutting was only undertaken during certain times in adherence with particular protocols surrounding death or other ritual circumstances. Read through a Lakota Sioux cultural lens, Bratley's threat to cut Kittie's hair was a direct threat to her spirit and identity. Reflecting on Turning

FIGURE 4.30. Bratley described the men in this photo as "patrons" of the Lower Cut Meat Creek Day School. If Bratley means these men were supporters of the school, the label is striking. Based on the names, it would seem that many of these men sent their own relatives to the school. Yet the image is rife with uneasy tension. While the men wear Western clothing and sit beneath an American flag, they also keep their hair long and have with them traditional accoutrements. Also, Turning Eagle's daughter, Kittie, attended the school, yet he became so upset about Bratley's treatment of her that he tried to attack the teacher. STANDING (LEFT TO RIGHT): George Steed, Chief Elk Teeth, Chief Otterman, and Horn. SEATED (LEFT TO RIGHT): One Wood, With Horns, Yellow Cloud, John Grey Eagle Tail, Turning Eagle, Fast Dog, Pulls the Arrow Out, and James Kills Plenty. Rosebud Reservation, 1897. (DMNS BR61-324)

CAT
WE ARE AMERICANS
3642
3
10,926

FIGURE 4.31. An artist, perhaps a friend of Bratley's, drew this cartoon of Turning Eagle attempting to kill Bratley because he had threatened to shore off Kittie Turning Eagle's hair. (DMNS AC.11680)

Eagle's motives, Clifford Broken Leg suggested that Bratley's threat to cut Kittie's hair was particularly offensive because it was not undertaken in the appropriate manner. "There is a certain protocol you use—like if you had lice," Broken Leg said, "I would go tell somebody close to you to tell you."[121] Broken Leg's comments suggest that Lakota Sioux people have a subtle way of dealing with social confrontation and that when non-relatives directly reprimand an individual, it undermines their status in the community.

Although it is difficult to know the intentions behind Turning Eagle's attack, it was met with harsh disciplinary measures. The chief's mercy on Bratley was repaid with strict reprisal; he was quickly arrested, placed in jail, and fed only bread and water for several weeks. Ultimately, the episode concluded with the triumph of Western authority: Kittie was given a final day to clean her hair, and the next morning she returned, Bratley recalled, "with a clean head of hair and it was kept clean thereafter."[122]

Although Bratley's encounter ended without harm to him, several years later a Lakota Sioux tribal member named George Bear shot Edward C. Tayloe, the teacher at Milk's Camp Day School on the Rosebud Reservation.[123] Whether successful or not, these acts of violent struggle reveal that federal policies did not completely succeed in reducing Native people to submissive citizens.

The opposition many older tribal members directed against the school often turned violent, as attested to by Bratley's account of being threatened with a knife by the grandmother of one of his students at Cantonment Boarding School. Bratley recorded: "This occurred at Thanksgiving in 1899, when there was to be no school and several of the students wanted to leave to go to their Indian camps. One student who was forbidden to go was later kidnapped by her grandmother and as I gave chase and cornered them, the old squaw raised her knife to stab me. I evaded the thrust and took the knife from her."[124] This altercation was not an isolated incident. His personal journal and account book from his time at Cantonment document a series of physical confrontations among Bratley, his pupils, and their parents (figure 4.32). Little explanation is documented in association with these episodes, which are only briefly listed, but they include an encounter in which Bratley was pulled down the stairs by a pupil, threatened with a knife by a man named Bob Finger, and forcibly kicked out of the schoolhouse by a man named White Face Bull.[125]

Bratley's official report from the 1900 school year never mentions these attacks. Instead, his report takes a strikingly positive tone, stating, "All of the children and most if not all of the older Indians went home from the closing of school with a good feeling toward it."[126] This official report contrasts with Bratley's personal journal, which not only documents these accounts of violence but also conveys a negative opinion of the Cheyenne and Arapaho—portraying them as stingy tricksters who asked for too many things and were constantly trying to assert their own authority over Bratley.[127]

For insurgents, the consequences could be severe, as the Hopi learned. In 1894, US troops arrested nineteen Hopi men for not complying with government orders.[128] Without a trial or formal proceedings, the men spent a year on the island prison of Alcatraz in California. Their imprisonment came after several years of severe tactics by Indian agents, including stopping ration goods, refusing to help build wells and houses (even during

FIGURE 4.32. Cheyenne men and children pose for a photo outside the Cantonment Boarding School. Given that they are dressed in Euro-American-style clothing, these Cheyenne and Arapaho might have given Bratley less trouble than others in the community. Cheyenne and Arapaho Reservation, 1899–1900. (DMNS BR61-363)

a violently cold winter), and sending soldiers to round up truant schoolchildren.[129] The direct link between the men's imprisonment and Indian education is documented in an article from *Call* magazine published in January 1895: "Uncle Sam has summarily arrested nineteen Moqui [Hopi] Indians . . . and taken them to Alcatraz Island, all because they would not let their children go to school. But he has not done it unkindly and the life of the burnt-umber natives is one of ease, comparatively speaking. They have not hardship aside from the fact that they have been rudely snatched from the bosom of their families and are prisoners and prisoners they shall stay until they have learned to appreciate the advantage of education."[130]

Four years after the Bratleys left the Hopi Reservation, US education became an even more divisive issue. Rival factions at Oraibi, the largest Hopi village, fought over whether to comply with the order for schooling (figure 4.33).[131] Those "hostiles" who refused the government's entreaties suffered various punishments, including work on a chain gang in Keams Canyon, imprisonment at Fort Huachuca in southern Arizona, and forced removal to attend Carlisle Indian School.[132] US government agents, upset at the turmoil, threatened the Oraibi village chief Tawaquaptewa with imprisonment if he did not agree to send children to an off-reservation boarding school.[133] Although seventy-one Hopi children subsequently went to the Sherman Institute in Riverside, California, many parents continued to refuse to send their children to school until 1911, when US troops were finally ordered to the area.[134]

While violent altercations between students and teachers seem to have been a common occurrence during the nineteenth and twentieth centuries, resistance to the Indian education system took other forms. For example, in a personal journal entry, Bratley recounts that

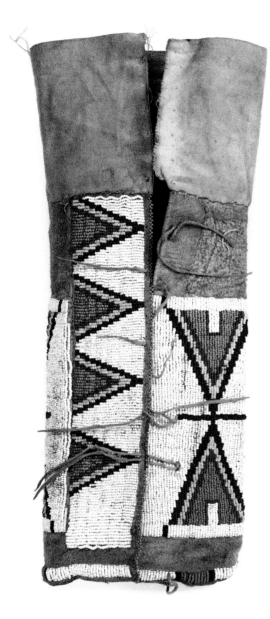
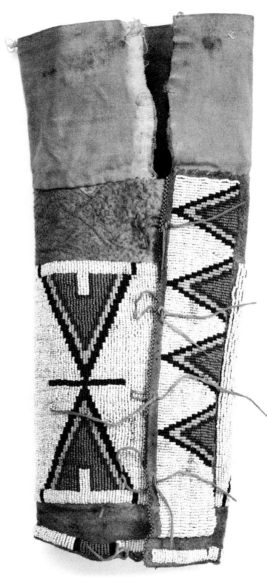

FIGURE 4.34. Subtle forms of resistance were practiced outside the educational sphere, too. Lakota Sioux families transitioned away from tipis, but the triangles in these leggings recall the centrality of this traditional house for the Lakota Sioux— ensuring that symbols of traditional life persisted. (DMNS AC.5740A-B)

upon arriving on the Havasupai Reservation, tribal members had "asked if I was a new man in the Service—they wanted new men so they could work him better."[135] Bratley's statement suggests that Havasupai tribal members exercised a kind of "soft power" in relation to BIA employees, using the naiveté of young, untested teachers to their own advantage.

Bratley experienced a similar form of contempt through manipulation at Cantonment, during which time Cheyenne and Arapaho parents undermined his authority by telling their children that he had been discharged (figure 4.34).[136] These examples point to the way Native people used persuasive rhetorical appeals rather than threats of physical violence to undercut the authority of teachers and exert control in situations of asymmetrical power.

In other instances, rebellion was expressed through deliberate acts of rule breaking. These more subtle acts of resistance took on many forms—as, for example, when female students at Chilocco Indian Agricultural School in Oklahoma slipped off their government-

FIGURE 4.35. The presence of a Cheyenne camp next to Cantonment Boarding School documents how some families refused to be separated from their children. Cheyenne and Arapaho Reservation, 1899–1900. (DMNS BR61-364)

issued bloomers and hid them in the bushes after passing the matron's inspection.[137] Accompanied by domestic training, school uniforms were part of a two-pronged effort to instill a Protestant ethic and aesthetic in Native women. During the early twentieth century, proper Euro-American clothing for girls included cotton stockings, long underwear for winter, bloomers, gingham and chambray dresses, and oxford shoes.[138] These changes in bodily comportment were intended to disempower Native girls by erasing their individual and tribal identity, which was often expressed through dress. The issuing and policing of proper dress further enforced the power of the government school system while reinforcing the White Victorian attitude of propriety. In removing their bloomers, Native girls at Chilocco and other schools challenged this symbol of power, effectively undermining the schools' efforts to mold their bodies and minds.

Complementary forms of willful disobedience were undertaken by Cheyenne and Arapaho parents, who would often camp around the Cantonment Boarding School despite government regulations intended to separate Native children from their tribal community. Other Native parents, such as among the Blackfeet, also used this strategy.[139] Families often refused to allow the school systems to break them apart.[140] Bratley captured this subversive tactic in a photograph taken of tipis raised near the school (figure 4.35).

Gordon Yellowman recounted hearing elders talk about how "some of our families would camp right there around the fort, around the sub agency, but they were not allowed to go and talk to them [their children]. Their parents would see them walking from class to class, but they couldn't wave."[141] Although teachers did not permit students to communicate with their families directly, the practice of camping around boarding schools reflects a conscious refusal to sever the ties that connected Native children and their parents. In many ways, the mere presence of Native parents encamped nearby would certainly have helped to ease the emotional trauma experienced by Native children who were forced to leave their families behind.

Although Bratley's experiences provide evidence for both overt and subtle forms of resistance, not all Native people opposed education. Some students reported being content, if not happy, with their educational experience.[142] Among several of the tribes Bratley worked with, divisions emerged between "conservative" members of the community who opposed the school system and other tribal members deemed "progressive" because they accepted it. This division is based largely on the perceptions of Indian agents who viewed Native individuals who adopted an agrarian lifestyle, lived in a house, sent their kids to school, and showed a willingness to dress, act, and speak like Whites as progressive. At times, the progressive-conservation divide also reflected the emergence of inter- and intra-band factionalism over leadership during the creation of reservations.[143]

For many of the communities Bratley worked with, these divisions were associated with families classified as "rebellious" or "hostile"—for example, members of the Wazazia band who resided along Lower Cut Meat Creek on the Rosebud Reservation. Lakota tribal member Leland Little Dog described this tension: "At first there was a lot of animosity, our people (Wazazia band) hated their people for living at the agencies . . . They were either treaty or non-treaty. When we first came over here my grandmother (Alice Rowles Holy Medicine) used to tell us, 'We are not from here so they don't like us, these are Spotted Tail people.'"[144] Little Dog's comments point to the emergence of a geopolitical division between the Lower Cut Meat Creek community and those tribal members who chose to live closer to the agency and adopt a more sedentary lifestyle. This division reflects political decisions made by key leaders in each community—families under the leadership of Spotted Tail, who advocated for peace with the United States Army—and those families who took an antagonistic approach toward White settlement.

Rosebud tribal member Travis High Pipe further explained the division between tribal members while describing his ancestor Chief High Pipe (figure 4.36): "He was a real good speaker. Put words into perspective. It was during that time [the 1890s] that some were thinking ahead and some still wanted to live the old ways; they didn't want to negotiate at all. But he [High Pipe] saw what was going to happen, that times changed. And I think a lot of them did too. A lot of them encouraged the language to be English, to learn that, education, modern day education."[145] Travis High Pipe's comments indicate that during the early reservation period, internal divisions emerged between those Lakota Sioux who continued to oppose the American government and those who more readily adapted to and negotiated that system. "Many old Indians look upon governmental schoolwork as hostile to them and the taking away of their children as hostages," Commissioner of Indian Affairs William A. Jones wrote in 1900, "others view it as a special mark of favor that their little ones should be permitted to attend school, and they demand payment for the favor."[146] Although the rhetoric of progressive-conservative factionalism continued, by the 1970s many tribal communities had bridged these divides.[147]

For many Native leaders during the early twentieth century, "progressive" strategies, including attending school, sending delegates to the seat of political power, petition drives, and alliance building with religious and philanthropic organizations, offered the best means of maintaining the values of their elders. Among the Cheyenne and Arapaho, many intermediary chiefs—individuals who acted on consensus of the people they represented and were elected based on performance—were proponents of farming, cattle raising, and school attendance during the late nineteenth century.[148]

For example, several Arapaho leaders, including Little Raven, Left Hand, Yellow Horse, and Row of Lodges, were early promoters of agriculture among their community members, planting 110 acres of corn and vegetables along the North Canadian River.[149] Many of these leaders, including Arapaho leaders Little Raven and Left Hand as well as Cheyenne leaders White Shield and Yellow Ear, went so far as to voluntarily send their children to off-reservation boarding schools such as Carlisle. A mere three years after Carlisle opened, seventy Cheyenne and Arapaho students attended the Pennsylvania school, and 27 percent of children on the reservation were enrolled in some form of school.[150]

While historians have often labeled these leaders as advocating for a "progressive" agenda, their behavior also reflects Indigenous goals. Specifically, their decision to support

FIGURE 4.36. Chief High Pipe's wife and four children. High Pipe is remembered today as a leader who grasped the possibilities for Indian education during this tumultuous period for the Lakota Sioux. Rosebud Reservation, 1895–1899. (DMNS BR61-302)

the government's civilization program was a strategic move intended to gain resources from the federal government. With the government's help, these leaders could then gain influence over official matters of central importance to the Cheyenne and Arapaho communities, such as the distribution of rations and allotments.[151]

In addition to gaining political influence, formal education at boarding schools like Carlisle and Hampton promised to provide students with skills they could bring home. Many of the boys who returned to Oklahoma were later employed in agency shops, and educated girls found work as assistant matrons in the kitchens and sewing rooms of on-reservation boarding schools like Cantonment.[152] These examples demonstrate how Native people used formal education to strengthen their own communities rather than simply assimilate into American society.

Other tribal leaders who were compelled to find new ways to protect their community's interests also chose to support certain aspects of the US government's assimilationist agenda. For example, activists on the Crow Creek Reservation in central South Dakota sought to integrate tribal members into leadership positions created by the federal government, such as police officers and tribal judges, in an effort to maintain control over ancestral lands, remove corrupt Indian agents, and promote community self-sufficiency and the recognition of treaty payments.[153] The Crow Creek activists had a diversity of identities and experiences, ranging from non-English speakers to Indian school graduates to church representatives.[154] Although this diverse group shared a commitment to fighting for their common rights as a tribe within the new political system of the reservation era, tribal members were not united on all aspects of the progressive agenda. For example, while some tribal members supported funding Catholic mission schools on the reservation, other progressive leaders rejected a Roman Catholic identity.[155]

The diversity that existed among so-called progressive and conservative groups has also been documented by historian Thomas G. Andrews, who has written about the disagreements that arose among Oglala Sioux leaders over the question of whether boarding schools or day schools best met the tribe's needs. While supporters of boarding schools tended to stress the superior education they provided, advocates for day schools viewed them as a middle path that would provide skills from Euro-American culture while protecting their children from infectious disease and maintaining the family home and Oglala community.[156] Although boarding school supporters have typically been labeled as "progressive" and day school supporters as "traditionalists," the fact that both sides perceived education as a tool of empowerment and survival indicates the inadequacy of these strict categories to capture the complex rationales behind Native adaptations to radical change at the turn of the century.

The division between progressive and conservative perspectives was complex and often blurry. Many leaders advocated for policies federal government agents labeled as pro-assimilation while maintaining what insiders interpreted as the interests of the community. Similar to High Pipe, the northern Ute leader William Walsh was considered by

FIGURE 4.37. This image of Hopi wedding jars and boilers filled with cornmeal illustrates ongoing traditional wedding practices in the face of American colonization. The bride must grind the mounds of cornmeal, which demonstrates her ability to prepare traditional foods, and it is then used to feed the wedding guests. Hopi Reservation, 1901–1902. (DMNS BR61-228)

Indian agents to be a "progressive" because he accumulated wealth in a White-approved manner by ranching and farming as well as promoting allotment. While Walsh's actions and politics certainly represented interests that aligned with government efforts, they were also intended to maintain traditional Ute cultural values. As historian David Lewis argues, Walsh viewed allotment as a means of maintaining the community's land base and independence from White homesteaders.[157] The actions of leaders like Little Raven, High Pipe, and Walsh demonstrate how variable Indigenous responses were to the federal government's assimilationist agenda and point to the ways individual actions transcend simplistic categories like conservative and progressive (figures 4.37 and 4.38).[158]

Reflecting on his varied experiences, in a 1901 newspaper interview Bratley stated that "the greatest difficulty is to overcome the influences of the old Indians who insist on keeping up tribal customs and use every effort to keep the young Indians who have been in school from practicing the ways of civilization."[159] Bratley's comment points to the underlying dichotomy between tradition and modernization on which the Indian education system was structured.

The supposed corroding effect of tribal customs on young minds was the primary rationale for removing Native children from homes and placing them in schools. Although the education system aimed to eradicate Native traditions, many of these practices were preserved through small acts of resistance, such as speaking tribal languages while out of earshot of teachers or continuing to perform dances and making traditional crafts in secret.[160]

Persistence

As an employee in the Indian Service, Bratley was tasked with what government officials at the time perceived to be the work of history—mainly, the complete and final eradication of what remained of Native culture. Bratley's experiences along with the photographs and artifacts he collected suggest otherwise. Although Indian schools certainly served as sites of cultural loss, from another viewpoint they were also sites of cultural persistence.[161]

Persistence is not stasis; no doubt Native American cultures of the twentieth century would not look the same as those of the nineteenth century (figure 4.39). Within a single generation, Native cultures fundamentally and forever changed. Yet persistence for Indigenous communities involved the perpetuation of many traditional practices and identities as well as their transformation and reinterpretation.[162] Bratley's collection offers a window into the ways Native traditions and identities evolved and survived during this period.

FIGURE 4.38. The wedding jars (in DMNS BR61-228) Bratley collected on the Hopi Reservation are physical evidence of Hopi living traditions. The jars are decorated with four images of the Katsina Palhik Mana (Butterfly Maiden). Bratley purchased them for $5.50 each. (DMNS AC.10472)

FIGURE 4.39. Bratley noted that this was the only Hopi silversmith on the reservation and that he made his jewelry out of Mexican silver money. Over the course of the twentieth century, a growing number of Hopi began to learn the silversmithing craft. While tourist demands for particular design aesthetics like arrows and thunderbirds influenced Hopi artisans, artists actively employed more subtle traditional motifs in their work. Hopi Reservation, 1902. (DMNS BR61-235)

While government-sponsored programs may have prompted the process of culture change, tribal members were largely responsible for shaping the changes that took place in Indian country.[163] The many Native communities for whom reservations came to represent a new form of communal identity are just one manifestation of this creative process of cultural adaptation. Following the close of the Indian Wars, reservations became the setting for a new kind of culture that adopted certain non-Indian institutions but also became a space where communal identity was solidified and traditional values and goals were defended.

Although initiated by federal administrators, tribal councils became central platforms through which Native politicians could hold on to un-allotted lands. The power of tribal councils is exemplified by the actions of Lakota activists on the Rosebud Reservation at the turn of the twentieth century. Following a 1903 ruling—known as the Gamble campaign—which determined that the federal government had ultimate authority over the disposition of all Indian lands, the Rosebud Reservation was opened for white settlement. Although the Lakota had actively resisted the creation of the reservation in 1889, increasing White settlement in the region led many leaders in the tribe to unite in favor of preserving their land base. The reservation business council led resistance to the Gamble campaign. Using this newly imposed governmental structure, the Lakota community passed a unanimous resolution opposing the measure and authorizing a delegation to go to Washington.[164] Similarly, tribal police provided protection against homesteaders, and schools offered educated Native people an alternative source of income.[165] The transformation of reservations from places of confinement into homelands demonstrates how the tools of assimilation were employed as mechanisms of empowerment.

The world Bratley entered into when he first stepped onto the Puget Sound region suggests that the government's expectation of cultural extinction was exaggerated. Although the S'Klallam were in the midst of a series of economic and political changes brought on by White settlement and milling interests, many of their traditional cultural practices continued to flourish (figure 4.40). The most persistent of these traditions revolved around subsistence. Bratley first became aware of these practices just two days after his arrival on the Spit. When he attempted to begin school, he quickly found that despite government attendance reports, there were few children around to teach. During this time, all of the able-bodied S'Klallam men, women, and children had left the village and were salmon fishing 25 miles south near Hood Canal.[166] Although unaware of this practice upon his arrival, Bratley would learn that while the S'Klallam were increasingly consuming commercial goods, the fall salmon run was an important subsistence practice that supplemented their daily diet of shellfish, wild game, and berries. Indeed, Bratley notes that the S'Klallam kept "a good supply of long slabs of smoked, dried salmon stored over the ceiling beams in their cabins."[167]

In addition to supplementing the villagers' diet, salmon were part of an annual cultural tradition in which the fish were carefully carried by children, prepared in a special way, eaten by the community, and their bones ritually returned to the water.[168] The S'Klallam believed salmon were spiritual beings that lived in their own world like people, annually coming to the human world as fish and giving their flesh to humans in exchange for proper respect and treatment.[169] Consideration of traditional persistence reveals the intimate relationship between subsistence and Native beliefs and social practices. This close connection likely played an important role in preserving traditional subsistence practices among

FIGURE 4.40. Played by many Indigenous communities across the Pacific Northwest, *sla-hal* is a team-based gambling game and was once used to determine territory and settle disputes. Archaeological evidence indicates that the game was developed over 13,000 years ago and according to oral tradition began as a competition between animals and humans to determine who would become the hunters and who would be food. (Children of Dr. Forrest G. Bratley)

the S'Klallam, despite the introduction of a cash economy and the influx of commercial foodstuffs.

Ironically, even though the US government employed Bratley to suppress his students' culture, in some measure he became enthralled by it, collecting several traditional objects and documenting cultural practices in his personal journals.[170] Bratley filled his autobiography with descriptions of the various events that defined S'Klallam traditional life, such as smelt fishing and clambakes. One such account discusses the clambake, which the S'Klallam often invited Bratley to participate in. "When the Indians had a clambake, they never failed to invite me to eat with them and I never turned them down," he wrote. "If they opened the mound of rocks and dirt where the shellfish had baked for twenty-four hours or more,[171] while school was in session, I would dismiss school so the pupils and teacher could partake. After the feast we would go back to school."[172]

This account offers one example of the amiable relationship that, at least at certain moments, formed between Bratley and the Native communities with which he worked. It also demonstrates Bratley's willingness to partake in and even encourage some traditional practices. But most important, Bratley's description of the clambake provides another example of the persistence of traditional subsistence practices among the S'Klallam. The continued practice of the clambake today demonstrates the survival of S'Klallam cultural life. Joshua Wisnowski, the former archaeologist for the Port Gamble S'Klallam Tribe, articulated the importance of this event; he commented to us that the clambake is "an awesome example of cultural continuity. The fact that he [Bratley] identifies clambakes as an important thing in 1893, and I would say that clambakes are an equally important thing in 2016."[173] The themes of adaptation and continuity embodied in the clambake are defining features of contemporary Native life and are shared across all of the tribal communities Bratley worked with.

As an instructor at Lower Cut Meat Creek Day School and the Cantonment Boarding School, one of Bratley's primary tasks had been to teach the Native pupils Euro-American methods of farming and ranching (figure 4.41). Not only was agriculture a foreign practice among the nineteenth-century Lakota Sioux, Arapaho, and Cheyenne, but their attempts at Euro-American farming was often stymied by the barren prairies of the Great Plains or drought. In contrast, the Havasupai had successfully farmed corn, beans, and squash for centuries, and their reservation encompassed approximately 350 acres of productive agricultural land. The natural abundance of the Havasupai's traditional territory is captured by the comments of a day school teacher who reported that the reservation had "the finest stream of pure spring water in Arizona for irrigating, [which] renders the cultivation of corn, pumpkins, beans, melons, and peaches an easy problem, even for the untutored mind of a savage."[174]

FIGURE 4.41. Bratley photographed children irrigating three acres of garden at the Lower Cut Meat Creek Day School. Agricultural training was a key part of the Indian school experience. The goal was to change not only Indian subsistence patterns but also their tastes and preferences. Bratley once declared, reflecting on the school garden, "I never saw such Irish potatoes, enough to feed the children for months, celery two feet tall, tomatoes that the fruit from two bushes would fill a 100 lb. grain bag and watermelons by the wagon load. The children like the potatoes and melons but at first did not care for celery or tomatoes. But by keeping a tub half full in the school yard of tomatoes they became fond of tomatoes." Rosebud Reservation, 1895–1899. (DMNS BR61-253)

The Havasupai's geographic location allowed the community to support itself entirely through agriculture—a unique occurrence during a time in which Native American dependency on government rations was widespread.[175] Bratley later remembered, with a hint of wonder, that the Havasupai's "knowledge of farming was not gained from whites, but passed down from one generation to the next."[176] Several of Bratley's photographs document the continuation of traditional farming techniques in the face of government efforts to supplant them with more industrial modes of agriculture. Bratley, for example, took several images of Havasupai men and women dressed in Euro-American clothing but using their customary method of a stick rather than a plow to plant seeds (figure 4.42).

FIGURE 4.42. Havasupai women continued to plant crops using traditional methods, despite encouragement during this period for Native Americans to adopt Western agricultural practices. Havasupai Reservation, 1900–1901. (DMNS BR61-003)

The continuation of traditional Havasupai agricultural methods was facilitated in part by the isolated location of the community, which could not easily obtain the plows and other modern implements intended to improve agricultural productivity according to Euro-American expectations. The Indian agent at Havasupai was well aware of this disjuncture, stating that "the teaching of improved methods of agriculture is rather more in name than in fact at Supai."[177] In addition to preventing the incorporation of Euro-American machines, the isolated location of the Havasupai facilitated the continuation of other cultural practices in spite of external pressures to adopt White educators' methods and practices. Bratley's photograph and artifact collection offers an intriguing glimpse into some of the Havasupai's traditional activities—activities that persisted among many Native communities—including basket making and the use of sweat lodges as part of ritual healing and purifying ceremonies (figures 4.43 and 4.44).

Much like the S'Klallam and Havasupai, Hopi cultural persistence was closely tied to the perpetuation of traditional subsistence practices (figure 4.45). Hopis supported themselves through the planting and harvesting of corn, beans, melons, squash, and other vegetables in the valley bottoms that surrounded the mesas on which they lived (figure 4.46). A system of shared labor called *na'ya* sustained their traditional subsistence.

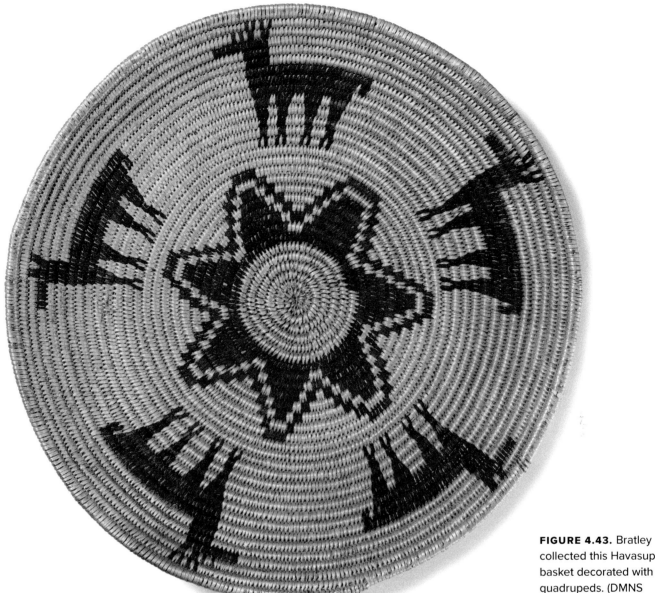

FIGURE 4.43. Bratley collected this Havasupai basket decorated with quadrupeds. (DMNS AC.5647)

FIGURE 4.44. The Lakota Sioux men's use of a sweat lodge shows the persistence of deeply important spiritual practices. Rosebud Reservation, 1898. (DMNS BR61-168).

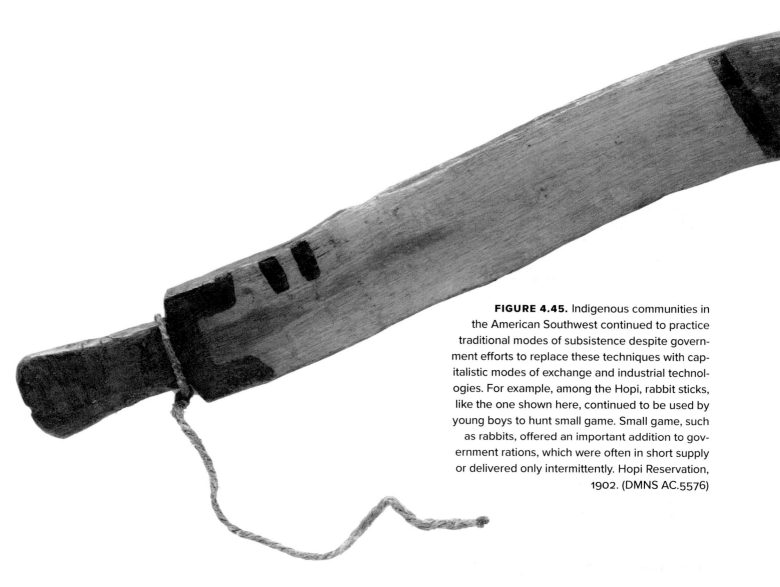

FIGURE 4.45. Indigenous communities in the American Southwest continued to practice traditional modes of subsistence despite government efforts to replace these techniques with capitalistic modes of exchange and industrial technologies. For example, among the Hopi, rabbit sticks, like the one shown here, continued to be used by young boys to hunt small game. Small game, such as rabbits, offered an important addition to government rations, which were often in short supply or delivered only intermittently. Hopi Reservation, 1902. (DMNS AC.5576)

Within this system, groups of men would work together to plant each other's fields.[178] During Bratley's tenure at Polacca, he recorded these traditional agricultural practices and collected a significant number of related ethnographic objects. Bratley's extensive photograph collection offers a fleeting but haunting glimpse into Hopi life a century ago, depicting social activities such as corn grinding, blanket weaving, and ritual running races (figures 4.47 and 4.48). In his autobiography Bratley describes several of these customary observances:

> The "squaw" corn raised by the Hopi has multi-colored kernels on each ear. They planted a handful of grains in shallow holes, which were nine feet apart, and often as many as twenty-seven stalks would grow from one hill. Usually four ears were produced by each stalk. When the corn is ground between stones, it is not like our cornmeal, but is more like starch. Batter for piki bread, made from the meal, is spread thinly on a huge flat stone, which is heated [figure 4.49]. When it is cooked it is rolled up on a stick and eaten at their leisure . . . An unusual annual ceremony, held in August, is the Snake Dance, using live rattlesnakes. The primary purpose of this ceremony is to bring rain. One unusual Hopi is Chaca, a young Indian runner. I took a picture of him for my collection after he finished running barefooted 85 miles to the railroad in one day and returning the next [figure 4.50].[179]

FIGURE 4.46 (top). Bratley noted that each garden plot north of the village of Walpi on First Mesa was approximately the size of a large extension table, with one terrace running water to another. The Hopi raised onions, chili peppers, melons, and more. Hopi Reservation, 1902. (DMNS BR61-147)

FIGURE 4.47 (bottom). This image depicts a group of Hopi men running in between corn plantings. After planting corn, Hopi farmers will race together to ensure a successful harvest. The persistence of traditional agricultural practices went beyond subsistence and was an important means of sustaining tribal identities and modes of community interaction. Hopi Reservation, 1902. (DMNS BR61-403)

FIGURE 4.48. Sixteen Hopi runners line up at sunrise to ritually race 3 miles before the Snake Dance. Hopi Reservation, 1902. (DMNS BR61-146)

FIGURE 4.49. Bratley diligently documented the process of baking bread during his time at Polacca and made the following comments during an educational slide show presentation, likely to accompany this image of Mrs. Chua (Rattlesnake) baking: "After the meal is ground it is roasted usually in a pottery jar which is set over a fire in one corner of the room. The meal is stirred about with a loose bundle of small grease wood sticks. The meal is then mixed into a batter using water which has filtered through a specially prepared charcoal. The baker dips her hand into the batter and gives it a rapid sweep over this flat stone which you see, and in four to six sweeps she has the stone covered with the batter coat. She then raises the bread sheet from the stone and rolls it up like this you see by her left hand. This is her batter bowl. This stone upon which she bakes the piki is about 20 × 30 inches, some are smaller and some are larger. There is a fireplace under the stone and here an escape for the smoke. They spend weeks in polishing a stone before using it. Generally several families use one bake stone." This image captures the continuation of traditional subsistence practices among the Hopi and reflects the important link among food, social practices, and identity. Hopi Reservation, 1902. (DMNS BR61-219)

Bratley's description and documentation of traditional practices offers evidence for the continuation of many cultural practices, particularly those around subsistence and religion, among the Hopi despite government efforts to replace them with modern farming techniques and Christianity.

For the nomadic tribes with whom Bratley worked, persistence required a series of culturally grounded adaptations to adjust to the new realities of life in the twentieth century. By the time Bratley entered the Indian Service, Euro-American hunters had systematically annihilated the bison herds on which Plains tribes depended for subsistence. Although scholars widely debate whether the extermination of bison herds was ever an explicit element of US Indian policy, it is clear that federal administrators actively promoted their destruction by hosting hunts for visiting dignitaries, permitting army troops to kill bison for sport, and promoting the expansion of a commercial market in buffalo hides.[180] The destruction of thousands of bison was devastatingly effective (figure 4.51). Starving and war-torn Plains tribes were forced onto reservations and came to rely largely on government-issued rations for survival. In his autobiography, Bratley testifies to these historical realities:

> White men killed them [bison] wantonly, but the Indians killed them for food and robes only. Thousands upon thousands of buffalo hides were brought to Dodge City. They were piled in great stacks as high as the tops of trains and for blocks long. I saw piles of hides after we moved out there. When the hides had all been shipped, then the homesteaders began to pick up the bleached buffalo bones and sell them to bone buyers, who had them piled up in long and high ricks where the buffalo hides were pilled a few years before. The bones were shipped east to be made into buckles, buttons, and fertilizers.[181]

Bratley's account documents the tremendous scale on which bison were destroyed and the essential disconnect between Anglo and Native approaches to buffalo hunting.

To fill the socioeconomic void created by the ruin of the bison and to supplement their meager government support, some Lakota Sioux began to sell traditional objects and pose for photographs. Bratley's account books from his years at Rosebud indicate that he acquired his curio collection through various means, including by direct purchase and by bartering his own photographs or ration goods, such as coffee and sugar (figure 4.52).[182]

FIGURE 4.50. Bratley recounted that Thomas Keam, the local trader, once paid Chaca the sum of two dollars to deliver a message to Winslow, Arizona, more than 80 miles away. Hopi Reservation, 1902. (DMNS BR61-227)

FIGURE 4.51 (above). Projectile points similar to this one were used by Plains people for hunting wild game such as bison. Rosebud Reservation, 1895–1899. (DMNS AC.11872)

FIGURE 4.52 (right). The traditional economic practice of bartering among Indigenous groups is captured in this photograph of a Havasupai woman named Yunosi wearing traditional clothing and carrying squash in a burden basket. Bratley reported that Yunosi brought the squash to trade with him for sugar. Bratley's account books are full of examples of bartering with tribal members and point to the continued importance of exchange as a mode of social and economic interaction. Havasupai Reservation, 1900–1901. (DMNS BR61-055)

Reflecting on Bratley's Lakota Sioux collection, Travis High Pipe explained to us the logic behind why his ancestors sold objects to collectors—objects that were often considered sacred or used in ceremonial activities: "I think a lot of it had to do with, because you know times changed. They killed all our buffalo at that time, so we had to rely on beef and commodities, you know canned stuff, so we had to barter. A couple of years back you know one of the store owners on the other side of Winner [South Dakota] gave a bonnet back to a family for food. He had to give up his bonnet for food."[183]

High Pipe's comments speak to the financial hardships Lakota Sioux people have faced and the sacrifices they made to survive (figure 4.53). Yet High Pipe's story also demonstrates the creative ways Lakota Sioux individuals adapted to the new economic realities of the period by capitalizing on the new monetary value of their traditional cultural possessions (figure 4.54).

Plains communities abandoned seasonal bison hunts, but they maintained other traditional cultural practices related to subsistence. Despite government efforts to introduce agriculture among nomadic communities, many Cheyenne, Arapaho, and Lakota men actively rejected agriculture. This resistance reflects in part the fact that farming was often difficult on the Plains because of sparse rainfall during the growing season, which made it difficult for crops such as corn to mature fast enough for harvesting.[184]

In addition to these practical issues, their reticence to take up agriculture reflects cultural differences in what constituted appropriate gender roles; among many nomadic communities, harvesting was considered unmanly and was categorized as "women's work." Ranching and hauling freight for the agency offered two alternative occupations that were both consistent with gendered subsistence practices and aligned with federal prohibitions on hunting-gathering.[185] In 1877, John D. Miles, the Indian agent on the Cheyenne-Arapaho Reservation, acknowledged this cultural inclination toward stock raising by allocating more agency funds to buying cattle. This shift in policy was further supported by altering the curriculum at the Cheyenne-Arapaho Manual Training and Labor School to include classes in animal husbandry.[186] Within a year, Miles's policy decision was recognized on a federal level through amendments to the Indian Appropriation Act, which dedicated

funds to the purchase of wagons, harnesses, and other hauling equipment that would allow Natives to transport supplies on behalf of the federal government. This amendment facilitated the formation of the Cheyenne-Arapaho Transportation Company, which freighted supplies to and from the Darlington Agency at a rate of $1.50 for every 100 pounds of freight.[187]

These practices represent an important culturally consistent adaptation to the reservation system. Still, the number of Cheyenne and Arapaho men willing to labor as freighters or ranchers remained a minority for much of the late nineteenth and early twentieth centuries.[188]

Many hunting-gathering communities did, in fact, embrace agriculture as a means of survival. For example, the formerly dispersed communities who came to occupy the Grand Ronde Reservation

FIGURE 4.53. Bratley collected this eagle feather bonnet on the Rosebud Reservation, where tribal members often sold personal items out of desperation for survival. (DMNS AC.5718)

THE
CIVILIZING
MACHINE

169

FIGURE 4.54. During an educational slide show presentation, Bratley commented that this store and stock of goods were owned and managed by Tommy Pavatya, the Hopi man in the photograph. Each month Pavatya would sell about two wagonloads of goods in exchange for crafts such as baskets, blankets, pottery, and pelts. Over the course of the twentieth century, Native communities were forced to abandon many of their traditional socioeconomic practices and become increasingly integrated into a larger commercial market. Many enterprising individuals embraced the new economy and used this system to support their families while preserving and promoting traditional crafts. These sorts of adaptations demonstrate the creative ways Indigenous people negotiated their position between two worlds, a capitalistic Western world and a traditional Indigenous one. Hopi Reservation, 1902. (DMNS BR61-062)

in western Oregon actively incorporated agriculture into their lives.[189] While agriculture was at first difficult for the Tualatin because of poor soil quality and inadequate training by government farmers, by the late nineteenth century Native farms were productive. In addition, traditional practices could still supplement the produce from these plots. Women sold handwoven baskets in patterns that appealed to White customers and continued to gather berries, dig roots, and collect seeds.[190] While on the surface the Grand Ronde community gave up aspects of their traditional system of hunting and gathering, they also developed new subsistence practices that included traditional foods and annual migrations to the Willamette Valley for community celebrations and trade. These adaptations involved both innovation and cultural continuity and indicate that Native people were neither passive objects of government policies nor victims of their changing social and economic conditions.[191]

The widespread practice among Plains tribes of requesting that their beef rations be "issued on the hoof" is yet another example of culturally consistent adaptation from the early years of the reservation period in the late 1800s. Every two weeks, people would travel from across the reservation to the central agency where cattle would be hunted, butchered by the women of the tribe, their hides removed, and the meat divided and issued to each family by the elder leader of each band (figure 4.55).[192] While the original basis of Plains subsistence had changed from bison to beef, what persisted were the social practices around hunting that regulated gender roles and communal power structures and were central to Lakota Sioux, Cheyenne, and Arapaho identity. This practice of receiving beef rations on the hoof points to the adaptability and resiliency of Native communities in the face of the federal government's rigorous efforts to snuff out such cultural practices.

Accompanying the maintenance of culturally appropriate hunting practices among nomadic groups was the use of seasonal mobility to maintain social ties and conduct ceremonies. Among Plains tribes, attendance at the day schools varied greatly as families continued to practice some level of seasonal mobility. For example, on Bratley's first day as superintendent at Cantonment Boarding School, only 15 of the 120 students the school could officially accommodate were enrolled. For the first three quarters of the school year, Cheyenne and Arapaho children accompanied their parents on seasonal hunting excursions and social visits to Utes and other neighboring tribal communities. Bratley's photograph of Cheyenne-Arapaho women traveling with a child on a horse-drawn travois captures the continued practice of seasonal mobility and the use of horses during these long journeys (see figure 3.14).

Bratley also unintentionally captured in his collecting efforts the centrality of the horse among Plains tribes through the continued production of horse tack (figure 4.56). After the Spanish brought horses into North America during the sixteenth century, the animals became integral to a large number of Indigenous societies—particularly nomadic communities on the northern and southern Plains. Over the course of the next several centuries, a rich corpus of material culture developed around the horse, including ornately decorated saddles, cowls, bridles, bits, blankets, and bags. Although the reservation system

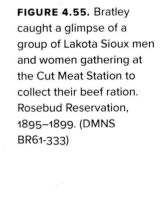

FIGURE 4.55. Bratley caught a glimpse of a group of Lakota Sioux men and women gathering at the Cut Meat Station to collect their beef ration. Rosebud Reservation, 1895–1899. (DMNS BR61-333)

and allotment program severely curtailed the mobility of Plains tribes, horses remained a staple of these societies, and Plains women continued to produce the decorative material culture associated with them.

Rosebud tribal member Leland Little Dog described to us the persistence of seasonal mobility into the twentieth century. "My grandpa's generation was all tents," Little Dog said, "they were still mobile, they were still hunting and gathering all the time for food . . . They would eat things like roasted skunk and porcupines."[193] Little Dog's comments were echoed by Sage Fast Dog in reference to his grandmother Mercy Fast Dog. "They would always travel, she said they would always travel by wagon," Fast Dog said. "And they would camp."[194] Little Dog's and Fast Dog's comments suggest that despite government efforts to force the tribe to be sedentary, many Lakota Sioux people not only maintained some aspects of their traditional mobility but incorporated modern technologies, such as wagons, into this system (figure 4.57).

This sort of innovation extends to a broad range of material culture, including architecture. In addition to decreasing mobility to control nomadic communities, allotment imposed a nuclear-focused family structure that disrupted the spiritual- and property-based systems surrounding the tipi.[195] The increasing use of American-style residences on the Rosebud Reservation is captured in an essay written by Bratley's student Maggie Otterman in 1899, which describes her home: "My father's house near close by the creek. My father has three houses and one barn. Three houses each has two windows and one chimney. And all it is made of log and dirty. My father's houses all around the tree and hill all around it. My father's houses one is large and two are small. Two beds in the house. Two dish pans in the house. One table is in the house."[196]

Although American-style houses became increasingly common on many reservations, they were not blindly accepted. For example, there is evidence that the Crow leader Plenty Coup incorporated many tipi-like features into his rectilinear home, including positioning the front door toward the east as opposed to facing the main road and placing the fireplace in the center as opposed to at the gable end, as was typical in American homes. In addition to these structural elements, Plenty Coup also furnished his home in a similar manner to a tipi, decorating the walls of his

cabin with hide liners documenting his accomplishments in battle, medicine bundles, and war accoutrements.[197] Accompanying these material elements were subtle social protocols associated with culturally appropriate behaviors, for instance, the association between house or tipi size and relative status.[198]

Although Bratley does not seem to have taken any images of the interior of Native homes, many Native cabins likely contained similar forms of stylistic melding, as seen in the image discussed above of Solomon Elk's sod home on the Rosebud Reservation (see figure 4.27). While the rectilinear form of Elk's house appears to conform to Euro-American standards, abutting the wooden structure is a large rack with dried hides, pointing to the family's continued negotiation between old and new traditions.

In addition to traditional subsistence and social practices, tribes continued to find ways to perpetuate their religious beliefs. Bratley photographed traditional rituals of the Hopi and adapted ones, such as the gatherings now associated with public holidays. The many religious objects Bratley collected could be read as a willingness of Native peoples to part with cherished ceremonial pieces—but their mere existence at the turn of the twentieth century also tangibly demonstrates that many religious practices continued.[199] In addition, Bratley was likely not privy to some of the most important ceremonies. The Courts of Indian Offenses, established in 1883, made feasts and dances, medicine men, circulating personal property in "giveaway" ceremonies, polygamy, hunting, and other cultural practices punishable criminal offenses—so many Native people took their rites underground.[200]

Native participation in pageants, plays, and parades does not actually tell us how the participants in these performances viewed those events.[201] From the perspective of anxious Whites trying to convince Native Americans to assimilate into American society, these performances were a cathartic moment that confirmed the success of assimilation. However, for some indigenous people, these public performances offered strategic opportunities to maintain a communal identity. For example, following the federal ban on the Sun Dance in the 1880s, many Plains communities, particularly the Lakota Sioux, continued

FIGURE 4.57. Bratley captured another example of the blending of traditional encampment practices with modern technologies in this picture, which depicts a large Cheyenne and Arapaho tipi encampment. Through the depiction of tipis alongside horse-drawn wagons, Bratley's photograph captures the merging of traditional encampment practices with Euro-American modes of transportation. In doing so, this image points to the dynamic ways Indigenous people negotiated the acculturation process, persisting in some practices while adapting others to accommodate new needs and materials. Cheyenne and Arapaho Reservation, 1899–1900. (DMNS BR61-362)

FIGURE 4.58. Bratley observed this Fourth of July parade. The procession was led by a mounted Lakota Sioux man wearing a large feather headdress and carrying an American flag. Many other American flags are visible at intervals along the procession. Rosebud Reservation, 1897. (DMNS BR61-265)

to gather in large groups in early July to celebrate (figure 4.58). During these celebrations, participants would build a dance ring and position a large pole in the center—as was common in the Sun Dance—and hang an American flag on it.

While these gatherings appeared to outsiders as appropriate expressions of American patriotism, for Lakotas the American flag was imbued with a series of Indigenous values associated with this ritual of thanksgiving, including bounty and protection. In the context of the Plains coup counting tradition, the American flag was also seen as a trophy that conveyed the power and honor of the warrior who wore it.[202] As suggested by Howard Bad Hand, "Through the flag, the individual warrior is honored, recognized and memorialize[d]; it symbolizes the prowess of the individual warrior[,] not patriotism."[203] These traditional meanings also took on a material form. Instead of the typical five-pointed star, the beaded American flags made by Lakota women often had four points, which was not only easier to make when beading but was intended to honor the four directions recognized by many tribal communities as sacred. The importance of the flag as a symbol of power for Lakota people has endured to the present day and continues to be used to honor veterans who have served in the US Army.

The tribes with which Bratley worked also protected and preserved traditional cultural values and associated social practices. One such practice was polygamy, which persisted into the twentieth century (figure 4.59). The Lakota Sioux particularly considered polygamy desirable, viewing the practice as lessening each wife's child-bearing and household duties.[204] Another crucial social practice that persisted among Plains tribes, was gift giving—a practice Bratley directly witnessed and benefited from. For the Arapaho, for instance, "an important way in which respect was expressed and relationships affirmed was through gift giving ceremonies in which one relative honored another or by gift exchange" (figure 4.60).[205]

Although many of Bratley's objects were purchased or bartered for, some of them were acquired as gifts. In reference to Bratley's collecting practices, Rosebud tribal member

FIGURE 4.59. Bratley took this image of a Lakota Sioux man with his wives. Among many Plains tribes, polygamy was an accepted cultural practice and was linked to a man's social status. A man could only marry additional women—often women related to his first wife—if he had acquired enough wealth to support them equally. Christian missionaries and educators discouraged polygamy, instead actively promoting the nuclear family as the correct domestic model among Indigenous communities. This image is notable for the fact that the Sioux man in this image is a policeman, a supposedly loyal employee of the American civilizing program, and yet he continues to participate in a banned social practice—polygamy. Bratley's photograph reveals that America's acculturation program was incomplete and that individuals maintained multiple and often contradictory identities and practices. Rosebud Reservation, 1895–1899. (DMNS BR61-476)

FIGURE 4.60. Bratley documented this massive gathering of women who sat in a circle to feast and give away presents. The gifts were piled in the center of the circle and included a trunk, washboards, metal tubs, bolts of cloth, and cups. Rosebud Reservation, 1897. (DMNS BR61-276)

Cathleen High Pipe discussed the common tradition of gift giving. "Say I have a gift, and I want to honor you and thank you for coming here," she said. "A lot of that goes on here . . . they thank the person that helped them and they give him a gift."[206] One example of probable gift giving within the Bratley collection occurred on October 31, 1895, when Bratley received a pair of women's moccasins from Edith Otterman (figure 4.61). The moccasins were likely intended as a gift to thank Bratley, who had given the Ottermans money several weeks earlier so they could rent a team of horses to drive to the Rosebud Agency.[207] Bratley's account books are filled with other instances of charity, such as buying bread, paying train fares for community members, or providing loans for travel to and from the agency. Although Bratley never explicitly recorded objects as gifts in his account books, his active participation in the community suggests that he was considered a valued member and may have received some of his extensive ethnographic collection through the form of gift giving.

Native people further maintained their unique Indigenous identities in material ways. Although the US government's efforts to ensure that all Native people wore "civilized dress" were largely effective, in many cases Indigenous people continued to make and wear traditional clothing (figure 4.62). In addition to producing traditional items of clothing for personal use, apparel such as moccasins and dresses became commodities that could be sold or bartered to obtain subsistence goods. While the production of traditional crafts persisted, their use-value evolved and diversified to fit the economic conditions of the twentieth century.

FIGURE 4.61. This beautiful pair of Lakota Sioux women's moccasins is decorated with quills and glass beads. (DMNS AC.5752 A-B)

No. 18.

Sioux Squaw.

As an educator and collector, Bratley occupied a somewhat ambiguous position with regard to these sorts of material expressions of identity. For example, a photo he took of Harry With Horns was most likely posed by Bratley and depicts two iconic elements of traditional Plains culture—the horse and the feather headdress (figure 4.63). While this photograph certainly fits within the romantic genre of Indian photography, it is notable

FIGURE 4.63. Harry With Horns, a Bratley student dressed in traditional regalia, sat astride a pinto pony for this portrait. Rosebud Reservation, 1895–1899. (DMNS BR61-169)

that the subject of the image is not only a young boy but one of Bratley's students. The image points to a slippage between Bratley's role as a civilizer and his hobby as a photographer. In having his pupil dress up and pose for this picture, Bratley seems to be actively promoting the continuation of non-Western traditions. The material preservation of identity is also captured in the domestic objects such as beaded utensils Bratley

collected (figure 4.64). The beaded fork, knife, and spoon reflect the creative melding together of Euro-American material culture with traditional forms of adornment among Plains tribes. These utensils are hybrid objects that demonstrate the diversity of forms Indigenous persistence could take, including continuation, accommodation, adaptation, or, in this case, amalgamation.

Bratley's experiences while living and working among Native Americans at the turn of the century reveal the widespread persistence of traditional cultural practices and identities in the face of the federal government's assimilationist policies. This is not to deny the radical changes Native communities underwent during the height of American colonialism. But many of the contemporary tribal members with whom we spoke emphasized not loss and ruin but resiliency and survival. S'Klallam tribal member Gene Jones captured this sentiment when discussing his parents', Foster and Clara Jones, experience at Tulalip Indian Boarding School, north of Seattle. "A lot of our people blame that boarding school for beating our culture and our traditions out of them," he said, "but my mom and dad both used to say that's bunk because they held on to all their traditions and culture."[208]

FIGURE 4.64. A beaded fork, knife, and spoon Bratley collected show the fusion of different forms and traditions on the Rosebud Reservation in the late 1800s. (DMNS AC.5617A-C)

Jones's statement suggests that Indian schools were places where Indigenous identities and practices were *both* stamped out and actively perpetuated.[209]

Although federal administrators and teachers believed in environmental determinism—that a group's surroundings, customs, dress, and food determined how they would behave—for many Native people having a short haircut or wearing "civilized dress" did not prevent them from "being Indians."[210] This perspective is reflected in a letter an Oglala man named Makes Enemy wrote to the commissioner of Indian affairs petitioning to allow his son to wear long hair to school: "Cutting the hair does not make us Indians like they [*sic*] ways of the white man any better and it does not keep us from being Indians."[211]

The continuation of tribal traditions in the face of government-sponsored education was also articulated by Leland Little Dog. "Just because you go to [school] doesn't mean you automatically lose your culture," he said.[212] Little Dog's comments suggest that for many tribal members, Euro-American education and even religion did not *replace* Lakota Sioux identity. Other Rosebud residents confirmed this sentiment, as they emphasized the survival of Lakota Sioux culture and the importance of family connections in helping to preserve their lifeways. This emphasis on familial history is both a deeply rooted part of Lakota Sioux knowledge systems and a means of redressing the destructive legacy of America's assimilationist policies.

"We carry on everything that we were taught," Cathleen High Pipe insisted, "that was handed down to us by our parents and from what their parents gave them."[213]

▼ ▽ ▼

Resistance and persistence converge at times. They are two sides of the same coin. Cultural tenacity as a form of rebellion is captured in Bratley's photograph collection from the Cheyenne and Arapaho Reservation—particularly an image depicting thirteen play tipis arranged in a typical U-shaped encampment in front of the Cantonment Boarding School (figure 4.65). Play tipis, along with dolls dressed in traditional clothes, were a standard part

FIGURE 4.65. Surprisingly, given the school's civilizing mission, these play tipis were allowed to be erected in front of Cantonment Boarding School. The tipis, likely only intended for child's play, would have allowed the students to continue a sense of connection to their traditional identities. Cheyenne and Arapaho Reservation, 1899–1900. (DMNS BR61-377)

FIGURE 4.66. This Indian doll, made of leather and decorated with glass seed beads, would have helped children imagine themselves and others as being Indian. Bratley gifted this doll to Margaret Mamet, his granddaughter, prior to 1944. Cheyenne and Arapaho Reservation, 1899–1900. (DMNS AN.2014.171.2)

of a Cheyenne or Arapaho child's upbringing and were used to teach young people proper conventions of behavior and dress (figure 4.66). The continued use of tipis and dolls, if only for play, reflects the often subtle ways in which Native traditions persisted despite educators' attempts to purge them. Such sedition could even be woven into subtle forms of material signaling—for example, the use of a morning star symbol (the cross) and a tipi representation (the triangles) on Lakota Sioux beaded hatbands—even when an Anglicized name is included on the hatband or an individual is dressed entirely in Western clothes (figures 4.67 and 4.68). Although it is unclear how intentional this signaling might have been, its existence shows at least an implicit desire to maintain traditional forms of knowledge and meaning making.

Spiritual practices and religious beliefs often continued in the midst of missionization. While the Christianization efforts of churches and day school instructors were in many cases successful, in other instances these attempts at conversion failed (figure 4.69). In spite of missionary efforts, the influence of Christianity on the Hopi Reservation where Bratley taught was less pronounced than in other parts of Indian country (figure 4.70). The Spanish had supported Catholic missionaries at Hopi for centuries, yet few converted. American Protestants undertook similar attempts at conversion; for example, between 1893 and 1902, the Mennonite Church, led by anthropologist cum missionary H. R. Voth, actively worked to convert Hopis at Oraibi.[214] Despite statements by Voth that the Hopi "more and more opened their kivas and their knowledge and their hearts to us,"[215] after a decade of work the Mennonite Church had managed to baptize only one village leader (figures 4.71 and 4.72). Tribal member Leigh J. Kuwanwisiwma told us about the general failure of missionary efforts at Hopi and noted that the Hopi are "still a non-Christian tribe and that helps us fight and retain our culture."[216]

S'Klallam tribal member Gene Jones recounted another example of persistence as a form of resistance to assimilation. Reflecting on his mother's schooling experience at Tulalip, he stated that "my mother was one of the last basket weavers so a lot of the kids

FIGURE 4.68. This Lakota Sioux man wearing Euro-American clothing, then referred to as "citizen's dress," still wore a beaded hatband with traditional symbols. Rosebud Reservation, 1895–1899 (DMNS BR61-277)

FIGURE 4.69. A bag with intricate beaded designs and quillwork, used to hold a pipe, illustrates the continuity of traditional religious practices amid attempts to turn the Lakota Sioux into Christians. (DMNS AC.5809)

FIGURE 4.70. Bratley photographed this kiva, the Hopi religious house. It is underground, reached by a long ladder. The image testifies to the Hopi weathering missionization. Hopi Reservation, 1902. (DMNS BR61-126)

would come and say, 'Clara will you show us how to make baskets?' It was made out of what we called cattail cordage. And she said, 'Oh yeah.' So they'd go out and pick cordage for the baskets." Eventually, Clara was caught teaching traditional basket making to other students and was punished by having her knuckles wrapped. According to Jones, the schoolteachers "hit her with that sharp edge of the ruler and she had three scars on her hand. And she would cry every time she'd think about that."[217]

Jones's story about his mother reveals the various ways Native children undermined the school system's acculturation program through the continued production of traditional crafts. Clara's story also reveals the often intense physical violence children experienced when caught practicing their culture. It was precisely these sorts of violent reprisals that Native parents feared and tried to prevent. Such resistance is deeply embedded in the will to survive, to persist.

FIGURE 4.71. Bratley was apparently granted access into Hopi kivas. He photographed two Hopi men in the ceremonial chamber, one spinning cotton and the other weaving a blanket. Weaving was an important but subtle means of defying the totalizing effects of colonization, as the kilts, capes, belts, and blankets were needed for traditional Hopi religious and cultural practices. Hopi Reservation, 1902. (DMNS BR61-225)

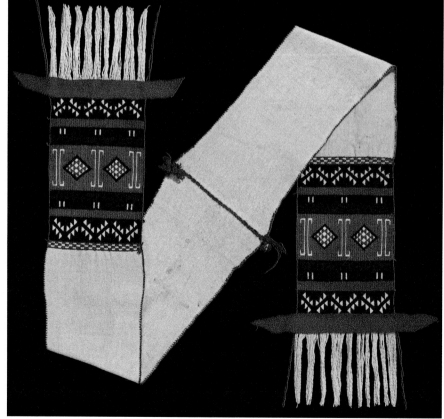

FIGURE 4.72. A woven belt Bratley collected demonstrates the ongoing religious practices among Hopi at the turn of the twentieth century. (DMNS AC.5580)

Notes

1. Adams 1997:27.
2. Abbott 1898; Miles 1879.
3. Cahill 2011:39.
4. Adams 1988:8.
5. Stuart 1978:29.
6. Genetin-Pilawa 2012; Kickingbird and Ducheneaux 1973.
7. Reel 1900:426.
8. Glancy 2014:13; Pratt 1967.
9. Richard Henry Pratt cited in Lookingbill 2006:159.
10. Lookingbill 2006.
11. Lookingbill 2006:162.
12. Glancy 2014:84.
13. Lookingbill 2006:150.
14. Stout 2012:28; see also Reddick 2000.
15. Pratt 1967.
16. Trennert 1988.
17. Pratt 1892:46.
18. Churchill 2004:88.
19. Ellis 1996:98–99.
20. Adams 1997:28.
21. Jones 1898:4.
22. Cahill 2011:83.
23. Emmerich 1991; Wright 1895:297.
24. Browning 1895a:23.
25. Standing Bear 1975:193.
26. Archuleta et al. 2000; DeJong 1993; Hoerig 2002; Lomawaima 1994.
27. Bratley n.d.a:107.
28. Bratley n.d.a:108–109.
29. Qoyawayma 1992:28.
30. Bratley n.d.b.
31. Duncan 1990:188.
32. Andrews 2002:418.
33. Black 2016.
34. Arthur 1998; Butler 2011; Foucault 1979, 1980; Shilling 2003.
35. Lomawaima 1993:236.
36. Farr 1984:39.

37. Burton 1902:153.
38. Bratley 1902d.
39. Bratley 1902d.
40. Jones 1898:3.
41. Hailmann 1896:343.
42. Bloom 2000.
43. See Klotz 2017.
44. Neuman 2008:180.
45. Gonzalez 2016.
46. Atkins 1886:xxiii.
47. Adams 1997:104.
48. Spack 2002:97.
49. Bratley n.d.a:98.
50. Charles et al. 2012:23.
51. Hebert 2016.
52. Sullivan 2016.
53. Hailmann 1896:8.
54. Bartelt 1991:188; Gram 2015:113.
55. Mosquida 2016.
56. Yellowman 2016.
57. Hailmann 1896:347.
58. Hutchinson 2009:57; Lomawaima 1994:83–87; Paxton 2006; Whalen 2016.
59. Valentine 1911.
60. Lomawaima 1993:230; Valentine 1911.
61. Trennert 1982.
62. Reel 1901b:450–451.
63. Bratley 1900:330.
64. Bratley 1900:330.
65. Andrews 2002:426–427.
66. Reel 1901b:457; Hailmann 1895:344.
67. Reel 1900:432.
68. Bentley 2010:188.
69. Bentley 2010:195.
70. Information on Pratt from Adams 2001:26.
71. Whiteman 2016b.
72. Bratley n.d.a:106.
73. See Bess 2013.
74. Reel 1908:14.
75. Lindsey 1995:xi.

76. Cooper 2015:3; Reel 1898:339.
77. Cahill 2011:105.
78. Bratley n.d.b:21.
79. Reel 1898:343.
80. Gere 2005.
81. Horne and McBeth 1998.
82. Qoyawayma 1992.
83. Enoch 2002.
84. Andrews 2002:423.
85. Standing Bear 1975:192–193.
86. Gonzalez 2016.
87. Markowitz 2002:12; Mead 1976.
88. Markowitz 2002:15.
89. In Butts 1996:242.
90. Devens 1992; Markowitz 2002:22.
91. Markowitz 2002:26.
92. Prucha 1986:481.
93. Prucha 1986:482.
94. Genetin-Pilawa 2012:95.
95. Genetin-Pilawa 2012:94.
96. Markowitz 2002:14.
97. Markowitz 2002:15–16.
98. Markowitz 2002:26.
99. Mihesuah 1993.
100. See Gerlach 1973.
101. Markowitz 2002.
102. Bratley 1893–1897.
103. High Pipe 2016c.
104. Markowitz 2002:5–6, 10.
105. Markowitz 2002:21.
106. Markowitz 2002:18–20.
107. Little Dog 2016.
108. Kuwanwisiwma 2016.
109. Davis 2001:20.
110. Adams 1997; Hyer 1990; Lomawaima 1994.
111. E.g., Butts 1996:245; Child 1996; Qoyawayma 1992:19.
112. Dorchester 1893.
113. Cahill 2011:77–78; Duncan 1990:166–167; McBeth 1983a, 1983b.
114. Bratley 1893–1897.

115. Bratley n.d.a:97.

116. George 2017.

117. Gilbert 2010:19.

118. Kittie is also often spelled Kitty in Bratley's records and notes.

119. Bratley n.d.a:108.

120. Little Dog 2016.

121. Broken Leg 2016.

122. Bratley n.d.a:108.

123. McChesney 1903:319.

124. Bratley n.d.a.:110.

125. Bratley 1897–1901:101.

126. Bratley 1900:329.

127. Bratley 1897–1901.

128. Gilbert 2010:16–18; Whiteley 2008; Williams 1895:119.

129. https://www.nps.gov/alca /learn/historyculture/hopi -prisoners-on-the-rock.htm, accessed July 24, 2017.

130. http://www.nps.gov/alca /learn/historyculture/hopi -prisoners-on-the-rock.htm, accessed May 21, 2016.

131. Whiteley 1988.

132. Whiteley 2008.

133. Gilbert 2005:3.

134. Adams 1979:342.

135. Bratley n.d.c.

136. Bratley 1897–1901:101.

137. Lomawaima 1993:233.

138. Lomawaima 1993:234.

139. Farr 1984:24.

140. Yellowman 2016.

141. Yellowman 2016.

142. Southwell and Lovett 2010:21.

143. Lewis 1991:126.

144. Little Dog 2016.

145. High Pipe 2016c.

146. Jones 1900a:33.

147. Fowler 2002:213, 221.

148. Fowler 2002:22–24.

149. Berthrong 1992:59.

150. Berthrong 1992:85.

151. Fowler 2002:25.

152. Berthrong 1992:87.

153. Galler 2017:212–213.

154. Galler 2017:206.

155. Galler 2017:217–219.

156. Andrews 2002:417–418.

157. Lewis 1991:131.

158. Lewis 1991:140.

159. N.A. 1901.

160. Adams 1997; Child 1999; Lomawaima 1994.

161. Davis 2001:20.

162. McBeth 1983; Panich 2013:107.

163. Hoxie 1985:61.

164. Hoxie 1985:65.

165. Hoxie 1985:71.

166. Bratley n.d.a:97.

167. Bratley n.d.a:99.

168. Suttles 1990:468.

169. Suttles 1990:468.

170. Bratley 1893–1897.

171. All the S'Klallam we interviewed said that clams only bake for about twenty minutes—not twenty-four hours or more.

172. Bratley n.d.a:98–99.

173. Wisnowski 2016.

174. Ewing 1900b:202.

175. Affairs 1948:198; White 2015:111.

176. Bratley n.d.a:110.

177. Ewing 1900b:203.

178. Polacca 2016.

179. Bratley n.d.a:111.

180. Isenberg 2000; Smits 1994.

181. Bratley n.d.a:69.

182. Bratley 1893–1897, 1897–1901.

183. High Pipe 2016c.

184. Berthrong 1992:68.

185. Lewis 1991:126.

186. Berthrong 1992:61.

187. Berthrong 1992:62.

188. Berthrong 1992:63.

189. Leavelle 1998:434.

190. Leavelle 1998:438.

191. Leavelle 1998:434.

192. Southwell and Lovett 2010:24.

193. Little Dog 2016.

194. Fast Dog 2016.

195. Carter et al. 2005:100.

196. Otterman, 1899.

197. Carter et al. 2005:103–104.

198. Carter et al. 2005:108.

199. Bernadin et al. 2003:14.

200. Corrigan and Neal 2010:143; Kerstetter 2015:145; Lazarus 1991:100; O'Brien 1993:150; Schmidt 2015:46–47.

201. Gram 2016:269.

202. https://www.nytimes.com /1999/11/28/nyregion/the -view-from-ledyard-the-flag -shows-up-in-american -indian-art.html, accessed July 11, 2018.

203. https://www.nytimes.com /1999/11/28/nyregion/the -view-from-ledyard-the-flag -shows-up-in-american -indian-art.html, accessed July 11, 2018.

204. Duncan 1990:114.

205. Fowler 2002:4.

206. High Pipe 2016a.

207. Bratley 1893–1897, 1897–1901.

208. Jones 2017.

209. Hutchinson 2009:88; Lomawaima 1994:xiv.

210. Carter et al. 2005:99.

211. Andrews 2002:420.

212. Little Dog 2016.

213. High Pipe 2016a.

214. Nicholas 1991.

215. James 1974.

216. Kuwanwisiwma 2016.

217. Jones 2017.

The colonial enterprise in America has been a collision—a violent smashup of peoples, cultures, languages, economies, religions, identities, possessions, desires, and aspirations. These collisions vary in scale—small and large, personal and structural. The responses by those subject to colonization shift over time, ranging from guerrilla warfare to diplomacy, accommodation to acculturation, defiance to acceptance. In turn, the colonizers may be reshaped by their subjects—taking on new foods, ideas, and politics. In the aftermath of such cataclysmic collisions, when the haze of the explosion has finally cleared, the participants are forced to look around, assess the damage, and pick up the pieces to begin anew. Like most crashes, the collision that occurred between Euro-American settlers and Native Americans in North America was in many ways unpredictable, its fallout unknowable.

Amid colonialism's ashes, settlers and Natives are left to make sense of the encounter and reconfigure their behavior and beliefs. Although many perceive the United States largely to be a postcolonial nation—the extraction of Indian resources and the threats to Native cultures a thing of the past—the colonial collision with Indigenous people persists to the present. A brief glimpse at today's news feed documents the continued clash of Western and Indigenous priorities and perspectives. From the fight over the Dakota Access Pipeline, which threatens sacred places and needed water for the Standing Rock Sioux and Cheyenne River Sioux, to the cruel stereotypes of Indians as sports mascots, Native Americans continue to battle over their natural resources, representations, and cultural patrimony.

Jesse H. Bratley's story is also a story of colliding worlds. As an Anglo-American man and employee of the Indian Service, he had to directly confront the Native people and cultures he was tasked with assimilating. The way educators like Bratley and the Native communities he worked with negotiated the realities of daily life during this transformative period in American history is complex. Scholars have drawn on a number of theoretical frameworks to make sense of the multifaceted relationships that formed among Indigenous people, colonial administrators, and settlers. This body of literature provides a helpful jumping-off point for working through and understanding Bratley's collection and the historical moment of which he was a part.

5

OBJECTS OF SURVIVANCE

Although a comprehensive engagement with this literature is not possible here, several theoretical perspectives seem to capture the experiences of Bratley and his Native pupils. To conclude this book, we briefly explore these theoretical framings as they apply to Bratley, the Indian education system, and the larger American colonial project. After grappling with these theories, we trace the legacy of America's acculturation policies, outlining how Native perspectives on education have evolved over the course of the twentieth and twenty-first centuries and highlighting the various ways contemporary Native communities have co-opted education for their own benefit.

▼ ▽ ▼

To make sense of the relationships that formed between Euro-American settlers and Native people in the aftermath of the colonial collision, some scholars have turned to the idea of *acculturation*.[1] The acculturation paradigm focuses on cultural transmission between two or more autonomous cultural systems.[2] The process of transmission is impacted by ecological factors, demography, the social position of the colonizer and colonized (e.g., missionary, military, or teacher), and the types of intercultural communication employed.[3] The result of these acculturative processes is multifaceted and can include substitution (both cultures replace an element from their culture), syncretism (blending of elements), compartmentalization (keeping separate particular cultural aspects), origination (creation of new elements), and assimilation (i.e., culture loss).[4]

One outgrowth of the acculturation literature is the notion of *transculturation*, first used by Cuban scholar Fernando Ortiz and popularized in American anthropology by A. Irving Hallowell.[5] The transculturation concept differs from acculturation models of colonial interaction through its emphasis on individual transformation rather than cultural systems. Hallowell defined transculturation as "the process whereby individuals under a variety of circumstances are temporarily or permanently detached from one group, enter the web of social relations that constitute another society, and come under the influence of its customs, ideas, and values to a greater or lesser degree."[6] The particular way or extent to which an individual's cultural practices and social identities might change is structured by various factors, such as the individual's age, length of contact with the different culture, previous perspectives, and whether the individual was willingly or forcibly involved with the new cultural group.[7] For some, this shift may be superficial, manifesting itself primarily through externally visible changes such as dress while their values and beliefs remain essentially unchanged. For others, transculturation may entail a profound psychological and behavioral transformation.

In many ways, the US Indian education system conforms to the acculturation and transculturation paradigms as explanatory frameworks.[8] Federal policymakers intended to speed up the rate of acculturation of Native people through the dissolution of traditional power structures and social units via allotment and reservations and through systematic

FIGURE 5.1. A Sioux woman poses in a shawl alongside an empty field. She wears a small cross around her neck, suggesting that she had embraced Christianity, at least in some ways. Rosebud Reservation, 1895–1899. (DMNS BR61-178)

instruction in Western thought and practice. Indian children experienced varying degrees of transculturation, some adopting only outward elements of Anglo-American identity such as English, trim hairstyles, and civilized dress, while others underwent deeper transitions—for example, those who embraced Christianity (figure 5.1).[9] The motivations behind both superficial and "deep" changes in Native behavior were diverse and complex, and they often more closely followed the goals and ideals of Indigenous actors than those of the colonialists. The material effects of acculturative processes can be seen, for instance, in a beaded blanket strip decorated with American flags, which Bratley collected (figure

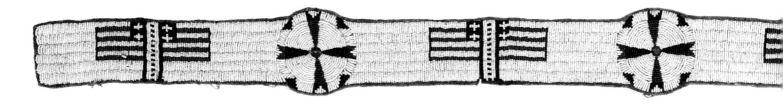

FIGURE 5.2. By incorporating the American flag into a traditional beaded blanket strip—and using the symbol for the morning star for stars on the American flag—this object that Bratley collected on the Rosebud Reservation helps reveal acculturative processes and syncretism. (DMNS AC.5676)

5.2). As discussed in chapter 4, by the 1890s, the American flag was widely incorporated into Native art across the Plains. For many Lakota, the American flag has taken on several different meanings. During the Plains Indian Wars, the flag was considered a trophy, but by the 1880s—the period when Bratley's blanket strip was made—the flag had become a symbol of protection and was used as a signal of peace.[10] As the tourist trade in Native crafts grew over the course of the twentieth century, the American flag took on a different role for bead workers, appealing to the patriotic sensibilities and aesthetics of Euro-American consumers. In merging a traditional form of craftsmanship with an image that symbolizes American power and unity, the blanket strip Bratley collected exemplifies the type of syncretism that emerged from the collision of Indigenous and American cultures.[11]

While providing a more nuanced explanation of individual experiences, the transcultural paradigm fails to capture all of what Bratley's life and collection reveal: transculturation approaches tend to focus on identity transformation within the subordinate community and assume a unidirectional movement of power in which the dominant colonizer transforms the colonized.[12] This emphasis on colonial power glosses over the ways cross-cultural interaction brought about change among the dominant group (figure 5.3). In other words, this theory is somewhat incomplete because not only did Bratley change the students he taught, they also changed him.

Bratley and other Indian Service employees occupied positions of power, but their identities were also altered—to varying degrees—by the relationships they formed with Native children and their communities. As historian Cathleen D. Cahill documented in her history of the Indian Service, after their work on the ground, many teachers "became less rigid in their expectations about cultural change, more appreciative of aspects of Native culture, and better able to see Indians as distinct human beings rather than a 'race' to be assimilated."[13] During his tenure on five different reservations, Bratley embraced the civilizing mission of the Indian Service, dutifully carrying out the charge of transforming Native children physically, intellectually, and morally.

However, his story is not a simple one of unidirectional power—of colonizer and colonized. In transforming Native children into "good Americans," Bratley was also transformed, describing his work among Native schoolchildren as one of "the biggest stepping stones to success in my life."[14] Bratley occupied multiple, sometimes conflicting worlds. He was both a devout Christian and immensely interested in documenting and attending ceremonies and festivities. He was a strict disciplinarian and devoted employee of the Indian Service, and yet he often blurred the lines between policy and practice, sometimes

FIGURE 5.3. Bratley photographed the Havasupai Agency farmer "Mr. Bushnel" holding gourds outside of his home, with corn drying on top of the roof. It is striking that the farmer depended on traditional Havasupai crops to feed agency employees and students, used traditional methods to process the crops, and himself occupied a traditional Havasupai brush and earth home. Havasupai Reservation, 1900. (DMNS BR61-109)

teaching students in their Native language and developing close relationships with some community members. By the time he retired, Bratley's educational goals with his collection reflected a changing current in mainstream America that increasingly acknowledged the realities of cultural pluralism and the value of Native America.[15]

Bratley's journals and collection lay bare critical slippages between policy and practice and point to the importance of individual experience in understanding the colonial process in nineteenth-century America. The Indian education system was structured around the notion that there was a unidirectional flow of culture from civilized teacher to savage Indian. This flow was often interrupted and occasionally reversed. This reversal is evidenced by several comments Corabelle Fellows made during her time as an instructor among the Lakota Sioux in the 1880s. "With something like consternation I realized how keenly I was enjoying myself, almost one with these Indians," she wrote, "that I was doing their way, not they mine."[16] A similar sentiment was captured in a statement Bratley made to a reporter regarding his son Homer, who "began to acquire so much of the various Indian dialects and songs that they decided to leave the service before the children became all 'Injun.'"[17] Bratley's fear over his children becoming Indian suggests that the overwhelming civilizing influence of Anglo-American culture was not as complete as policymakers trusted it was (figure 5.4).

Acculturation and transculturation paradigms also tend to obscure the ways Native people actively confronted assimilationist policies. The focus can be on how colonialism successfully changed colonial subjects compared to how those subjects worked against the colonialist enterprise's entire premise. Many of the Native community members we interviewed impressed upon us that the transformation of Native life did not consist of an even and progressive top-down replacement of traditions and material practices with European customs.[18] The fact that there was nothing inevitable about the trajectory of colonialism in America is revealed by the variety of ways Native people responded to American policies. In contrast to acculturation and transculturation models, the framework of *resistance* shifts our focus away from elites and conceptualizes the colonial landscape as a dynamic patchwork of domination, antagonism, accommodation, and negotiation.[19]

The ways Indigenous and American people negotiated the fallout of colonialism were varied.[20] As with most human collisions, the period of Indian education entailed violence—both emotional and physical. American teachers enacted this violence on the bodies and minds of Native children; Indigenous people who spurned incorporation by physically threatening or harming teachers also faced martial consequences. For example, in 1897, Elizabeth Flanders (Menomini) and Fannie Eaglehorn (Sioux) set the girl's dormitory at Carlisle boarding school on fire, later receiving an eighteen-month sentence in the penitentiary and a $2,000 fine.[21] In addition to these blatant acts of violence, Indigenous people negotiated federal policy in more subtle ways, including running away,

FIGURE 5.5. Later in life, Jesse and Della Bratley visited Charlie Black Calf, who was a student of theirs at the Lower Cut Meat Creek Day School. Together at Black Calf's home, they reminisced about the school garden, watermelons, and ice cream. Rosebud Reservation, date unknown. (Children of Dr. Forrest G. Bratley)

refusing to speak English, breaking rules, and continuing to practice traditional customs in covert ways.[22]

Resistance studies have often focused on historical instances of armed conflict and Native manipulations of economic and judicial systems.[23] Applying resistance theory to the Indian education experience offers compelling insights into how it works in a different social frame. However, in focusing on a bottom-up understanding of colonialism, resistance approaches may ignore the fact that colonial power structures—particularly in the case of boarding schools—remained intact after these acts of rebellion had passed. In Indian schools, these acts of dissent no doubt changed the system's trajectory, but ultimately the system did change the lives of Indian communities. Hence, while transculturation glosses over modes of resistance, in turn, focusing only on resistance avoids the ways in which transculturation did unfold.

Furthermore, while studies of resistance capture the nuanced ways Native people responded to and negotiated colonial systems, in doing so we lose some clarity on Bratley's role and the experience of other employees in the Indian Service. Indian Service employees were not always violent. The division between civilizer and civilized was not always rigid. During this period, some employees developed friendships with the members of the Indigenous community they were tasked with civilizing—attending celebrations, exchanging goods and services, and sometimes even marrying (figure 5.5).[24] In addition to revealing moments of resistance, Bratley's experiences also expose an "intimate colonialism," which "created complex webs of power on the reservations and in the schools" where "the lines of administrative authority often became confused because of the personal or intimate links between family members."[25] While resistance is an important part of the story, it is not the only story.

One concept that seeks this fuller story is that of the *contact zone*, which scholars have used to tack between individual experiences and the larger cultural systems present within colonial contexts. As originally conceptualized by Mary Louise Pratt, contact zones are

"social spaces where cultures meet, clash, and grapple with each other, often in contexts of highly asymmetrical relations of power, such as colonialism, slavery, or their aftermaths as they are lived out in many parts of the world today."[26] Within the contact zone, the dominant power—in this case, the United States—creates a negotiated space for cultural exchanges and transactions, a space that is needed to maintain imperial power.[27]

While recognizing the systemic and persistent nature of colonial power, the contact zone approach also draws on the notion of transculturation, which is conceptualized in this context as the process marginalized groups use to select and invent from materials the dominant society transmits.[28] In emphasizing cross-cultural negotiation and translation, the contact zone approach recognizes that power relations are unequal while allowing for Indigenous negotiations, challenges, and manipulations of that power.

The contact zone paradigm provides a productive lens for understanding the Indian school system and Bratley's role within it. Bratley regularly created negotiated spaces of cross-cultural interaction—for example, when he exchanged photographs and ration goods with Native Americans for the artifacts they owned or produced.[29] Although the Native communities Bratley worked among engaged in selective exchanges from which they often benefited, the legitimacy and appropriateness of these acts was always framed from the point of view of the party in authority (figure 5.6).[30] As Leland Little Dog, a Rosebud tribal member, succinctly stated to us, despite any of Bratley's good intentions, "this guy was under government orders to get them to knock it off, to stop being Indian."[31] The asymmetry of the contact zone is captured by the fact that Bratley appears to have never officially reported any of the instances of violent opposition he faced while teaching. In refusing to even acknowledge these acts of defiance as legitimate or of real cause for concern, Bratley rendered them effectively invisible. At its essence, the contact zone approach tends to produce a narrative in which dominance inevitably wins.

Although the interactions between Native Americans and Indian Service employees were inherently unequal, emphasizing the US government's overwhelming dominance leaves little room for the stories of resistance and persistence contemporary tribal members shared and which are reflected in many of the photographs and accounts Bratley made himself. Understanding what Native people think they were doing within colonial contexts is just as important as understanding how dominant power structures operate to constrain people's choices and interactions.

▼ ▽ ▼

For us, the key concept is *survivance*, which scholars have used to understand how Indigenous people were able to preserve traditional practices and identities within contexts of asymmetrical power.[32] Developed by Anishinaabe scholar Gerald Vizenor, the concept of survivance goes beyond mere survival.[33] Unlike the term *survival*—which presents an image of Indigenous people holding on to tradition for dear life—survivance entails creative and dynamic adaptions to current circumstances that ensure future possibilities.[34] In other words, survivance denies stasis and inaction, focusing on movement and action. Survivance is fluid; it captures how Native Americans often take a flexible approach to traumatizing change in an effort to counter colonization (figure 5.7). Native Americans who became teachers in the early Indian school system could be considered the embodiment of this concept—individuals who had to overcome colonial dominance by living within it.[35] These early trailblazers developed innovative ways of adapting to American society while maintaining a sense of communal identity; "those feelings of identity and strength, which overrode the horrors of the past, shaped the activities of those who were drawn to the new reservation institutions."[36] In this sense, the framework of survivance captures both survival and resistance.[37]

Most scholars have deployed Vizenor's concept of survivance in the realm of literature, rhetoric, and storytelling—including in the context of the Indian school experience.[38] Sharing stories about education gives Native people "an active sense of presence" in the world and is a medium through which contemporary descendants can renounce and replace colonial narratives of dominance, tragedy, and victimhood.[39] Fewer scholars have attended to the material embodiment and expression of the intersection between survival and resistance. Photography is one area that has pushed researchers to consider how Native Americans are not merely passive subjects but dynamic actors. As the American studies professor Steven D. Hoelscher has argued, "A camera may have been a tool of domination, but it could also be turned into a technology of survivance."[40]

Anthropologist Amy Lonetree saw this when she gazed at a collection of historic images of her Ho-Chunk ancestors. Many of these images, taken in Black River Falls, Wisconsin,

FIGURE 5.7A/B. Bratley took this photo of Red Hill, Watonga, Oklahoma (TOP). During an interview, Cheyenne tribal member Marie Whiteman explained that Red Hill was traditionally used as a sacred place for fasting by Cheyenne people. The hill had to be abandoned as a sacred site during the 1940s because of interference from road traffic and farming (BOTTOM). However, the religious practices associated with Red Hill continued but were relocated to a different place. Oklahoma, 1899–1900. (DMNS BR61-383/Chip Colwell)

and dating between 1879 and 1942, were taken at the request of the Ho-Chunk themselves—essentially, they are family photographs. In some images, the subjects are romantic in traditional regalia. In other images, they wear modern clothing—sometimes intensely dapper, other times more plain. But all of them radiate strength and resiliency during a period of intense colonial turmoil, what the Ho-Chunk remember as the "dark ages."[41] Lonetree argues that viewers today should reflect on how "every encounter with the images should begin with the recognition that you are not just looking at Indians; you are looking at survivors whose presence in the frame speaks to a larger story of Ho-Chunk survivance."[42] Art historian Brittany Watson has further solidified this notion of "objects of survivance" by articulating how historic photographs—and by implication any artifact— allow us to trace the complex presence of actual Indians in spaces from which they have been erased.[43]

How to trace survivance through material evidence? Looking at Native settlements in New England through the eighteenth and nineteenth centuries, archaeologist Stephen W.

Silliman has investigated how Indigenous peoples sought "to change in order to stay the same."[44] In other words, how did Native Americans both accept and elude colonialism, as seen through the technology they adopted or rejected? Analyzing artifacts from Eastern Pequot settlements, Silliman points out how the prevalence of European artifacts found there could be read as evidence of culture change—or, alternately, the continued use of Indigenous tools could be interpreted as resistance. Silliman insists that this is a false dichotomy because "survivance for the Eastern Pequot meant always negotiating what it meant to be Native in post-1600 New England."[45] The result for the Eastern Pequot was a form of "hybridity, a blending of new and old cultural materialities" that "situates community identities and authenticities in unique historical trajectories that involve community members looking back (social memory) and moving forward (intentional acts and repetitive practice)."[46]

Silliman's work has been expanded by his colleague Matthew A. Beaudoin, who works in Ontario, Canada. He similarly saw how European artifacts at Mohawk sites did not result from the inhabitants' different identities but rather how multiple "identities (ethnic, social, colonial, gender) are simultaneously expressed, contested, denied, and revealed in daily choices."[47] The Mohawk use of European tools and technology was a choice "to incorporate and change their materials and dispositions without losing essential connections to identities, communities, or their respective pasts."[48]

The Indian artifacts and images in Bratley's collection are objects of survivance—objects that overcome colonial hegemony by finding ways to live within the colonial frame. The objects in this collection are the products of the colonial moment, yet they also escape that moment and transcend them; they are objects that encapsulate domination *and* opposition; they are objects of change *and* continuity; they are objects of impotence *and* strength; they are objects of loss *and* profit; they are objects of shame *and* honor.

Many of the objects Bratley collected show how tribal artisans continued to express deep value for the very things that were being lost in this colonial moment. For example, a Lakota Sioux bag Bratley obtained includes a prominent image of a bison (figure 5.8). By the time Bratley was living in South Dakota, the great bison herds had long passed. But the bag's maker was inserting the image of this revered animal back into the present, insisting on its importance, even though the bison was nearly extinct and the hunters were confined to the reservation. Although Lakota Sioux men could no longer stalk the bison they revered, the animal took on a new role as a nostalgic icon that appealed to Western fantasies of the burgeoning tourist trade in Indigenous crafts. In this new world, the bison was still a source of subsistence.

Or consider the artifacts in the Bratley collection that relate to Christian imagery and practices. Most striking to us is a Bible cover adorned with colorful quillwork (figure 5.9).

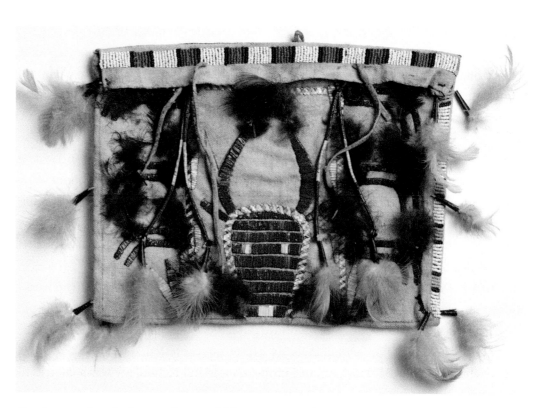

On the one hand, this artifact could be interpreted as evidence of conversion, a capitulation to the foreign doctrines of Christianity. On the other hand, the book cover could be interpreted as evidence of resistance, a subtle refusal to accept Christianity, materially marked by literally covering up and clothing the foreign book in traditional materials. Perhaps the book cover is not an either-or object, not representing change or continuity but a means to achieve both. An insistence on labeling people as changed or not, as modern or traditional, is a false dichotomy. If we consider the book cover as an object of survivance, we can reimagine how it might have provided its maker with a means of navigating the foreign beliefs on her own terms.

We might also reconsider Bratley's photograph of a young Lakota Sioux woman wearing a cross around her neck (see figure 5.1). Other photographs suggest that Christian converts prominently wore the cross—for example, Solomon Elk, an Episcopal convert, wearing a large cross (see figure 4.27). So the young woman might have been a convert. If this is the case, then we might imagine how her choice to visibly wear a cross allowed her to more easily navigate the authorities on the Rosebud Reservation at the time and so perhaps instilled a sense of control and calm during such tumultuous days. However, it is also possible that what appealed to this young woman had nothing to do with Christianity. Whether conscious or unconscious, many converts recast elements of Christianity to reflect aspects of traditional Lakota spirituality, for example, the substitution of a morning catechism for prayers to the four winds.[49] From this perspective, the woman in Bratley's photos may have worn the cross because of its resonance as a traditional symbol of the four directions. If this is the case, then it could have been a sly move in this colonial moment, to

FIGURE 5.9. Bratley received this quilled book cover from Grey Eagle Tail on January 4, 1898, in exchange for a photograph. (DMNS AC.5773)

outwardly display an image that would suggest conversion, while the object in fact served to reinforce traditional beliefs. Of course, we will never know what really motivated this young woman. The point is that seeing this image through the lens of survivance opens up a window into the ways Native Americans *chose* to persevere.

Other Bratley images capture these active choices. Among the most powerful for us is the image of the Cheyenne camp next to Cantonment Boarding School around 1899–1900 (see figure 4.34). Here we see how Cheyenne parents and elders released their children to colonial authorities—and yet they also simultaneously thwarted that move by inserting themselves into the scene. The Cheyenne are letting go and holding on, all at once. Furthermore, camping alongside the boarding schools can be read as an assertion of power by Native parents; in close proximity, these parents could better monitor the activities of their children and the teachers.

And to return to the most iconic depiction of culture change: the dual portrait. In one Bratley version of this image, Chauncey Yellow Robe, dressed in Euro-American-style clothing, stands next to his father, Chief Yellow Robe, who is wearing a mix of clothing styles (see figure 1.6). Within a frame such as acculturation, we would be tempted to see the image as proof of how one generation refuses transformation while the next accepts it. But a view of survivance would encourage us to dive deeper into the behavior and intentions of the Yellow Robe family.

For many Native people, there was a core hypocrisy in the belief that what one wore influenced how one thought. "I have been among white people and have seen that they are permitted to wear their hair as they choose," Makes Enemy, an Oglala, once said, "and have seen boys and even men among the whites that wear their hair long."[50] Instead of seeing their outward appearance as evidence of change or loss, this image offers proof of the possibilities of survival. Perhaps they did not see themselves as victims but as people embracing the opportunities fate gave them in the face of colonialism's terrors.

▼ ▽ ▼

As artifacts now in a museum, Bratley's collection can be considered "objects of survivance" in two ways. As the examples discussed above demonstrate, these are objects of survivance because their material form reflects specific choices made by Native people during a moment that required both survival and resistance. Second, these are objects of survivance because they can help communities in the here and now maintain connections to their history and heritage. As the Ho-Chunk anthropologist Amy Lonetree wrote about seeing boxes of photographs of her ancestors stored at the Jackson County Historical Society, "I will never forget the moment when I found them—individuals whom I have heard about all my life, people whose names I carry and who are the source of the fierce pride I hold within me."[51] Even more, these photographs sparked conversations with her elders, and "through these conversations I came to know my own family history and tribal history in ways that strengthen me to this day."[52] As Lonetree suggests, ethnographic objects are material witnesses to a dynamic past, provocateurs of deep conversations about that past.

What role can these objects of survivance from the Indian school experience play for us today as a material memory of the colonial past?

First, documentation. The objects Bratley collected and the photographs he took record one of the most difficult, tumultuous moments in Native American history. At their nadir, many tribes were faced with the possibility of extermination. Instead, many persisted and survived. Like objects and images from other moments of historical violence—from racial violence in the United States to the Jewish Holocaust in Europe—Bratley's collection gives proof of and testimony to both what Native peoples suffered and how they survived.[53] The documentation of the Indian school experience has been particularly useful for Canada's Truth and Reconciliation Commission. In response to a class action lawsuit by survivors, the government established the Indian Residential Schools Truth and Reconciliation Commission (TRC) in 2006, which was charged with assessing the history of its residential school system and promoting "the healing of Aboriginal communities and reconciliation between Aboriginal peoples and non-Aboriginal Canadians."[54] Canada's TRC marked the first formal acknowledgment and investigation of a country's entire Indian school system and its legacy.

The TRC saw documentation as a vital means of interpreting past actions and determining responsibilities for the school system. It struggled to obtain access to 3.5 million documents from the government's archives.[55] Although largely unsuccessful in gaining access, the TRC insisted that this history lived as much in the experiences of its students as in the documents and items that recorded what transpired.[56] As further evidence of the importance of archives, the TRC was mandated with creating a national research center, which was considered "one element contributing to a fair, comprehensive, and lasting resolution of the legacy of the residential schools."[57]

In 2013, the TRC established a national research center at the University of Manitoba for former students and their families, the public, educators, and researchers. The center houses thousands of statements, millions of digitized archival documents and photographs, works of art, and more.[58] The power of this archive is that the paper it holds itself becomes a witness. Consider how in moments of war, when a losing side knows it is doomed, often its last act is destroying archives, the material evidence of its misdeeds.[59] As public historian Krista McCracken argues, "Archives play a crucial role in ensuring all sides of the past are documented and archivists need to look at their practices to ensure Indigenous voices are being preserved in a complete and respectful way."[60]

Second, education. Objects of survivance have a key role to play in learning about this past so that we can learn *from* this history. Several exhibits on the Indian school experience, which depend heavily on authentic artifacts and photographs, have already successfully shaped public conversations about confronting that history and asking what can be learned from it. For example, in 2000, the Heard Museum in Phoenix opened *Remembering Our Indian School Days: The Boarding School Experience*. It was supposed to run for 3 years, but because of overwhelming response from visitors, instead it has not closed since and now has a traveling component.[61] The National Museum of the American Indian (NMAI) in Washington, DC, stands as another example of an institution that has tackled these histories and even incorporated survivance as a key concept underlying its permanent exhibit halls.[62] (Although, notably, critiques of the NMAI include Sonya Atalay's argument that the NMAI exhibits emphasize survival at the expense of the *struggle* to survive, Amy Lonetree's suggestion that the museum "silences" the full tragedy of the American holocaust, and Steven Conn's barbed claim that the museum fails to present artifacts that tangibly prove actual survivance . . . But we'd suggest that these critiques do not mean that museums should not use objects of survivance but rather that we must still work toward better, more effective museum practices.)[63]

Other exhibits, documentaries, books, and public archaeology projects have all brought light to this little-known corner of US history for the public.[64] These projects are especially important because, as Canada's TRC found, too often curators and scholars "have interpreted the past in ways that have excluded or marginalized Aboriginal peoples' cultural perspectives and historical experience."[65] As such, the TRC continued to argue, there is an urgent need "to develop historically literate citizens who understand why and how the past is relevant to their own lives and the future of the country."[66]

Third, reconciliation. The emotional legacy of unresolved grief, shame, and self-hatred produced by US colonialism is directly linked to addiction and other social problems, such as suicide and sexual violence.[67] Over time, these events create "a pathway that results in the current generation being at an increased risk of experiencing mental and physical distress."[68] By creating a culture of unresolved distress, the historical trauma caused by the Indian education system has directly contributed to the current social, environmental, psychological, and physiological torment present in many contemporary Native American communities.[69] Healing and forgiveness, buttressed by concrete action, are needed.[70]

Each colonial settler state that sought to civilize and educate its Indigenous peoples has its own unique history—and its own way of finding recompense today.[71] In 2000, the US assistant secretary for Indian affairs, Kevin Gover, apologized in a speech for the government's "legacy of racism and inhumanity" and acknowledged the need for the government to "accept responsibility to putting things right."[72] He simply called US Indian policy one of "ethnic cleansing."[73] "Worst of all," he admitted, "the Bureau of Indian Affairs committed these acts against children entrusted to its boarding schools, brutalizing them emotionally, psychologically, physically, and spiritually."[74] While the apology was significant, some victims of the Indian school system sought more direct reparations. In 2003, a $25 billion class action lawsuit was pursued against the US government for the abuses it rendered on Native American boarding school students.[75] The case was dismissed. But the argument for some type of corrective action is clear.[76]

The devastating effects of the residential school system on Indigenous communities have been more directly addressed in Canada.[77] In 1996, the Canadian government closed its last residential school, and in 2008 the prime minister formally apologized for the physical and psychological damages it had wrought upon First Nations children; it budgeted $350 million to a "healing fund" for victims.[78] And, as noted, between 2008 and 2015, Canada's Indian Residential Schools Truth and Reconciliation Commission pursued its work, which, in turn, led to dozens of recommendations for reconciliation that will be undertaken in the decades ahead.

Objects of survivance can play a role in turning the public from passive learners to active agents of change by forcing them to confront the past, cultivating empathy for Indian students' anguish, and inspiring them to seek remedy for the harms leveled against Indian communities. In some cases, objects can be returned and reinserted into Native communities for them to reconnect to ancestors and share their stories with a broader public.

For example, in 2008, the family of Canadian artist Robert Aller donated to the University of Victoria more than 700 paintings made by Indigenous children (primarily Algonquin and Ojibwa) between the 1950s and 1970s, when Aller taught at summer camps. The university has transformed this collection from mere art objects into objects that can heal by turning them into a kind of "witness" used during the truth and reconciliation process.[79] In other cases, consideration of the material can lead to more direct forms of reparation. For example, in 2017, the remains of several children who died at Carlisle Indian School were exhumed and returned home; dozens of tribes are still waiting their turn to claim ancestors.[80] The magnitude of the Carlisle repatriation is clear. As Christine Diindiisi McCleave, a member of the Turtle Mountain Ojibwe Tribe, said, "So as the flagship school—the icon and model of all boarding schools—it makes sense that Carlisle would also be the model for healing and genesis of truth, reconciliation, and healing."[81] In all these cases, it is the physical remains, the tangible objects, that may allow the generations to reconnect, to honor those who perished, and to inspire us to make amends.

In the end, documentation, education, and reconciliation converge. Each goal supports the other. Documentation feeds education; education fosters healing; healing requires proof of what has transpired. As Canada's Truth and Reconciliation Commission found:

> Educating Canadians for reconciliation involves not only schools and post-secondary institutions, but also dialogue forums and public history institutions such as museums and archives. Education must remedy the gaps in historical knowledge that perpetuate ignorance and racism.
>
> But education for reconciliation must do even more. Survivors told us that Canadians must learn about the history and legacy of residential schools in ways that change both minds and hearts. At the Manitoba National Event in Winnipeg, Allan Sutherland [a Canadian residential schools survivor] said, "There are still a lot of emotions [that are] unresolved. People need to tell their stories . . . We need the ability to move forward together but you have to understand how it all began [starting with] Christopher Columbus, from Christianization, then colonization, and then assimilation . . . If we put our minds and hearts to it, we can [change] the status quo."[82]

This is true not just for Canada but in all places where we can remember, confront, and heal from the Indian school experience.

Survivance matters because the Native communities Bratley lived in more than a century ago did not disappear. Instead, they found ways to persist. This is not to say that the impacts of Indian schools were innocuous—trauma has been real and intergenerational—but that adaption is also part of the story. Although individuals in these communities experienced the education system differently—depending on when they attended school, the type of school they attended (day, boarding, or mission school), and the particularities of their familial and tribal histories—over the twentieth century a notable shift in attitudes toward education occurred.

In the early 1900s, Indian schools began to increasingly accept the value of some parts of Native culture, and after 1915 widespread educational reforms unfolded in the wake of John Dewey's influential work on children and education.[83] It would seem that by the 1930s many Native community members began to accept and seek out Euro-American-style education.[84] The changing relationship between tribal communities and federal education was caused by several interrelated historical events, including the growing number of White settlers on and surrounding reservations, enduring economic hardship, and the fracturing of communal ties through allotment.

Although life in federally funded day and boarding schools continued to be physically and emotionally difficult for many students, there was a gradual improvement in living conditions as the result of the 1928 Meriam Report, formally known as "The Problem of Indian Administration." After surveying conditions on Indian reservations throughout the country, the Meriam Report set out a series of prescriptions intended to overhaul the education system—implementing measures for training better teachers, revising the curriculum, and improving the deplorable health conditions at most schools.[85] Corporeal punishment was reigned in.[86] The Indian Reorganization Act of 1934, a reform law amid the New Deal, swung the pendulum of tribal sovereignty toward self-government and provided tribal authorities with more autonomy and control.[87] Followed by the 1969 Kennedy Report, titled "Indian Education: A National Tragedy—a National Challenge," small but not insignificant changes to improve education on reservations continued.[88]

By the second half of the twentieth century, many tribal communities had embraced Euro-American-style education and actively sought to shape the curricula taught in schools.[89] One survey of Indian students who attended boarding schools between 1950 and 2004 found that some emphasized negative experiences such as loneliness, but many spoke about positive aspects such as friendships.[90] Most reported a complex mix of emotions, which, while not entirely affirmative, at least suggests improvement from the largely unbearable experiences of previous generations. As an Alaska Native who was a boarding school student not long ago said in another study, "It was bad or it was good and I could say both."[91]

The evolution of Native attitudes toward education is epitomized by the Hopi. Throughout the late nineteenth century, Hopi parents vehemently opposed the Indian education system, particularly compulsory attendance and the forced removal of children to boarding schools. Reflecting on his grandparents' stories, Leigh J. Kuwanwisiwma recounted the trauma of early encounters between parents and government officials. "If kids were found, they were physically accosted and in some cases ripped out of their mothers' hands," he said. "And as they were marched down here [to Oraibi Day School], my grandpa and grandmother in particular would talk about how the mothers would be crying after them to not take the kids."[92] Over the course of the twentieth century, Hopi antipathy decreased in response to the changing realities of life on the reservation (figure 5.10).

FIGURE 5.10. The area where the Polacca Day School buildings once stood is used by Hopi families today, a symbol of how life continues on even after the trauma of the early Indian school experience. Hopi Reservation, 2016. (Chip Colwell)

Although some Hopis actively impugned formal education, as early as 1890, some tribal members had begun to accept and even actively participate in the American system. In 1890, a delegation of Hopi leaders was sent to Washington, DC.[93] According to oral history, told to us by Kuwanwisiwma, the federal government paid for leaders from the Hopi villages of Walpi, Songoopavi, and Oraibi to take a cross-country journey to impress upon them the grandeur of Western civilization and the inevitability of White settlement. The first stop along this journey was Fort Leavenworth in Kansas. There, the Hopi leaders were given a tour of the prisons, speaking with some of the Plains chiefs being held in captivity for fighting the government. Shocked and dismayed by the sight of Native leaders behind bars, the Hopi leaders continued across the prairies, amazed by the endless stretches of corn and agricultural fields they passed along the way. When they arrived in the capital, they were once again awestruck by the vast numbers of White people who surrounded them. The leaders returned home. They convened a large meeting in one of the Third Mesa kivas to express the futility of truculence. One leader first picked up a pinch of sand and said, "This is the Hopi." He then picked up a fistful of sand. Then another. Then another. Picking up another and yet another he said, "This is the Americans."[94]

Following the 1890 visit, some Hopis gradually began to view education as a tool of empowerment. For many Hopi parents, English proficiency in particular was seen as providing their children with the tools to persist as Indigenous people in a nation Whites controlled.[95] William Preston remembers that his uncles and grandfather encouraged him to "go to school, learn their ways, learn their language, and become whatever it takes to stand up to them. So that when the time comes . . . young people will stand up and say, 'No. We know your ways. No more. This is where it ends.'"[96] The belief that education offered a means of combatting oppression and facilitating cultural survival has informed generations of Hopi youth, who began actively pursuing education. Instead of rejecting outright Euro-American ways, people began to accept a middle way. As Kuwanwisiwma said:

> Collectively that was our decision. We got to look at the White man's ways, then look at the future. How the Hopi people are going to survive . . . And this is how it is going to happen. The best of the White man's world, and he [a Hopi elder during the kiva meeting following the 1890 trip] took up a twine. The Hopi is this other string. Put them together and we will be twice as strong. So out of that the chief said, "Future generations, learn the White man's way. Learn how he thinks. Learn how he speaks. Because one day, the future generation will become our eyes, our ears, and our tongues. And with the White man's knowledge we can do good things. And with the White man's knowledge we can fight for the culture."[97]

This is a variation of a story we heard among all the tribes we visited. The S'Klallam also slowly accepted the Indian education system. As tribal member Lloyd Fulton stated, "The difference [today] is that people want education—our elders and a bigger majority of the moms and dads—they want their kids to have an education. They push for it, even going to college. They want to do it and I think it's a real good thing."[98]

Similarly, among the Cheyenne, Gordon Yellowman told us that in the early years education "wasn't taken advantage of because it was feared. We saw it as a separation. A tool used against us to separate the children and the parent."[99] The gradual acceptance of formal schooling was in large part a response to the poor economic opportunities available to tribal people isolated on reservations. Today, when a student graduates from high school, Yellowman said, the community celebrates the accomplishment by hosting "dances for them, dinners for them, receptions for them, and they'd have big giveaways."[100]

A similar shift in attitude toward education is present among the Rosebud tribal members we interviewed (figure 5.11). Luella High Pipe, a seventy-year-old tribal member, stated that her mother, Sarah High Pipe, who attended St. Francis Mission School, always "spoke real highly about them, 'cause that is where she learned how to crochet, and she learned how to do all kinds of sewing . . . I have no bad things to say about them [Indian schools] . . . I never once got hit with a board or ruler or anything."[101] These statements suggest that Indian education had its bright spots and that the acceptance of Euro-American education is viewed by some as a successful adaptation to changing conditions.[102]

Today, ironically, a revamped educational experience offers one of the principal means through which these tribal communities have sought to redress the violence of US colonization and regain a sense of control and connection.[103] By developing culturally specific curricula and offering Indigenous language classes, these communities have usurped the tools of the colonizer and taken an important step toward healing the individual and collective wounds that are the legacy of the US Indian education system.[104]

FIGURE 5.11. The stone foundation of the blacksmith shop at the Lower Cut Meat Creek Day School in 2016 reveals the fading memories of the school. Rosebud Reservation, 2016. (Lindsay M. Montgomery)

FIGURE 5.12. Ghosts, many believe, haunt the landscape surrounding the ruined remains of Indian schools, such as the Cantonment Boarding School. Cheyenne and Arapaho Reservation, 2016. (Chip Colwell)

Indian schools are not historical artifacts; they continue to be part of reservations and Native communities. As of 2017, the BIA oversees 185 elementary, secondary, residential, and postsecondary schools across twenty-three states.[105] Of these, tribes control 130 schools, while the Bureau of Indian Education manages the rest. The work of educating Native youth goes on.[106]

In the end, the past is present (figure 5.12). The search for Indian education continues. Because the past shapes the present, we must remember what has gone before to understand where we are now and what may lie ahead. And so, Jesse H. Bratley's collection of objects and images is one means for all of us to remember. Through Bratley we can reflect on the historical moment when Native Americans were annihilated but also survived; how the forces of transculturation and acculturation, assimilation and resistance work in practice; the effect of Indian education on Indian communities; and how we have the opportunity for reconciliation and restorative justice. Through Bratley, we remember the vanished who endured.

Notes

1. Elkin 1940; Farnsworth 1989; Hoover 1989; Kessel 1987; Lurie 1968; Redfield et al. 1936; Spicer 1961; Teske and Nelson 1974.
2. Council 1967:257.
3. Council 1967:270.
4. Orser 2002:4.
5. Emmerich 1991; Ervin 1980; Hallowell 1963; Huffman 2008; Kadar 2012; Mignolo and Schiwy 2003; Ortiz 1947:98; Phillips 1998; Pratt 1992.
6. Hallowell 1963:523.
7. Hallowell 1963:523.
8. Fear-Segal 2007.
9. Emmerich 1991; Spack 2002:131.
10. https://www.nytimes.com/1999/11/28/nyregion/the-view-from-ledyard-the-flag-shows-up-in-american-indian-art.html, accessed July 11, 2018.
11. See Carroll 1998.
12. Stein 2005:16.
13. Cahill 2011:151.
14. Bratley n.d.a:101.
15. Hutchinson 2009:54.
16. Duncan 1990:192.
17. Page 1924.
18. Spicer 1962:1–4.
19. Liebmann 2012; Ruuska 2011; Scott 1985; Wachtel 1977; Wilcox 2009.

20. DeJong 1993; Ellis 1996; Trafzer 2009.
21. Adams 1997:229–230.
22. Adams 1997:209–270; Archuleta et al. 2000:47; Haig-Brown 1988:48, 57; Lomawaima 1994:96, 101, 118.
23. Borah 1983; Farriss 1984; Liebmann and Murphy 2011:6; Stern 1982.
24. Cahill 2011.
25. Cahill 2011:98.
26. Pratt 1991:34.
27. Boast 2011:57.
28. Pratt 1991:35.
29. See also Riney 1999:193–215.
30. Boast 2011:62.
31. Little Dog 2016.
32. Carson 2009; Powell 2004.
33. Vizenor 1994, 2008, 2009.
34. Stromberg 2006:1; Vizenor and Lee 1999; Wantanabe 2015:42.
35. Gere 2004.
36. Hoxie 1985:71.
37. Powell 2004; Vizenor 1994.
38. Eigenbrod 2012; Klotz 2017.
39. Vizenor 2008:19.
40. Hoelscher 2008:136.
41. Lonetree 2011:22.
42. Lonetree 2011:22.
43. Watson 2016:29.
44. Silliman 2014:60.
45. Silliman 2014:69.
46. Silliman 2014:60.

47. Beaudoin 2017:53.
48. Beaudoin 2017:47–48.
49. Markowitz 2012:15–16.
50. Andrews 2002: 420.
51. Lonetree 2011:14.
52. Lonetree 2011:14.
53. Linenthal 1995; Wood 2009.
54. Bradley and Nahwegahbow 2018:7; Walker 2009:2.
55. http://www.nationnews.ca/federal-budget-cuts-to-the-library-archives-of-canada-stall-truth-and-reconciliation-commission/, accessed May 11, 2018.
56. Sinclair et al. 2015:27–29.
57. http://www.oag-bvg.gc.ca/internet/English/parl_oag_201304_e_38212.html, accessed May 11, 2018.
58. http://www.trc.ca/websites/trcinstitution/index.php?p=815, accessed May 11, 2018.
59. Jockusch 2012; Riedlmayer 1995.
60. http://activehistory.ca/2015/06/the-role-of-canadas-museums-and-archives-in-reconciliation/, accessed May 11, 2018.
61. https://indiancountrymedianetwork.com/news/museum-exhibit-and-book-hope-to-ignite-dialogue-over-boarding-school-experience/, accessed April 30, 2018; www.azcentral.com/story/news

/local/phoenix/contributor/2015/10/06/heard-museums-american-indian-boarding-school-exhibit-gets-updates/73021296/, accessed May 1, 2018.

62. Lonetree and Cobb 2008; Shannon 2014.

63. Atalay 2006; Conn 2010:39; Lonetree 2012:110.

64. http://www.pbs.org/video/unspoken-americas-native-american-boarding-schools-oobt1r/, accessed May 15, 2018; https://www.wm.edu/news/stories/2016/the-legacy-of-americas-indian-school-remembering-a-forgotten-history.php, accessed May 15, 2018; https://www.peabody.harvard.edu/exhibits/current?q=node/282, accessed May 15, 2018.

65. Sinclair et al. 2015:246.

66. Sinclair et al. 2015:251.

67. Aguiar and Halseth 2015a; Ross 1996.

68. Brown-Rice 2013:123; Big-Foot and Braden 2007.

69. Brave Heart et al. 2011; Brown-Rice 2013; Evans-Campbell 2008; Garrett and

Pichette 2000; Whitebeck et al. 2004.

70. Lajimodiere 2012.

71. Armitage 1995; Dawson 2012.

72. Tsosie 2006:193.

73. Tsosie 2006:189.

74. Tsosie 2006:194.

75. Stout 2012:130.

76. Smith 2004.

77. Miller 1996.

78. http://www.bctf.ca/HiddenHistory/eBook.pdf, accessed August 9, 2017; Bradley and Nahwegahbow 2018:8.

79. http://uvac.uvic.ca/gallery/truth/, accessed May 10, 2018.

80. http://www.pennlive.com/news/2017/10/could_more_remains_of_native_a.html, accessed May 11, 2018.

81. http://www.boardingschoolhealing.org/join-the-call-for-carlisle-boarding-school-to-send-the-children-home, accessed June 27, 2016.

82. Sinclair et al. 2015:234.

83. Adams 1997:316; Cooper 2015:7, 85; Hutchinson 2009:73.

84. Ellis 1996:131–152.

85. Szasz 1999:16–36.

86. Trennert 1989.

87. Reyhner and Eder 2004:205–231.

88. Reyhner and Eder 2004:252–253; Szasz 1999:151–153.

89. Klug 2012.

90. Colmant et al. 2004.

91. Hirshberg 2008:28.

92. Kuwanwisiwma 2016.

93. Cameron 1999:37; Reyhner and Eder 2004:172.

94. Kuwanwisiwma 2016.

95. Andrews 2002:425.

96. Preston 2016.

97. Kuwanwisiwma 2016.

98. Fulton 2017.

99. Yellowman 2016.

100. Yellowman 2016.

101. High Pipe 2016b.

102. Adams 2006; Child 1999:1; Ellis 2006.

103. Kirmayer 2004.

104. Aguiar and Halseth 2015b; Horseman 2004.

105. https://bie.edu/Schools/, accessed August 8, 2017.

106. Sanchez and Stuckey 1999.

From the first, we would like to thank the Bratley family members for their gracious support of this project in various ways. The Bratley family has been an admirable steward of Jesse H. Bratley's legacy. We deeply appreciate Forrest G. Bratley Jr. opening his home to us and being so eager to see his grandfather's life understood and remembered. We further thank him and his siblings, Mary Ann McCurley and William M. Bratley, for sharing the parts of the collection that remain in their hands and giving us permission to study them and include them in this volume. We are also grateful to Margaret Bratley Mamet (one of the three daughters of Cyril Oliver Bratley, Jesse's third child) for her munificent donation of additional items Bratley collected to the Denver Museum of Nature & Science in 2011.

We are fortunate to have had the Denver Museum of Nature & Science as an incomparable institutional supporter of this project. For 2015–2016, the museum awarded Lindsay a Native American Postdoctoral Research Fellowship, during which she was able to work with Chip to research and complete this manuscript. Research was generously supported by the Avenir Foundation. The museum's Phipps Anthropology Fund and KT Challenge Grant Program provided additional vital funding for travel, interviews, and publication. We are especially grateful for material and moral support provided by Steve Nash, Carla Bradmon, Taylor Hitte, Kathy Honda, Michelle D'Ippolito, Scott Sampson, Gabriela Chavarria, and George Sparks.

Colleagues at other institutions were also helpful in answering our inquiries and providing information on Jesse Bratley: the Smithsonian's National Anthropological Archives, the US National Archives and Records Administration, the National Cowboy & Western Heritage Museum, and the South Dakota State Historical Society.

We are indebted to the patient and consistent support of the University Press of Colorado staff—particularly Jessica d'Arbonne, Charlotte Steinhardt, Beth Svinarich, Laura Furney, Daniel Pratt, and Darrin Pratt. Cheryl Carnahan embodied the word *perfection* in her amazing copyedit.

Finally, we are profoundly appreciative of tribal community members and officials across the United States who agreed to be interviewed. Their voices and experiences contributed enormously to this project, greatly enriching our interpretations of

Acknowledgments

history and culture. We thank Effie J. Beatty, Luella Begay, Rita Black, Clifford Broken Leg, Elidia S. Chapella, Ronald Charles, Sage Fast Dog, Lloyd Fulton, Ted George, Patricia Gonzales, Kaitlyn Gutierrez, Marie Hebert, Aaron Travis High Pipe, Kathleen High Pipe, Wilfred Huma, Wilson Huma Sr., Ruby James, Gene R. Jones Sr., Gerald Jones, June A. Jones, Leigh Kuwanwisiwma, Leland Little Dog, Lee Wayne Lomayestewa, Fred Mosqueda Sr., Ray Mosqueda, Lyman W. Polacca, Bill Preston, Laura Price, Rose E. Purser, Conrad Sullivan, Kelly Sullivan, Chester Whiteman, Marie Whiteman, Ferrell Lee Wilson, Josh Wisniewski, and Gordon Yellowman.

ACKNOWLEDGMENTS

Abbott, Lyman. 1898. "Our Indian Problem." *North American Review* 167 (505):719–728.

Adams, David Wallace. 1977. "Education in Hues: Red and Black at Hampton Institute, 1878–1893." *South Atlantic Quarterly* 76 (Spring):159–176.

Adams, David Wallace. 1979. "Schooling the Hopi: Federal Indian Policy Writ Small, 1887–1917." *Pacific Historical Review* 48 (3):335–356.

Adams, David Wallace. 1988. "Fundamental Considerations: The Deep Meaning of Native American Schooling, 1880–1900." *Harvard Educational Review* 58 (11):1–28.

Adams, David Wallace. 1997. *Education for Extinction: American Indians and the Boarding School Experience, 1875–1928*. Lawrence: University Press of Kansas.

Adams, David Wallace. 2001. "More Than a Game: The Carlisle Indians Take to the Gridiron, 1893–1917." *Western Historical Quarterly* 32 (1):25–53.

Adams, David Wallace. 2006. "Beyond Bleakness: The Brighter Side of Indian Boarding Schools, 1870–1940." In *Boarding School Blues: Revisiting American Indian Educational Experiences*, edited by C. E. Trafzer, J. A. Keller, and L. Sisquoc, 35–64. Lincoln: University of Nebraska Press.

Affairs, Bureau of Indian. 1904. "Visitor's Remarks." *Indian School Journal* 4 (1):54–56.

Affairs, Office of Indian. 1948. *Indian Education*. Washington, DC: Government Printing Office.

Aguiar, William, and Regine Halseth. 2015a. *Aboriginal Peoples and Historical Trauma: The Process of Intergenerational Transmission*. Prince George, BC: National Collaborating Center for Aboriginal Health.

Aguiar, William, and Regine Halseth. 2015b. *Addressing the Healing of Aboriginal Adults and Families within a Community-Owned College Model*. Prince George, BC: National Collaborating Center for Aboriginal Health.

Andrews, Thomas G. 2002. "Turning the Tables on Assimilation: Oglala Lakotas and the Pine Ridge Day Schools, 1889–1920s." *Western Historical Quarterly* 33 (4):407–430.

Archuleta, Margaret L., Brenda J. Child, and K. Tsianina Lomawaima. 2000. *Away from Home: American Indian Boarding School Experiences, 1879–2000*. Phoenix, AZ: Heard Museum.

Armitage, Andrew. 1995. *Comparing the Policy of Aboriginal Assimilation: Australia, Canada, and New Zealand*. Vancouver, BC: University of British Columbia Press.

Arthur, Linda B. 1998. "Deviance, Agency, and the Social Control of Women's Bodies in a Mennonite Community." *NWSA Journal* 10 (2):75–99.

Atalay, Sonya. 2006. "No Sense of the Struggle: Creating a Context for Survivance at the NMAI." *American Indian Quarterly* 30 (3–4):597–618.

Atencio, Ernest. 1996. "Havasupai Traditional and Historical Use of the Grand Canyon Village Area." In *Havasupai Oral History Project*, 1–36. Grand Canyon, AZ: Grand Canyon National Park.

Atkins, J.D.C. 1886. "Report of the Commissioner of Indian Affairs." In *Annual Report of the Commissioner of Indian Affairs*, III–LVI. Washington, DC: Government Printing Office.

Auerbach, Jeffrey A. 1999. *The Great Exhibition of 1851: A Nation on Display*. New Haven, CT: Yale University Press.

Badger, Reid. 1979. *The Great American Fair: The World's Columbian Exposition and American Culture*. Chicago: Taylor Trade Publications.

Bartelt, Guillermo. 1991. "The Early Spread of English among American Indians." *Anthropos* 86 (1–3):187–192.

Bauer, William J., Jr. 2010. "Family Matters: Round Valley Indian Families at the Sherman Indian Institute, 1900–1945." *Southern California Quarterly* 92 (4):393–421.

Beadle, J. H. 1897. *Five Years in the Territories*. Washington, DC: National Publishing Company.

Beaudoin, Matthew A. 2017. "A Tale of Two Settlements: Consumption and the Historical Archaeology of Natives and Newcomers in the 19th-Century Great Lakes Region." In *Foreign Objects: Rethinking Indigenous Consumption in American Archaeology*, edited by Craig N. Cipolla, 44–58. Tucson: University of Arizona Press.

Bennett, Tony. 2013. *The Birth of the Museum: History, Theory, Politics*. London: Routledge.

Bentley, Matthew. 2010. "Playing White Men: American Football and Manhood at the Carlisle Indian School, 1893–1904." *Journal of the History of Childhood and Youth* 3 (2):187–209.

Berlo, Janet C. 1992. "Introduction: The Formative Years of Native American Art History." In *The Early Years of Native American Art History: The Politics of Scholarship and Collecting*, edited by Janet C. Berlo, 1–21. Seattle: University of Washington Press.

Bernadin, Susan, Melody Graulich, Lisa MacFarlane, Nicole Tonkovich, and Louis Owens. 2003. *Trading Gazes: Euro-American Women Photographers and Native North Americans, 1880–1940*. New Brunswick, NJ: Rutgers University Press.

Berthrong, Donald J. 1992. *The Cheyenne and Arapaho Ordeal: Reservation and Agency Life in the Indian Territory, 1875–1907*. Norman: University of Oklahoma Press.

Bess, Jennifer. 2013. "Indigenizing the Safety Zone: Contesting Ideologies in Foodways at the Chilocco Indian Industrial School, 1902–1918." *Journal of the Southwest* 55 (2):193–244.

BigFoot, Delores, and Janie Braden. 2007. "Adapting Evidence-Based Treatments for Use with American Indian and Native Alaskan Children and Youth." *Focal Point* 21 (1):19–22.

Black, Rita. 2016. Interview with Authors. Denver: Denver Museum of Nature & Science Archives.

Blackhawk, Ned. 2004. "Confronting Indian Imagery in Contemporary America: A Personal Account." In *Beyond the Reach of Time and Change: Native American Reflections on the Frank A. Rinehart Photograph Collection*, edited by Simon J. Ortiz, 27–38. Tucson: University of Arizona Press.

Blalock-Moore, Nicole. 2012. "*Piper v. Big Pine School District of Inyo County*: Indigenous Schooling and Resistance in the Early Twentieth Century." *Southern California Quarterly* 94 (3):346–377.

Bloom, John. 2000. *To Show What an Indian Can Do: Sports at Native American Boarding Schools.* Minneapolis: University of Minnesota Press.

Boas, Franz. 1974. *A Franz Boas Reader: The Shaping of American Anthropology, 1883–1911.* Chicago: University of Chicago Press.

Boast, Robin. 2011. "Neocolonial Collaboration: Museum as Contact Zone Revisited." *Museum Anthropology* 34 (1):56–70.

Borah, Woodrow Wilson. 1983. *Justice by Insurance: The General Indian Court of Colonial Mexico and the Legal Aides of the Half-Real.* Berkeley: University of California Press.

Bradley, Berg, and David C. Nahwegahbow. 2018. *Guide for Lawyers Working with Indigenous People.* Toronto Law Society of Ontario.

Bratley, Forrest G. 1992. Letter from Dr. Forrest G. Bratley to Mr. Donald Reeves. Oklahoma City: National Cowboy & Western Heritage Museum.

Bratley, Hommer. 1961. The Bratley Collection. Marathon, FL: Southeast Museum of the North American Indian.

Bratley, Jesse H. 1893–1897. Account book and personal journal. Courtesy of the children of Dr. Forrest G. Bratley.

Bratley, Jesse H. 1897–1901. Account book and personal journal. Courtesy of the children of Dr. Forrest G. Bratley.

Bratley, Jesse H. 1898a. Letter from Bratley to F. W. Hodge, Bureau of American Ethnology. Washington, DC: Records of the Bureau of American Ethnology.

Bratley, Jesse H. 1898b. Letter from Bratley to J. W. Powell, Bureau of American Ethnology. Washington, DC: Records of the Bureau of American Ethnology.

Bratley, Jesse H. 1900. "Report of the Superintendent of Cantonment School." In *Annual Report of the Commissioner of Indian Affairs*, 329–330. Washington, DC: Government Printing Office.

Bratley, Jesse H. 1901. Letter from Bratley to S. P. Langley, Secretary of the Smithsonian Institution. Washington, DC: Records of the Bureau of American Ethnology.

Bratley, Jesse H. 1902a. Letter from Bratley to J. W. Powell, Bureau of American Ethnology. Washington, DC: Records of the Bureau of American Ethnology.

Bratley, Jesse H. 1902b. Letter from Bratley to W. A. Jones, Superintendent of Indian Schools. Washington, DC: National Archives Record Administration.

Bratley, Jesse H. 1902c. Letter from Bratley to W. A. Jones, Superintendent of Indian Schools. Washington, DC: National Archives Record Administration.

Bratley, Jesse H. 1902d. "Report of the Teacher of Polacca Day School." In *Annual Report of the Commissioner of Indian Affairs*, 154. Washintgon, DC: Government Printing Office.

Bratley, Jesse H. 1904. Letter from Bratley to W. H. Holmes, Bureau of American Ethnology. Washington, DC: Records of the Bureau of American Ethnology.

Bratley, Jesse H. 1932. Our Trip to Yellowstone Park. Courtesy of the children of Dr. Forrest G. Bratley.

Bratley, Jesse H. 1938. "Indian's Belief." *Miami Herald.* Courtesy of the children of Dr. Forrest G. Bratley.

Bratley, Jesse H. n.d.a. Autobiography of Jesse Hastings Bratley. Denver: Denver Museum of Nature & Science Archives.

Bratley, Jesse H. n.d.b. Personal Journal. Courtesy of the children of Dr. Forrest G. Bratley.

Bratley, Jesse H. n.d.c. Personal Journal. Courtesy of the children of Dr. Forrest G. Bratley.

Brave Heart, Maria Y.H., Josephine Chase, Jennifer Elkins, and Deborah B. Altschul. 2011. "Historical Trauma among Indigenous Peoples of the Americas: Concepts, Research, and Clinical Considerations." *Journal of Psychoactive Drugs* 43 (4):282–290.

Breckenridge, Carol A. 1989. "The Aesthetics and Politics of Colonial Collecting: India at the World Fairs." *Comparative Studies in Society and History* 31 (2):195–216.

Brew, J. O. 1979. "Hopi Prehistory and History to 1850." In *Handbook of North American Indians*, edited by Alfonso Ortiz, 514–523. Washington, DC: Smithsonian Institution Press.

Broken Leg, Clifford. 2016. Interview with Authors. Denver: Denver Museum of Nature & Science Archives.

Brooks, James F. 2016. *Mesa of Sorrows: A History of the Awat'ovi Massacre*. New York: W. W. Norton.

Brown, Julie K. 2001. *Making Culture Visible: Photography and Display at Industrial Fairs, International Expositions and Institutional Exhibitions in the US, 1847–1900*. Amsterdam: Hardwood Academy.

Brown-Rice, Kathleen. 2013. "Examining the Theory of Historical Trauma among Native Americans." *Professional Counselor* 3 (3):117–130.

Browning, Daniel M. 1893. "Education." In *Annual Report of the Commissioner of Indian Affairs*, 5–102. Washington, DC: Government Printing Office.

Browning, Daniel M. 1895a. "Education." In *Annual Report of the Commissioner of Indian Affairs*, 1–110. Washington, DC: Government Printing Office.

Browning, Daniel M. 1895b. Letter of Transfer, number 34089-1895. Washington, DC: National Archives.

Bsumek, Erika Marie. 2008. *Indian-Made: Navajo Culture in the Marketplace, 1868–1940*. Lawrence: University Press of Kansas.

Burton, C. E. 1902. "Report of School Superintendent in Charge of Moqui." In *Annual Report of the Commissioner of Indian Affairs*, 151–154. Washington, DC: Government Printing Office.

Butler, Judith. 2011. *Bodies That Matter: On the Discursive Limits of Sex*. New York: Routledge.

Butts, Michèle. 1996. "Native American Resistance and Presbyterian Missions in Post–Civil War New Mexico, 1867–1912." *American Presbyterians* 74 (4):241–252.

Cahill, Cathleen D. 2011. *Federal Fathers and Mothers: A Social History of the United States Indian Service, 1869–1933*. Chapel Hill: University of North Carolina Press.

Calloway, Colin G. 2010. *The Indian History of an American Institution: Native Americans and Dartmouth*. Hanover, NH: Dartmouth College Press.

Cameron, Catherine M. 1999. *Hopi Dwellings: Architectural Change at Orayvi*. Tucson: University of Arizona Press.

Carroll, James. 1998. "Self-Direction, Activity, and Syncretism: Catholic Indian Boarding Schools on the Northern Great Plains in Contact." *US Catholic Historian* 16 (2):78–89.

Carson, Benjamin D., ed. 2009. *Sovereignty, Separatism, and Survivance: Ideological Encounters in the Literature of Native North America*. Newcastle upon Tyne, UK: Cambridge Scholars Publishing.

Carter, Thomas, Edward Chappell, and Timothy McCleary. 2005. "In the Lodge of the Chickadee: Architecture and Cultural Resistance on the Crow Indian Reservation, 1884–1920." *Perspectives in Vernacular Architecture* 10:97–111.

Charles, Ron, Ted George, Ron Hirschi, Emily Mansfield, Laurie Mattson, Sharon Purser, Gina Stevens, and Greg Anderson, eds. 2012. *The Strong People: A History of the Port Gamble S'klallam Tribe*. Kingston, WA: Port Gamble S'Kllalam Tribe.

Child, Brenda J. 1996. "Runaway Boys, Resistant Girls: Rebellion at Flandreau and Haskell, 1900–1940." *Journal of American Indian Education* 35 (3):49–57.

Child, Brenda J. 1999. *Boarding School Seasons: American Indian Families, 1900–1940*. Lincoln: University of Nebraska Press.

Churchill, Ward. 2004. "Genocide by Any Other Name: North American Indian Residential Schools in Context." In *Genocide, War Crimes, and the West: History and Complicity*, edited by Adam Jones, 78–115. London: Zed Books.

Clifford, James. 1987. "Of Other Peoples: Beyond the 'Salvage' Paradigm." In *Discussions in Contemporary Culture*, edited by Hal Foster, 121–130. Seattle: Bay Press.

Clifford, James. 1988. "On Ethnographic Authority." In *The Predicament of Culture: Twentieth-Century Ethnography, Literature, and Art*, edited by James Clifford, 21–54. Cambridge, MA: Harvard University Press.

Cole, Douglas. 1999. *Franz Boas: The Early Years, 1858–1906*. Seattle: University of Washington Press.

Collins, Cary C. 2000. "The Broken Crucible of Assimilation: Forest Grove Indian School and the Origins of Off-Reservation Boarding-School Education in the West." *Oregon Historical Quarterly* 101 (4):466–507.

Collins, Cary C., ed. 2004. *Assimilation's Agent: My Life as a Superintendent in the Indian Boarding School System by Edwin L. Chalcraft*. Lincoln: University of Nebraska Press.

Colmant, Stephen, Lahoma Schultz, Rockey Robbins, Peter Ciali, Julie Dorton, and Yvette Rivera-Colmant. 2004. "Constructing Meaning to the Indian Boarding School Experience." *Journal of American Indian Education* 43 (3):22–40.

Colwell-Chanthaphonh, Chip, Stephen E. Nash, Steven R. Holen, and Marc N. Levine. 2013. "Anthropology: Unearthing the Human Experience." *Denver Museum of Nature and Science Annals* 4:283–335.

Conn, Steven. 2004. *History's Shadow: Native Americans and Historical Consciousness in the Nineteenth Century*. Chicago: University of Chicago Press.

Conn, Steven. 2010. *Do Museums Still Need Objects?* Philadelphia: University of Pennsylvania Press.

Cooley, D. N. 1866. *Annual Report of the Commissioner of Indian Affairs*, edited by Department of the Interior. Washington, DC: Government Printing Office.

Cooper, Tova. 2015. *The Autobiography of Citizenship: Assimilation and Resistance in US Education*. New Brunswick, NJ: Rutgers University Press.

Corrigan, John, and Lynn S. Neal. 2010. *Religious Intolerance in America: A Documentary History*. Chapel Hill: University of North Carolina Press.

Coues, Elliott. 1897. *New Light on the Early History of the Greater Northwest: Exploration and Adventure among the Indians of the Red, Saskatchewan, Missouri, and Columbia Rivers*. New York: Francis P. Harper.

Council, Social Science Research. 1967. "Acculturation: An Exploratory Formulation." In *Beyond the Frontier: Social Process and Cultural Change*, edited by Paul Bohannon and Fred Plog, 255–286. Garden City, NY: American Museum of Natural History Press.

Darnell, Regna. 2000. "Reenvisioning Boas and Boasian Anthropology." *American Anthropologist* 102 (4):896–910.

Davis, Julie. 2001. "American Indian Boarding School Experiences: Recent Studies from Native Perspectives." *OAH Magazine of History* 15 (2):20–22.

Dawson, Alexander S. 2012. "Histories and Memories of the Indian Boarding Schools in Mexico, Canada, and the United States." *Latin American Perspectives* 39 (5):80–99.

DeJong, David H. 1993. *Promises of the Past: A History of Indian Education*. Golden, CO: North American Press.

DeJong, David H. 2007. "'Unless They Are Kept Alive': Federal Indian Schools and Student Health, 1878–1918." *American Indian Quarterly* 31 (2):256–282.

Deloria, Philip. 1998. *Playing Indian*. New Haven, CT: Yale University Press.

DeMallie, Raymond J. 2001a. "Sioux until 1850." In *Handbook of North American Indians*, edited by Raymond J. DeMallie, 718–760. Washington, DC: Smithsonian Institution Press.

DeMallie, Raymond J. 2001b. "Teton." In *Handbook of North American Indians*, edited by Raymond J. DeMallie, 794–820. Washington, DC: Smithsonian Institution Press.

Devens, Carol. 1992. "'If We Get the Girls, We Get the Race': Missionary Education of Native American Girls." *Journal of World History* 3 (2):219–237.

Dobyns, Henry F., and Robert C. Euler. 1971. *The Havasupai People*. Phoenix: Indian Tribal Series.

Dockstader, Frederick J. 1979. "Hopi History 1850–1940." In *Handbook of North American Indians*, edited by Alfonso Ortiz, 524–532. Washington, DC: Smithsonian Institution Press.

Dodge, Richard Irving, and W. Rogers. 2000. *The Indian Territory Journals of Colonel Richard Irving Dodge*. Norman: University of Oklahoma Press.

Dolan, Veronica. 1977. "Life on the Reservation." *Empire Magazine*. Courtesy of the children of Dr. Forrest G. Bratley.

Dole, W. P. 1861. "Report." In *Annual Report of the Commissioner of Indian Affairs*, 8–30. Washington, DC: Government Printing Office.

Donaldson, Thomas. 1890. "Moqui Pueblo Indians of Arizona and Pueblos of New Mexico." In *Extra Census Bulletin*, edited by R. P. Porter, 13–48. Washington, DC: United States Census Office.

Dorchester, D. 1893. "Report of the Superintendent of Indian Schools." In *Annual Report of the Commissioner of Indian Affairs*, 360–399. Washington, DC: Government Printing Office.

Duncan, Kunigunde, ed. 1990. *Blue Star: The Story of Corabelle Fellows, Teacher at Dakota Missions, 1884–1888*. St. Paul: Minnesota Historical Society Press.

Dyck, Paul. 1971. *The Sioux People of the Rosebud*. Flagstaff, AZ: Northland.

Edwards, Elizabeth. 2001. *Raw Histories: Photographs, Anthropology, and Museums*. New York: Bloomsbury Academic.

Edwards, Elizabeth. 2008. "Anthropology." In *Encyclopedia of Nineteenth-Century Photography*, edited by John Hannavy, 50–54. New York: Routledge.

Edwards, Laurie J. 2012. *U-X-L Encyclopedia of Native American Tribes*. Farmington Hill, MI: Gale Publishing.

Eells, Edwin. 1893. "Report of the Agents in Washington." In *Annual Report to the Commissioner of Indian Affairs*, 320–341. Washington, DC: Government Printing Office.

Eells, Edwin. 1894. "Report of Agents in Washington." In *Annual Report to the Commissioner of Indian Affairs*, 311–327. Washington, DC: Government Printing Office.

Egan, Timothy. 2012. *Short Nights of the Shadow Catcher: The Epic Life and Immortal Photographs of Edward Curtis*. Boston: Houghton Mifflin Harcourt.

Eigenbrod, Renate. 2012. "'For the Child Taken, for the Parent Left Behind': Residential School Narratives as Acts of 'Survivance.'" *English Studies in Canada* 38 (3–4):277–297.

Eisler, Benita. 2013. *The Red Man's Bones: George Catlin, Artist and Showman*. New York: W. W. Norton.

Ekquist, Karla L. 1999. *Federal Indian Policy and the St. Francis Mission School on Rosebud Reservation, South Dakota: 1886–1908*. Ames: Agricultural History and Rural Studies, Iowa State University.

Elkin, Henry. 1940. "The Northern Arapaho of Wyoming." In *Acculturation in Seven American Indian Tribes*, edited by Ralph Linton, 207–229. New York: Appleton-Century.

Ellis, Clyde. 1996. *To Change Them Forever: Indian Education at the Rainy Mountain Boarding School, 1893–1920*. Norman: University of Oklahoma Press.

Ellis, Clyde. 2006. "'We Had a Lot of Fun, but of Course, That Wasn't the School Part': Life at the Rainy Mountain Boarding School, 1893–1920." In *Boarding School Blues: Revisiting American Indian Educational Experiences*, edited by Clifford E. Trafzer, Jean A. Keller, and Lorene Sisquoc, 65–98. Lincoln: University of Nebraska Press.

Emmerich, Lisa E. 1991. "'Civilization' and Transculturation: The Field Matron Program and Cross-Cultural Contact." *American Indian Culture and Research Journal* 15 (4):33–48.

Enoch, Jessica. 2002. "Resisting the Script of Indian Education: Zitkala Ša and the Carlisle Indian School." *College English* 65 (2):117–141.

Ervin, Alexander M. 1980. "A Review of the Acculturation Approach in Anthropology with Special Reference to Recent Change in Native Alaska." *Journal of Anthropological Research* 36 (1):49–70.

Evans-Campbell, Teresa. 2008. "Historical Trauma in American Indian/Native Alaska Communities: A Multilevel Framework for Exploring Impacts on Individuals, Families, and Communities." *Journal of Interpersonal Violence* 23 (3):316–338.

Ewing, Henry P. 1900a. Letter from Henry P. Ewing, Dept. of Interior Indian School Service, to Miss Estelle Reel, Supt. Indian Schools, Hualapai Agency, Arizona. Washington, DC: National Archives Records Administration.

Ewing, Henry P. 1900b. *Report of the Industrial Teacher in Charge of Walapai and Havasupai Indians and Day Schools*. In *Annual Report to the Commissioner of Indian Affairs*, 201–203. Washington, DC: Government Printing Office.

Ewing, Henry P. 1901. Letter from Henry P. Ewing to W. A. Jones. Washington, DC: National Archive Record Administration.

Farnsworth, Paul. 1989. "The Economics of Acculturation in the Spanish Missions of Alta California." *Research in Economic Anthropology* 11:217–249.

Farr, William E. 1984. *The Reservation Blackfeet, 1882–1945: Photographic History of Cultural Survival*. Seattle: University of Washington Press.

Farriss, Nancy M. 1984. *Maya Society under Colonial Rule: The Collective Enterprise of Survival*. Princeton, NJ: Princeton University Press.

Fast Dog, Sage. 2016. Interview with Authors. Denver: Denver Museum of Nature & Science Archives.

Fear-Segal, Jacqueline. 2007. *White Man's Club: Schools, Race, and the Struggle of Indian Acculturation*. Lincoln: University of Nebraska Press.

Fenelon, James V. 2014. *Culturicide, Resistance, and Survival of the Lakota ("Sioux Nation")*. New York: Routledge.

Fewkes, Jesse W. 1880. "Tusayan Katcinas." In *15th Annual Report of the Bureau of Ethnology*, edited by J. W. Powell, 251–320. Washington, DC: Smithsonian Institution.

Foley, Thomas W. 2002. *Father Francis M. Craft: Missionary to the Sioux*. Lincoln: University of Nebraska Press.

Foucault, Michel. 1979. *Discipline and Punishment: The Birth of the Prison*. Translated by A. Sheridan. London: Penguin.

Foucault, Michel. 1980. "Body/Power." In *Power/Knowledge, Selected Interviews and Other Writings, 1972–1977*, edited by Colin Gordge, 55–63. New York: Pantheon Books.

Fowler, Loretta. 1982. *Arapahoe Politics, 1851–1978: Symbols in Crisis of Authority*. Lincoln: University of Nebraska Press.

Fowler, Loretta. 2001. "Arapaho." In *Handbook of North American Indians*, edited by Raymond J. DeMallie, 840–862. Washington, DC: Smithsonian Institution Press.

Fowler, Loretta. 2002. *Tribal Sovereignty and the Historical Imagination: Cheyenne-Arapaho Politics*. Lincoln: University of Nebraska Press.

Frehill, Lisa M. 1996. "Occupational Segmentation in Kansas and Nebraska, 1890–1900." *Great Plains Research* 6:213–244.

Frigout, Arlette. 1979. "Hopi Ceremonial Organization." In *Handbook of North American Indians*, edited by Alfonso Ortiz, 564–580. Washington, DC: Smithsonian Institution Press.

Fulton, Lloyd. 2017. Interview with Authors. Denver: Denver Museum of Nature & Science Archives.

Galler, Robert. 2017. "Councils, Petitions, and Delegations: Crow Creek Activism and the Progressive Era in Central South Dakota." *Journal of the Gilded Age and Progressive Era* 16 (2):206–227.

Ganz, Cheryl. 2008. *The 1933 Chicago World's Fair: A Century of Progress*. Urbana: University of Illinois Press.

Garrett, Michael Tlanusta, and Eugene F. Pichette. 2000. "Red as an Apple: Native American Acculturation and Counseling with or without Reservation." *Journal of Counseling and Development* 78 (1):3–13.

Genetin-Pilawa, C. Joseph. 2012. *Crooked Paths to Allotment: The Fight over Federal Indian Policy after the Civil War*. Chapel Hill: University of North Carolina Press.

George, Ted. 2017. Interview with Authors. Denver: Denver Museum of Nature & Science Archives.

Gere, Anne Ruggles. 2004. "An Art of Survivance: Angel DeCora at Carlisle." *American Indian Quarterly* 28 (3–4):649–684.

Gere, Anne Ruggles. 2005. "Indian Heart/White Man's Head: Native-American Teachers in Indian Schools, 1880–1930." *History of Education Quarterly* 45 (1):38–65.

Gerlach, Dominic B. 1973. "St. Joseph's Indian Normal School, 1888–1896." *Indiana Magazine of History* 69 (1):1–42.

Gilbert, Matthew Sakiestewa. 2005. "'The Hopi Followers': Chief Tawaquaptewa and Hopi Student Advancement at Sherman Institute, 1906–1909." *Journal of American Indian Education* 44 (2):1–23.

Gilbert, Matthew Sakiestewa. 2010. *Education beyond the Mesas: Hopi Students at Sherman Institute, 1902–1929*. Lincoln: University of Nebraska Press.

Glancy, Diane. 2014. *Fort Marion Prisoners and the Trauma of Indian Education*. Lincoln: University of Nebraska Press.

Gmelch, Sharon Bohn. 2008. *The Tlingit Encounter with Photography*. Philadelphia: University of Pennsylvania, University Museum of Archaeology and Anthropology.

Gonzalez, Mario, and Elizabeth Cook-Lynn. 1999. *The Politics of Hallowed Ground: Wounded Knee and the Struggle for Indian Sovereignty*. Urbana-Champaign: University of Illinois Press.

Gonzalez, Patricia. 2016. Interview with Authors. Denver: Denver Museum of Nature & Science Archives.

Gram, John R. 2015. *Education at the Edge of Empire: Negotiating Pueblo Identity in New Mexico's Boarding Schools*. Seattle: University of Washington Press.

Gram, John R. 2016. "Playing Indian and Becoming American in the Federal Indian Boarding Schools." *American Indian Quarterly* 40 (3):251–273.

Greene, Jerome A. 1970. "The Sioux Land Commission of 1889: Prelude to Wounded Knee." *South Dakota State Historical Society* 1 (1):41–72.

Grinde, Donald A., Jr. 2004. "Taking the Indian out of the Indian: US Policies of Ethnocide through Education." *Wicazo Sa Review* 19 (2):25–32.

Grossman, James E., ed. 1994. *The Frontier in American Culture*. Berkeley: University of California Press.

Gruber, Jacob W. 1970. "Ethnographic Salvage and the Shaping of Anthropology." *American Anthropologist* 72 (6):1289–1299.

Haig-Brown, Celia. 1988. *Resistance and Renewal: Surviving the Indian Residential School*. Vancouver, BC: Tillacum Library.

Hailmann, William N. 1895. "Report of the Superintendent of Indian Schools." In *Annual Report of the Commissioner of Indian Affairs*, 337–355. Washington, DC: Government Printing Office.

Hailmann, William N. 1896. "Report of the Superintendent of Indian Schools." In *Annual Report of the Commissioner of Indian Affairs*, 339–357. Washington, DC: Government Printing Office.

Hallowell, A. Irving. 1963. "Papers in Honor of Melville J. Herskovits: American Indians, White and Black: The Phenomenon of Transculturalization." *Current Anthropology* 4 (5):519–531.

Hamilton, S. S. 1827. *Documents from the War Department, Accompanying the President's Message to Congress*. Washington, DC: Government Printing Office.

Heater, Derek. 2004. *A History of Education for Citizenship*. London: Routledge Farmer.

Hebert, Marie. 2016. Interview with Authors. Denver: Denver Museum of Nature & Science Archives.

Heckwelder, John. 1819. *An Account of the History, Manners, and Customs of the Indian Nations*. Philadelphia: Transaction of the Committee of History, Moral Science and General Literature of the American Philosophical Society.

Herold, Joyce. 1999. "Grand Amateur Collecting in the Mid-Twentieth Century: The Mary W.A. and Francis V. Crane American Indian Collection." In *Collecting Native America, 1870–1960*, edited by Shepard Krech III, 259–291. Washington, DC: Smithsonian Institution Press.

High Pipe, Cathleen. 2016a. Interview with Authors. Denver: Denver Museum of Nature & Science Archives.

High Pipe, Luella. 2016b. Interview with Authors. Denver: Denver Museum of Nature & Science Archives.

High Pipe, Travis. 2016c. Interview with Authors. Denver: Denver Museum of Nature & Science Archives.

Hill, Richmond C. 1912. *A Great White Indian Chief: A Thrilling and Romantic Story of the Remarkable Career, Extraordinary Experiences Hunting, Scouting, and Indian Adventures of Col. Fred Cummins "Chief La-Ko-Ta."* Ossining, NY: Rand, McNaily.

Hinsley, Curtis M. 1981. *Savages and Scientists: The Smithsonian Institution and the Development of American Anthropology, 1846–1910.* Washington, DC: Smithsonian Institution Press.

Hinsley, Curtis M., and David R. Wilcox, eds. 2016. *Coming of Age in Chicago: The 1893 World's Fair and the Coalescence of American Anthropology.* Lincoln: University of Nebraska Press.

Hirshberg, Diane. 2008. "'It Was Bad or It Was Good': Alaska Natives in Past Boarding Schools." *Journal of American Indian Education* 47 (3):5–30.

Hirst, Stephen. 1985. *Havsuw 'Baaja: People of the Blue Green Water.* Havasupai, AZ: Havasupai Tribal Council.

Hoag, Enoch. 1875. Letters Received by the Office of Indian Affairs, vol. 119, no. 234. Washington, DC: National Archives and Records Service.

Hodge, Frederick. W. 1907. *Handbook of American Indians North of Mexico.* Bureau of American Ethnology Bulletin 30. Washington, DC: Smithsonian Institution.

Hoelscher, Steven D. 2008. *Picturing Indians: Photographic Encounters and Tourist Fantasies in H. H. Bennett's Wisconsin Dells.* Madison: University of Wisconsin Press.

Hoerig, Karl A. 2002. "Remembering Our Indian School Days: The Boarding School Experience." *American Anthropologist* 104 (2):642–646.

Hoffenberg, Peter H. 2001. *An Empire on Display: English, Indian, and Australian Exhibitions from the Crystal Palace to the Great War.* Berkeley: University of California Press.

Hoig, Stan. 1974. *The Sand Creek Massacre.* Norman: University of Oklahoma Press.

Hoover, Robert. 1989. "Spanish-Native Interaction and Acculturation in the Alta California Missions." In *Columbian Consequences*, edited by David H. Thomas, 395–406. Washington, DC: Smithsonian Institution Press.

Horne, Esther Burnett, and Sally McBeth. 1998. *Essie's Story: The Life and Legacy of a Shoshone Teacher.* Lincoln: University of Nebraska Press.

Horseman, Jenny. 2004. "But Is It Education? The Challenge of Creating Effective Learning for Survivors of Trauma." *Women's Studies Quarterly* 32 (1–2):130–146.

Hoxie, Frederick E. 1984. *A Final Promise: The Campaign to Assimilate the Indians, 1880–1920.* Lincoln: University of Nebraska Press.

Hoxie, Frederick E. 1985. "From Prison to Homeland: The Cheyenne River Indian Reservation before World War I." In *The Plains Indians of the Twentieth Century*, edited by Peter Iverson, 55–75. Norman, OK: University of Oklahoma Press.

Hoyt, J. L. 1902. Letter of Recommendation. Courtesy of the children of Dr. Forrest G. Bratley.

Huff, Delores J. 1997. *To Live Heroically: Institutional Racism and American Indian Education.* Albany: State University of New York Press.

Huffman, Terry E. 2008. *American Indian Higher Educational Experiences: Cultural Visions and Personal Journeys.* New York: Peter Lang.

Hutchinson, Elizabeth. 2009. *The Indian Craze: Primitivism, Modernism, and Transculturation in American Indian Art, 1890–1915.* Durham, NC: Duke University Press.

Hyer, Sally. 1990. *One House, One Voice, One Heart: Native American Education at the Santa Fe Indian School.* Santa Fe: Museum of New Mexico.

Isenberg, Andrew C. 2000. *The Destruction of the Bison*. Cambridge: Cambridge University Press.

Jacknis, Ira. 1984. "Franz Boas and Photography." *Studies in Visual Communication* 10 (1):2–60.

Jacknis, Ira. 2002. "The First Boasian: Alfred Kroeber and Franz Boas, 1896–1905." *American Anthropologist* 104 (2):520–532.

Jacobson, Claes H. 2009. "John Anderson: A Swedish Immigrant and Pioneer Photographer among the Rosebud Sioux Indians." *Swedish-American Historical Society* 60 (2):59–71.

James, Harry C. 1974. *Pages from Hopi History*. Tucson: University of Arizona Press.

Jockusch, Laura. 2012. *Collect and Record! Jewish Holocaust Documentation in Early Postwar Europe*. Oxford: University of Oxford Press.

Jones, A. A. 1913. *Rules for the Indian School Service, Records of the Education Division*. Washington, DC: Government Printing Office.

Jones, Gene. 2017. Interview with Authors. Denver: Denver Museum of Nature & Science Archives.

Jones, Tom, Michael Schmudlach, Matthew Daniel Mason, Amy Lonetree, and George A. Greendeer. 2011. *People of the Big Voice: Photographs of Ho-Chunk Families by Charles Van Schaick, 1879–1942*. Madison: Wisconsin Historical Society Press.

Jones, William A. 1898. "Education." In *Annual Report of the Commissioner of Indian Affairs*, 1–108. Washington, DC: Government Printing Office.

Jones, William A. 1899. "Statistics as to Indian Schools during the Year Ending on June 30, 1899." In *Annual Report of the Commissioner of Indian Affairs*, 549–561. Washington, DC: Government Printing Office.

Jones, William A. 1900a. "Education." In *Annual Report of the Commissioner of Indian Affairs*, 1–182. Washington, DC: Government Printing Office.

Jones, William A. 1900b. "Statistics as to Indian Schools during the Year Ended June 30, 1900." In *Annual Report of the Commissioner of Indian Affairs*, 622–635. Washington, DC: Government Printing Office.

Jones, William A. 1900c. "Employees in Indian School Service." In *Annual Report of the Commissioner of Indian Affairs*, 703–741. Washington, DC: Government Printing Office.

Jones, William A. 1901. "Education." In *Annual Report of the Commissioner of Indian Affairs*, 1–172. Washington, DC: Government Printing Office.

Jones, William A. 1902a. "Schedule Showing the Names of Indian Reservations in the United States, Agencies, Tribes Occupying or Belonging to the Reservation." In *Annual Report of the Commissioner of Indian Affairs*, 594–595. Washington, DC: Government Printing Office.

Jones, William A. 1902b. "Statistics as to Indian Schools during the Fiscal Year Ended June 30, 1902." In *Annual Report of the Commissioner of Indian Affairs*, 616–617. Washington, DC: Government Printing Office.

Jordan, Michael Paul. 2012. "Striving for Recognition: Ledger Drawings and the Construction and Maintenance of Social Status during the Reservation Period." In *Ledger Narratives: The Plains Indian Drawings of the Lansburgh Collection at Dartmouth College*, edited by Colin G. Calloway, 20–33. Norman: University of Oklahoma Press.

Kadar, Judit Agnes. 2012. *Going Indian: Cultural Appropriation in Recent North American Literature*. Valencia, Spain: Universitat de Valencia.

Kargon, Robert H., Karen Fiss, Morris Low, and Arthur P. Molella. 2015. *World's Fairs on the Eve of War: Science, Technology, and Modernity, 1937–1942*. Pittsburgh: University of Pittsburgh Press.

Katakis, Michael, ed. 1998. *Excavating Voices: Listening to Photographs of Native Americans.* Philadelphia: University of Pennsylvania, University Museum of Archaeology and Anthropology.

Katzive, David, ed. 1981. *Buffalo Bill and the Wild West.* Pittsburgh: University of Pittsburgh Press.

Kennard, E. A. 1979. "Hopi Economy and Subsistence." In *Handbook of North American Indians,* edited by Alfonso Ortiz, 554–563. Washington, DC: Smithsonian Institution Press.

Kerstetter, Todd M. 2015. *Inspiration and Innovation: Religion in the American West.* Malden, MA: Wiley Blackwell.

Kessel, James L. 1987. *Kiva, Cross, and Crown: The Pecos Indians and New Mexico, 1540–1840.* Albuquerque: University of New Mexico Press.

Kickingbird, Kirke, and Karen Ducheneaux. 1973. *One Hundred Million Acres.* New York: Macmillan.

King, J.C.H. 1986. "Tradition in Native American Art." In *The Arts of the North American Indian: Native Traditions in Evolution,* edited by Edwin Wade, 65–92. New York: Hudson Hills.

Kirmayer, Lawrence J. 2004. "The Cultural Diversity of Healing: Meaning, Metaphor, and Mechanism." *British Medical Bulletin* 69:33–48.

Klotz, Sarah. 2017. "Impossible Rhetorics of Survivance at the Carlisle School, 1879–1883." *College Composition and Communication* 69 (2):208–229.

Klug, Beverly J. 2012. *Standing Together: American Indian Education as Culturally Responsive Pedagogy.* Lanham, MD: Rowman and Littlefield.

Knox, J. T. 1867. "Washington Superintendency." In *Annual Report of the Commissioner of Indian Affairs,* 30–61. Washington, DC: Government Printing Office.

Kosmider, Alexia. 2001. "Refracting the Imperial Gaze onto the Colonizers: Geronimo Poses for the Empire." *ATQ (American Transcendental Quarterly)* 14 (4):317–332.

Kroeber, Alfred L. 1902. "The Arapaho." *Bulletin of the American Museum of Natural History* 18 (1):3–35.

Kuwanwisiwma, Leigh J. 2016. Interview with Authors. Denver: Denver Museum of Nature & Science Archives.

Lajimodiere, Denise. 2012. "A Healing Journey." *Wicazo Sa Review* 27 (2):5–19.

Lane, Robert B., and Barbara Lane. 1977. *Treaties of the Puget Sound: 1854–1855.* Washington, DC: Institute for the Development of Indian Law.

Lazarus, Edward. 1991. *Black Hills White Justice: The Sioux Nation versus the United States, 1775 to the Present.* Lincoln: University of Nebraska Press.

Leavelle, Tracy Neal. 1998. "We Will Make It Our Own Place: Agriculture and Adaptation at the Grand Ronde Reservation, 1856–1887." *American Indian Quarterly* 22 (4):433–456.

Lewis, David Rich. 1991. "Reservation Leadership and the Progressive-Traditional Dichotomy: William Wash and the Northern Utes, 1865–1928." *Ethnohistory* 38 (2):124–148.

Liebmann, Matthew. 2012. *Revolt: An Archaeological History of Pueblo Resistance and Revitalization in 17th-Century New Mexico.* Tucson: University of Arizona Press.

Liebmann, Matthew, and Melissa S. Murphy, eds. 2011. *Enduring Conquests: Rethinking the Archaeology of Resistance to Spanish Colonialism in the Americas.* Santa Fe, NM: School for Advanced Research Press.

Lindsey, Donal F. 1995. *Indians at Hampton Institute, 1877–1923.* Urbana: University of Illinois Press.

Linenthal, Edward T. 1995. *Preserving Memory: The Struggle to Create America's Holocaust Museum.* New York: Columbia University Press.

Lippard, Lucy, ed. 1992. *Partial Recall.* New York: New Press.

Little Dog, Leland. 2016. Interview with Authors. Denver: Denver Museum of Nature & Science Archives.

Lomawaima, K. Tsianina. 1993. "Domesticity in the Federal Indian Schools: The Power of Authority over Mind and Body." *American Ethnologist* 20 (2):227–250.

Lomawaima, K. Tsianina. 1994. *They Called It Prairie Light: The Story of Chilocco Indian School.* Lincoln: University of Nebraska Press.

Lomawaima, K. Tsianina. 1996. "Estelle Reel, Superintendent of Indian Schools, 1898–1910: Politics, Curriculum, and Land." *Journal of American Indian Education* 35 (3):5–31.

Lomawaima, K. Tsianina. 2006. *"To Remain an Indian": Lessons in Democracy from a Century of Native American Education.* New York: Teachers College Press.

Lomayestewa, Lee Wayne. 2016. Interview with Authors. Denver: Denver Museum of Nature & Science Archives.

Lonetree, Amy. 2011. "Visualizing Native Survivance: Encounters with My Ho-Chunk Ancestors in the Family Photographs of Charles Van Schaick." In *People of the Big Voice: Photographs of Ho-Chunk Families by Charles Van Schaick, 1879–1942*, edited by Tom Jones, Michael Schmudlach, Matthew Daniel Mason, Amy Lonetree, and George A. Greendeer, 13–22. Madison: Wisconsin Historical Society Press.

Lonetree, Amy. 2012. *Decolonizing Museums: Representing Native America in National and Tribal Museums.* Chapel Hill: University of North Carolina Press.

Lonetree, Amy, and Amanda J. Cobb, eds. 2008. *The National Museum of the American Indian: Critical Conversations.* Lincoln: University of Nebraska Press.

Lookingbill, Brad. 2006. *War Dance at Fort Marion: Plains Indian War Prisoner.* Norman: University of Oklahoma Press.

Lurie, Nancy O. 1968. "Culture Change." In *Introduction to Cultural Anthropology: Essays in the Scope and Methods of the Science of Man*, edited by James A. Clifton, 275–303. Boston: Houghton Mifflin.

Mann, Henrietta. 1997. *Cheyenne-Arapaho Education, 1871–1982.* Boulder: University Press of Colorado.

Markowitz, Harvey. 2002. *A Culture History of Catholic Mission and the Sicangu Lakotas, 1886–1916.* Chicago: Divinity School, University of Chicago.

Markowitz, Harvey. 2012. "Converting the Rosebud: Sicangu Lakota Catholicism in the Late Nineteenth and Early Twentieth Centuries." *Great Plains Quarterly* 32 (1):3–24.

Matthes, Francois E. 1905. "Topographic Methods Used for the New Detail Maps of the Grand Canyon of the Colorado." In *Report of the Eighth International Congress*, 801. Washington, DC: Government Printing Office.

Maurer, E. M. 2000a. "Presenting the American Indian: From Europe to America." In *The Changing Presentation of the American Indian: Museums and Native Cultures*, edited by W. Richard West, 15–28. Washington, DC: Smithsonian Institution Press.

McBeth, Sally. 1983a. *Ethnic Identity and the Boarding School Experience of West-Central Oklahoma Indians.* Washington, DC: University Press of America.

McBeth, Sally. 1983b. "Indian Boarding Schools and Ethnic Identity: An Example from the Southern Plains Tribes of Oklahoma." *Plains Anthropologist* 28 (100):119–128.

McChesney, Charles E. 1900. "Report of Agent for Rosebud Agency." In *Annual Report of the Commissioner of Indian Affairs*, 371–389. Washington, DC: Government Printing Office.

McChesney, Charles E. 1903. "Report of Day School Inspector, Rosebud Agency." In *Annual Report of the Commissioner of Indian Affairs*, 318–319. Washington, DC: Government Printing Office.

McCowan, S. M. 1899. "Report of School at Phoenix, Arizona." In *Annual Report of the Commissioner of Indian Affairs*, 381–436. Washington, DC: Government Printing Office.

McGee, William J. 1897. "Bureau of American Ethnology." In *The Smithsonian Institution, 1846–1896*, edited by George Brown Goode, 367–396. Washington, DC: Smithsonian Institution.

McKellips, Karen K. 1992. "Educational Practices in Two Nineteenth Century American Indian Mission Schools." *Journal of American Indian Education* 32 (1):12–20.

Mead, Sidney E. 1976. *The Lively Experiment: The Shaping of Christianity in America*. New York: Harper and Row.

Mignolo, Walter D., and Freya Schiwy. 2003. "Transculturation and the Colonial Difference: Double Translation." In *Translation and Ethnography: The Anthropological Challenge of Intercultural Understanding*, edited by Tullio Maranko and Bernhard Streck, 3–29. Tucson: University of Arizona Press.

Mihesuah, Devon A. 1993. *Cultivating the Rosebuds: The Education of Women at the Cherokee Female Seminary, 1851–1909*. Urbana: University of Illinois Press.

Miles, John D. 1878a. Monthly Report to E. Hayt, vol. 123, no. 234. Washington, DC: National Archives and Records Services.

Miles, John D. 1878b. "Reports of Agents in Indian Territory." In *Annual Report of the Commissioner of Indian Affairs*, 54–70. Washington, DC: Government Printing Office.

Miles, Nelson A. 1879. "The Indian Problem." *North American Review* 128 (268):304–314.

Miller, James Rodger. 1996. *Shingwauk's Vision: A History of Native Residential Schools*. Toronto: University of Toronto Press.

Mindeleff, Victor. 1891. "A Study of Pueblo Architecture: Tusayan and Cibola." In *Eighth Annual Report of the Bureau of Ethnology to the Secretary of the Smithsonian Institution 1886–87*, edited by John W. Powell, 3–228. Washington, DC: Bureau of Ethnology.

Mithlo, Nancy Marie. 2014. *For a Love of His People: The Photography of Horace Poolaw*. Washington, DC: National Museum of the American Indian.

Mooney, James. 1907. "Arapaho." In *Handbook of American Indians North of Mexico*, edited by Frederick W. Hodge, 72–74. Washington, DC: Government Printing Office.

Moore, John H. 1996. *The Cheyenne*. Cambridge, MA: Blackwell.

Morgan, Lewis H. 1901. *League of the Ho-de-no-sau-nee*. 2 vols. New York: Dodd, Mead.

Morgan, T. J. 1891. "Education." In *Annual Report of the Commissioner of Indian Affairs*, 3–146. Washington, DC: Government Printing Office.

Moses, L. G. 1996. *Wild West Shows and the Images of American Indians, 1883–1933*. Albuquerque: University of New Mexico Press.

Mosquida, Fred. 2016. Interview with Authors. Denver: Denver Museum of Nature & Science Archives.

Murdock, V. 1939. "Slightly Turned Foot Which Gave a Wichitan the Sioux Name of Si-ok-mi." *Miami Herald*. Courtesy of the children of Dr. Forrest G. Bratley.

N.A. 1901. "Had Experience in Teaching Indians." *Beacon*. Courtesy of the children of Dr. Forrest G. Bratley.

N.A. n.d. *First Camera Inadequate.* Courtesy of the children of Dr. Forrest G. Bratley.

Nash, S. E., and G. M. Feinman, eds. 2003. "Curators, Collections, and Contexts: Anthropology at the Field Museum, 1893–2002." Special issue of *Fieldiana*, Anthropology, New Series. Chicago: Field Museum of Natural History.

Neuman, Lisa K. 2008. "Indian Play: Students, Wordplay, and Ideologies of Indianness at a School for Native Americans." *American Indian Quarterly* 32 (2):178–203.

Nicholas, Sheilah E. 1991. *Hopi Education: A Look at the History, the Present, and the Future.* Tucson: American Indian Studies, University of Arizona.

O'Brien, Sharon. 1993. *American Indian Tribal Governments.* Norman: University of Oklahoma Press.

Oberly, J. H. 1885. "Report of the Superintendent of Indian Schools." In *Annual Report of the Commissioner of Indian Affairs*, LXXV–CCXXV. Washington, DC: Government Printing Office.

Orser, Charles E., Jr. 2002. *Encyclopedia of Historical Archaeology.* London: Routledge.

Ortiz, Fernando. 1947. *Cuban Counter-Points: Tobacco and Sugar.* New York: Alfred A. Knopf.

Ostler, Jeffrey. 2004. *The Plains Sioux and US Colonialism from Lewis and Clark to Wounded Knee.* Cambridge: Cambridge University Press.

Otteman, M. 1899. "My Home." Essay in Denver Museum of Nature & Science Archives.

Page, C. Clinton. 1924. "Miamian Spent Years Teaching the Indians." Article clipping in Denver Museum of Nature & Science Archives.

Panich, Lee M. 2013. "Archaeologies of Persistence: Reconsidering the Legacies of Colonialism in Native North America." *American Antiquity* 78 (1):105–122.

Parezo, Nancy J., and Don Fowler. 2007. *Anthropology Goes to the Fair: The 1904 Louisiana Purchase Exposition.* Lincoln: University of Nebraska Press.

Parker, Ely S. 1869. "Education." In *Annual Report of the Commissioner of Indian Affairs*, 3–42 Washington, DC: Government Printing Office.

Patterson, Thomas C. 2003. *A Social History of Anthropology in the United States.* New York: Bloomsbury Academic.

Paxton, Katrina A. 2006. "Learning Gender: Female Students at the Sherman Institute, 1907–1925." In *Boarding School Blues: Revisiting American Indian Educational Experiences*, edited by Clifford E. Trafzer, Jean A. Keller, and Lorene Sisquoc, 174–186. Lincoln: University of Nebraska Press.

Phillips, Ruth B. 1998. *Trading Identities: The Souvenir in Native North American Art from the Northeast, 1700–1900.* Seattle: University of Washington Press.

Polacca, Lyman. 2016. Interview with Authors. Denver: Denver Museum of Nature & Science Archives.

Powell, John Wesley. 1882. *Second Annual Report of the United States Geological Survey to the Secretary of the Interior, 1880–1881.* Washington, DC: Department of the Interior.

Powell, John Wesley. 1987. *The Exploration of the Colorado River and Its Canyons.* New York: Penguin.

Powell, Malea. 2004. "Down by the River, or How Susan La Flesche Picotte Can Teach Us about Alliance as a Practice of Survivance." *College English* 67 (1):38–60.

Pratt, Mary Louise. 1991. "The Arts of the Contact Zone." *Profession* 91:33–40.

Pratt, Mary Louise. 1992. *Imperial Eyes: Travel Writing and Transculturation.* London: Routledge.

Pratt, Richard Henry. 1967. *Battlefield and Classroom: Four Decades with the American Indian, 1867–1904*, edited by Robert M. Utley. New Haven, CT: Yale University Press.

Pratt, Richard Henry. 1892. "The Advantages of Mingling Indians with Whites." In *Proceedings and Addresses of the National Conference of Charities and Correction at the Nineteenth Annual Session Held in Denver, COL., June 23–29, 1892*, edited by Isabel C. Barrows, 45–58. Boston: Press of Geo. H. Ellis.

Preston, William. 2016. Interview with Authors. Denver: Denver Museum of Nature & Science Archives.

Prucha, Francis Paul. 1984. *The Great Father: The United States Government and the American Indian*. Vols. 1 and 2. Lincoln: University of Nebraska Press.

Prucha, Francis Paul. 1986. *The Great Father: The United States Government and the American Indians*. Abridged edition. Lincoln: University of Nebraska Press.

Purser, Sharon. 2012. "Education." In *The Strong People: A History of the Port Gamble S'klallam Tribe*, edited by Ron Charles, Ted George, Ron Hirschi, Emily Mansfield, Laurie Mattson, Sharon Purser, Gina Stevens, and Greg Anderson, 183–199. Kingston, WA: Port Gamble S'Kllalam Tribe.

Qoyawayma, Polingaysi. 1992 [1964]. *No Turning Back: A True Account of a Hopi Indian Girl's Struggle to Live in Two Worlds*. Albuquerque: University of New Mexico Press.

Rahder, Bobbi. 2004. "Introduction." In *Beyond the Reach of Time and Change: Native American Reflections on the Frank A. Rinehart Photograph Collection*, edited by Simon J. Ortiz, ix–xii. Tucson: University of Arizona Press.

Reddick, SuAnn M. 2000. "The Evolution of Chemawa Indian School: From Red River to Salem, 1825–1885." *Oregon Historical Quarterly* 101 (4):444–465.

Redfield, Ralph Linton, and Melville J. Herskovits. 1936. "Memorandum for the Study of Acculturation." *American Anthropologist* 38:149–152.

Reel, Estelle. 1898. "Report of the Superintendent of Indian Schools." In *Annual Report of the Commissioner of Indian Affairs*, 334–349. Washington, DC: Government Printing Office.

Reel, Estelle. 1900. "Report of the Superintendent of Indian Schools." In *Annual Report of the Commissioner of Indian Affairs*, 417–471. Washington, DC: Government Printing Office.

Reel, Estelle. 1901a. Course of Study for the Indian Schools of the United States: Industrial and Literary. Records of the Education Division, Bureau of Indian Affairs. Washington, DC: Government Printing Office.

Reel, Estelle. 1901b. "Report of the Superintendent of Indian Schools." In *Annual Report of the Commissioner of Indian Affairs*, 412–515. Washington, DC: Government Printing Office.

Reel, Estelle. 1903. "Report of the Superintendent of Indian Schools." In *Annual Report of the Commissioner of Indian Affairs*, 367–410. Washington, DC: Government Printing Office.

Reel, Estelle. 1908. "Report of the Commissioner of Indian Affairs." In *Annual Report of the Commissioner of Indian Affairs*, 1–186. Washington, DC: Government Printing Office.

Reutter, P., and W. Reutter. 1962. *Early Dakota Days: Stories and Pictures of Pioneers, Cowboys, and Indians*. White River, SD: Self-published.

Reyhner, Jon, and Jeanne Eder. 2004. *American Indian Education: A History*. Norman: University of Oklahoma Press.

Riding In, James. 2004. "Legacy of Resistance." In *Beyond the Reach of Time and Change: Native American Reflections on the Frank A. Rinehart Photograph Collection*, edited by Simon J. Ortiz, 52–63. Tucson: University of Arizona Press.

Riedlmayer, András. 1995. "Erasing the Past: The Destruction of Libraries and Archives in Bosnia-Herzegovina." *Middle East Studies Association Bulletin* 29 (1):7–11.

Riggs, Stephen R., and John Wesley Powell. 1890. *Contributions to North American Ethnology: A Dakota-English Dictionary*. Washington, DC: Smithsonian Institution.

Riney, Scott. 1999. *The Rapid City Indian School, 1898–1933*. Norman: University of Oklahoma Press.

Rockwell, Stephen J. 2010. *Indian Affairs and the Administrative State in the Nineteenth Century*. Cambridge: Cambridge University Press.

Rosaldo, Renato. 1989. "Imperialist Nostalgia." *Representations* 26:107–122.

Ross, Rupert. 1996. *Returning to the Teachings: Exploring Aboriginal Justice*. Toronto: Penguin Canada.

Royce, C. C., and C. Thomas. 1895. "Indian Land Cessions in the United States." In *18th Annual Report of the Bureau of American Ethnology*, edited by John W. Powell, 527–648. Washington, DC: Smithsonian Institution.

Rudy, D. G. 1891. "Report of Agents in Washington." In *Annual Report of the Commissioner of Indian Affairs*, 440–463. Washington, DC: Government Printing Office.

Russell, Don. 1970. *The Wild West: A History of the Wild West Shows*. Fort Worth, TX: Amon Carter Museum of Western Art.

Ruuska, Alex. 2011. "Ghost Dancing and the Iron Horse: Surviving through Tradition and Technology." *Technology and Culture* 52 (3):574–597.

Rydell, Robert W. 1984. *All the World's a Fair: Visions of Empire at American International Expositions, 1876–1916*. Chicago: University of Chicago Press.

Sanchez, John, and Mary E. Stuckey. 1999. "From Boarding Schools to the Multicultural Classroom: The Intercultural Politics of Education, Assimilation, and American Indians." *Teacher Education Quarterly* 26 (3):83–96.

Schmidt, Andrea. 2015. *Christian Missions and Indian Assimilation: Role and Effects upon the Lakota Sioux of Pine Ridge Indian Reservation and Their Institutions*. Norderstedt, Germany: Deutschen Nationalbibliografie.

Schwartz, Douglas W. 1983. "Havasupai." In *Handbook of North American Indians*, edited by Alfonso Ortiz, 13–24. Washington, DC: Smithsonian Institution Press.

Scott, James C. 1985. *Weapons of the Weak: Everyday Forms of Peasant Resistance*. New Haven, CT: Yale University Press.

Scott, R. 2009. *Blood at Sand Creek: The Massacre Revisited*. Caldwell, ID: Caxton.

Seniors, Paula Marie. 2008. "Cole and Johnson's 'The Red Moon,' 1908–1910: Reimagining African American and Native American Female Education at Hampton Institute." *Journal of African American History* 93 (1):21–35.

Shakespeare, Tom. 1971. *The Sky People*. New York: Vantage.

Shannon, Heather A. 2015. "Sacred Stories: Photography's Indigenous Origins." In *Photography and Its Origins*, edited by Tanya Sheehan and Andres Zervigón, 104–117. New York: Routledge.

Shannon, Jennifer A. 2014. *Our Lives: Collaboration, Native Voice, and the Making of the National Museum of the American Indian*. Santa Fe, NM: School for Advanced Research Press.

Shilling, C. 2003. *The Body and Social Theory*. London: Sage.

Silliman, Stephen W. 2014. "Archaeologies of Indigenous Survivance and Residence: Navigating Colonial and Scholarly Dualities." In *Rethinking Colonial Pasts through Archaeology*, edited by Neal Ferris, Rodney Harrison, and Michael V. Wilcox, 57–75. Oxford: University of Oxford Press.

Sinclair, Murray, Wilton Littlechild, and Marie Wilson. 2015. *Final Report of the Truth and Reconciliation Commission of Canada*, vol. 1: *Summary*. Toronto: James Lorimer and Company Publishers.

Slivka, Kevin. 2011. "Art, Craft, and Assimilation: Curriculum for Native Students during the Boarding School Era." *Studies in Art Education* 52 (3):225–242.

Slotkin, Richard. 1992. *Gunfighter Nation: The Myth of the Frontier in Twentieth-Century America*. Norman: University of Oklahoma Press.

Smith, Andrea. 2004. "Boarding School Abuses, Human Rights, and Reparations." *Social Justice* 31 (4):89–102.

Smith, Laura E. 2016. *Horace Poolaw, Photographer of American Indian Modernity*. Lincoln: University of Nebraska Press.

Smits, David D. 1994. "The Frontier Army and the Destruction of the Buffalo: 1865–1883." *Western Historical Quarterly* 25 (3):312–338.

Sontag, Susan. 1977. *On Photography*. New York: Farrar, Straus and Giroux.

Southwell, Kristina L., and John R. Lovett. 2010. *The Photographs of Annette Ross Hume: Life at the Kiowa, Comanche, and Wichita Agency*. Norman: University of Oklahoma Press.

Spack, Ruth. 2002. *America's Second Tongue: American Indian Education and the Ownership of English, 1860–1900*. Lincoln: University of Nebraska Press.

Spicer, Edward N. 1962. *Cycles of Conquest: The Impact of Spain, Mexico, and the United States on the Indians of the Southwest, 1533–1960*. Tucson: University of Arizona Press.

Spicer, Edward N., ed. 1961. *Perspectives in American Indian Culture Change*. Chicago: University of Chicago Press.

Standing Bear, Luther. 1975 [1928]. *My People the Sioux*. Lincoln: University of Nebraska Press.

Stein, Gil J. 2005. *The Archaeology of Colonial Encounters*. Santa Fe, NM: School of American Research Press.

Stern, Steven J. 1982. *Peru's Indian Peoples and the Challenge of Spanish Conquest: Huamanga to 1640*. Madison: University of Wisconsin Press.

Stocking, George W., Jr., ed. 1985. *Objects and Others: Essays on Museums and Material Culture*. Madison: University of Wisconsin Press.

Stouch, G.W.H. 1900. "Report of Agent for Cheyenne and Arapaho Agency." In *Annual Report of the Commissioner of Indian Affairs*, 325–327. Washington, DC: Government Printing Office.

Stout, Mary A. 2012. *Native American Boarding Schools*. Santa Barbara, CA: Greenwood.

Strathman, Nicole Dawn. 2002. "Through Native Lenses: American Indian Vernacular Photographies and Performances of Memories, 1890–1940." PhD dissertation, Culture and Performance Studies, University of California, Los Angeles.

Stromberg, Ernest. 2006. "Rhetoric and American Indians: An Introduction." In *American Indian Rhetorics of Survivance: Word Medicine, Word Magic*, edited by Ernest Stromberg, 1–12. Pittsburgh: University of Pittsburgh Press.

Stuart, Paul. 1978. "The US Office of Indian Affairs, 1865–1900: The Institutionalization of a Formal Organization." PhD dissertation, History, University of Wisconsin, Madison.

Sullivan, Kelly. 2016. Interview with Authors. Denver: Denver Museum of Nature & Science Archives.

Suttles, Wayne. 1990. "Central Coast Salish." In *Handbook of North American Indians*, edited by Wayne Suttles, 453–480. Washington, DC: Smithsonian Institution Press.

Suttles, Wayne, and Barbara Lane. 1990. "Southern Coast Salish." In *Handbook of North American Indians*, edited by Wayne Suttles, 485–502. Washington, DC: Smithsonian Institution Press.

Szasz, Margaret C. 1999. *Education and the American Indian: The Road to Self-Determination since 1928*. 3rd ed. Albuquerque: University of New Mexico Press.

Szasz, Margaret C. 2006. "Through a Wide-Angle Lens: Acquiring and Maintaining Power, Position, and Knowledge through Boarding Schools." In *Boarding School Blues: Revisiting American Indian Educational Experiences*, edited by Clifford E. Trafzer, Jean A. Keller, and Lorene Sisquoc, 187–201. Lincoln: University of Nebraska Press.

Szasz, Margaret C. 2007. *Indian Education in the American Colonies, 1607–1783*. Lincoln: University of Nebraska Press.

Szasz, Margaret C., and Carmelita Ryan. 1978. "American Indian Education." In *Handbook of North American Indians*, edited by William C. Sturtevant, 284–299. Washington, DC: Government Printing Office.

Tagg, John. 1993. *The Burden of Representation: Essays on Photographies and Histories*. Minneapolis: University of Minnesota Press.

Taylor, N. G. 1868. "Education." In *Annual Report of the Commissioner of Indian Affairs*, 1–22. Washington, DC: Government Printing Office.

Teske, Raymond, Jr., and Bardin H. Nelson. 1974. "Acculturation and Assimilation: A Clarification." *American Ethnologist* 1:351–369.

Theodossopoulos, Dimitrios. 2013. "Laying Claim to Authenticity: Anthropological Dilemmas." *Anthropological Quarterly* 86 (2):337–360.

Trafzer, Clifford E. 2009. *American Indians/American Presidents: A History*. Washington, DC: Smithsonian Institution Press.

Trennert, Robert A. 1982. "Educating Indian Girls at Nonreservation Boarding Schools, 1878–1920." *Western Historical Quarterly* 13 (3):271–290.

Trennert, Robert A. 1987. "Selling Indian Education at World's Fairs and Expositions, 1893–1904." *American Indian Quarterly* 11 (3):203–220.

Trennert, Robert A. 1988. *The Phoenix Indian School: Forced Assimilation in Arizona, 1891–1935*. Norman: University of Oklahoma Press.

Trennert, Robert A. 1989. "Corporal Punishment and the Politics of Indian Reform." *History of Education Quarterly* 29 (4):595–617.

Tsosie, Rebecca. 2006. "The BIA's Apology to Native Americans: An Essay on Collective Memory and Collective Conscience." In *Taking Wrongs Seriously: Apologies and Reconciliation*, edited by Elazar Barkan and Alexander Karn, 185–212. Stanford, CA: Stanford University Press.

Turcheneske, John A., Jr. 1979. "John G. Bourke—Troubled Scientist." *Journal of Arizona History* 20 (3):323–344.

Turner, Frederick Jackson. 1893. *The Significance of the Frontier in American History*. Chicago: American Historical Association.

Valentine, R. G. 1911. *Some Things That Girls Should Know How to Do and Hence Should Learn How to Do in School*. Records of the Education Division. Washington, DC: Government Printing Office.

Vizenor, Gerald. 1994. *Manifest Manners: Narratives on Postindian Survivance*. Lincoln: University of Nebraska Press.

Vizenor, Gerald. 1998. "Fugitive Poses." In *Excavating Voices: Listening to Photographs of Native Americans*, edited by Michael Katakis, 7–16. Philadelphia: University of Pennsylvania, University Museum of Archaeology and Anthropology.

Vizenor, Gerald. 2009. *Native Liberty: Natural Reason and Cultural Survivance*. Lincoln: University of Nebraska Press.

Vizenor, Gerald, ed. 2008. *Survivance: Narratives of Native Presence*. Lincoln: University of Nebraska Press.

Vizenor, Gerald, and A. Robert Lee. 1999. *Postindian Conversations*. Lincoln: University of Nebraska Press.

Wachtel, Nathan. 1977. *The Vision of the Vanquished: The Spanish Conquest of Peru through Indian Eyes, 1530–1570*. New York: Harper and Row.

Waggoner, Josephine. 2013. *Witness: A Hunkpapha Historian's Strong-Heart Song of the Lakotas*. Lincoln: University of Nebraska Press.

Walker, F. A. 1871. "Education." In *Annual Report of the Commissioner of Indian Affairs*, 1–8. Washington, DC: Government Printing Office.

Walker, J. 2009. *The Indian Residential Schools Truth and Reconciliation Commission*. Ottowa: Library of Parliament, Legal and Legislative Affairs.

Wantanabe, Sunday. 2015. "Socioacupuncture Pedagogy: Troubling Containment and Erasure in a Multimodal Composition Classroom." In *Survivance, Sovereignty, and Story: Teaching American Indian Rhetorics*, edited by Lisa King, Rose Gubele, and Joyce Rain Anderson, 35–56. Logan: Utah State University Press.

Warren, David M., and W. H. Brewer. 1890. *Warren's New Physical Geography*. Philadelphia: E. H. Butler.

Warren, Louis S. 2007. *Buffalo Bill's America: William Cody and the Wild West Show*. New York: Vintage.

Watson, Brittany. 2016. "Rethinking Photographic Histories: Indigenous Representation in the Bryon Harmon Collection." MA thesis in Art History, Carleton University.

West, Nancy Martha. 2000. *Kodak and the Lens of Nostalgia*. Charlottesville: University Press of Virginia.

Whalen, Kevin. 2016. *Native Students at Work: American Indian Labor and Sherman Institute's Outing Program, 1900–1945*. Seattle: University of Washington Press.

White, Richard. 2015. *It's Your Misfortune and None of My Own: A New History of the American West*. Norman: University of Oklahoma Press.

Whitebeck, Les B., Gary W. Adams, Dan R. Hoyt, and Xiaojin Chen. 2004. "Conceptualizing and Measuring Historical Trauma among American Indian People." *American Journal of Community Psychology* 33 (3–4):119–130.

Whiteley, Peter M. 1988. *Deliberate Acts: Changing Hopi Culture through the Oraibi Split*. Tucson: University of Arizona Press.

Whiteley, Peter M. 2008. *The Orayvi Split: A Hopi Transformation*. New York: American Museum of Natural History.

Whiteman, Chester. 2016a. Interview with Authors. Denver: Denver Museum of Nature & Science Archives.

Whiteman, Marie. 2016b. Interview with Authors. Denver: Denver Museum of Nature & Science Archives.

Whitman, Walt. 1900. *Leaves of Grass*. Philadelphia: David McKay.

Wilcox, Michael. 2009. *The Pueblo Revolt and the Mythology of Conquest: An Indigenous Archaeology of Contact*. Berkeley: University of California Press.

Williams, C. 1895. "Report of Navajo Agency." In *Annual Report of the Commissioner of Indian Affairs*, 118–119. Washington, DC: Government Printing Office.

Williams, Carol J. 2003. *Framing the West: Race, Gender, and the Photographic Frontier in the Pacific Northwest*. Oxford: Oxford University Press.

Wisnowski, Joshua. 2016. Interview with Authors. Denver: Denver Museum of Nature & Science Archives.

Wissler, Clark. 1912. "Societies and Ceremonial Associations in the Oglala Division of the Teton-Dakota." *American Museum of Natural History Anthropological Papers* 11 (1):1–100.

Wood, Amy Louise. 2009. *Lynching and Spectacle: Witnessing Racial Violence in America, 1890–1940*. Chapel Hill: University of North Carolina Press.

Wright, James G. 1883. "Reports of Agents in Dakota." In *Annual Report of the Commissioner of Indian Affairs*, 21–53. Washington, DC: Government Printing Office.

Wright, James G. 1895. "Reports of Agents in Dakota." In *Annual Report of the Commissioner of Indian Affairs*, 293–299. Washington, DC: Government Printing Office.

Yellowman, Gordon. 2016. Interview with Authors. Denver: Denver Museum of Nature & Science Archives.

Index

Page numbers in italic indicate illustrations.

Abbott, Ms., 103
acculturation, 194; process of, 190–92. *See also* assimilation
addiction, 204
African Americans, education of, 40, 41
agriculture, *12*, 168; Cheyenne and Arapaho, 93, 154; on Grand Ronde Reservation, 169–70; Havasupai, 161–62, *193*; Hopi, *48*, 162, 164; Indian school training in, 131–32; Lakota Sioux, 135, *136, 161*
Alcatraz, Hopi imprisonment on, 149, 150
Aller, Robert, 204–5
allotment, 116, 117, 156
Among the Sioux. See Anderson, John Alvin
Anderson, John Alvin, *Among the Sioux,* 89
Andrews, Thomas G., 155
animal husbandry, 168–69
Anna, 129, 130
annuities, 24; in Treaty of Fort Laramie, 86
Antelope Mesa, 108
anthropology, 25, 43–44, 59
Appling, Agent, 20
Arapaho, *4, 7,* 37, 91, 118, 151, 161, 171, 174; boarding schools, 92–93; cultural adaptations, 168–69; intermediary chiefs, 153–55
archaeological sites, *109;* evidence of survivance at, 198–99; at Hopi, 107–8
Arkansas River, 110
arrow bundles, *15*
Arthur, Chester A., 103
arts and crafts, 60, 136; adaptation and persistence through, 158, 185; American flag used in, *192–93;* commercialization of, 54–55. *See also* basketry; beadwork
assimilation, 3, 37, 54, 116, 159, 194; Christian reformers and, 140–41; and community preservation, 155–56; through dress, *137, 183;* through education, 25, 38–39, 40–41, 118–19, 120–24, 189, 190–92
Atalay, Sonya, 203
athletics, 133–34
Atkins, John, 128–29
authenticity, 54
Awat'ovi, 108

Bad Hand, Howard, 174
BAE. *See* Bureau of American Ethnology
bags, Lakota Sioux, *142, 184, 200*
Bailey, Artie, 93
Bailey, Ms., *139*
Baptist missionaries, 143
Barnes, Louise, 103
Barnes, Richard, 103
bartering, 167, *168*
basketry, *102;* Havasupai, *100, 163;* Hopi, *49;* S'Klallam, *182, 185*
bathing, at Lower Cut Meat Creek school, 122–23
beadwork, *142, 172, 179;* American flags in, 191, *192–93;* traditional designs in, *151, 182, 184*
Bear, George, 148
Bear Kicks, 20
Bear Looking, depiction of, *24*
Beaudoin, Matthew A., 199
beef rations, for Plains Indians, 170–71
belief systems: Hopi, 173, 182, *185, 186;* Lakota Sioux, 143, 200–201
Bentley, Matthew, 133–34
BIA. *See* Bureau of Indian Affairs
Bible cover, quillwork, 199–200, *201*
Big Foot (Spotted Female Elk), in Winter Count, *23;* saddle of, *123*
Big Crow, *17*
bison: decimation of, 92, 167; as icon, 199, *200;* in Winter Count, *12, 13, 17, 18*
Black, Rita, 124
Black Calf, Charles, *86, 124, 195*
Blackfeet, *17,* 152
Black Hills, 21, 81
Black Kettle, Dana, 124
blankets, Navajo, *19*
blanket strips, beaded, 191, *192*
Blue Horse, Claudie, *86*
Blue Lightning, depiction of, *24*
boarding schools, 39, *61, 75,* 155, 206; camps around, *152;* Cheyenne and Arapaho at, 92; assimilationist role of, 117, 118–19; effects of, 204–5; Havasupai and Walapai, 96, 98; Hopi, 103, 150; World's Fair replicas, 60, 63–64. *See also* Cantonment Boarding School; Carlisle Indian School
Boas, Franz, 25
bodily transformation, of students, *121,* 122–23, 124–25, 127–28
bonnets, eagle feather, *169*
Bourke, John G., 25
Bowman, Ella, 70
Bratley, Cyril, *5, 6,* 110, 111, *112*
Bratley, Della Ranson, *5, 57, 65, 77, 78,* 111, 121, 131, *132, 195;* as BIA

employee, 79–*80*, 81; at Cantonment Boarding School, 91, 93–95; at Havasupai, 95, 96, 98, *103*; at Hopi, 101, 103, 104–10; on Rosebud Reservation, 84–85, 86–89, 122, 146

Bratley, Etta, 5

Bratley, Forrest G., *5*, 6, 7, 110, 111, *112*

Bratley, Hazel, *5*, 6, 65, 88, *89*, 99, *101*, 111, *112*

Bratley, Homer (Na ta ska), *5*, 6, *57*, *69*, 88, 99, *101*, 111, *112*, 147, *193*, *194*

Bratley, Hugh, 70

Bratley, Jesse Hastings, 3, *6*, 7, 34, 79, 99, 141, *192–93*, *195*; and anthropology, 4–5, 43–44; at Cantonment Boarding School, 91, 93–95, *139*, 144–49; collecting and photography practices of, 26, 32, 41–43, 44–45, 65, 167–68; at Columbian Exposition, 59, 60, 61; as educator, 25, 36, 72–73; early career of, 70–72; early life of, 68–70; in Florida, 110–12; gifts to, 174, 176; at Havasupai, 95, 96, 98, *103*; at Hopi, 101, 103, 104–10; and Indian craze, 56, 57–58; and Indian school system, 196–97; on landscape, 51–53; lectures by, 49–50; note-taking by, 46–47, *48*, 50–51; at Port Gamble Day School, 73–78; on Rosebud Reservation, 84–85, 86–89, 122–23

Bratley, Joseph, 4, *5*, 68

Bratley, Leoni, 72

Bratley, Mary Emma Hastings, 4, *5*, 68

Bratley, Theresa, 5

Brave, Benjamin, family of, *137*

Brave Bear, in Winter Count, *17*

bridles, Lakota Sioux, *172*

Briscoe, Delia, 93

Broken Leg, Annie, 147

Browning, Daniel M., 62

Brulé Sioux, 83

buffalo. *See* bison

Buffalo Head, in Winter Count, *20*

buffalo medicine, in Winter Count, *17*

Burbank, Edward Everett, 56

Burbank, Elbridge Ayer, 56

Bureau of American Ethnology (BAE; Bureau of Ethnology), 25, 43–44, 50–51, 59

Bureau of Indian Affairs (BIA), 38, 39, 192, 209; Bratley's relationship with, 98–99, 110; community transformation by, 135–36; employment by, 137–38; on

language use, 128–29; paternalism of, 62–63; at St. Louis World's Fair, 63–64; school curricula, 126–27; summer institutes of, 78–79; at World's Columbian Exposition, 60, 61–62. *See also various schools by name*

Bureau of Indian Commissioners (BIC), 140–41

Bureau of Indian Education, 209

Burton, Charles E., 103

butterfly whorl hairstyle, *127*

Caddo, 117

Cahill, Cathleen D., 192

Canada: residential schools in, 204–5; Truth and Reconciliation Commission, 34–35, 202–3

canteen, Hopi, *105*

Cantonment Boarding School, *4*, 40, *61*, *119*, *139*, *209*; agricultural training at, 131–32, *133*, 161; Bratleys at, 91, 93–95, *111*; Cheyenne camp at, 152, 201; resistance at, 148–49, 151, *180*, 182; students at, 127–28, 171

Carlisle Indian School, 26, 27, 40, 118, 134, 150, 155, 194, 205; Cheyenne and Arapaho at, 92, 154

Caruthers, Amy, 118

Catholic Church: Indian schools, 75, 155; missionaries, 143, 182

Catholic Congress, and Lakota Sun Dance, 143

Catlin, George, *Wi-jn-jon, Pigeon's Egg Head (the Light) Going to and Returning from Washington*, 26

cattle, 19, federal issue of, 24, 170–71

Centennial International Exhibition (Philadelphia), 59

ceremonies: Cheyenne, *51*; outlawing, 173

Chaca, *167*

Chapella, Elidia S., 32

Cherokee Strip run, 72, 73

Cheyenne, 4, 7, 15, 37, *51*, 91, 118, 151, 161, 171; cultural adaptations, 168–69; education, 92–93, 201, 208; intermediary chiefs, 153–55

Cheyenne-Arapaho Manual Training and Labor School, animal husbandry, 168–69

Cheyenne and Arapaho (Cheyenne-Arapaho) Reservation, 92, *209*; animal husbandry, 168–69; Cantonment Boarding School at, *4*, 40, *61*, 91, *111*, *119*, *133*, *139*, 148–49; play tipis, *180*, 182; "progressive" decisions on, 153–55

Cheyenne-Arapaho Transportation Company, 169

Chicago, world's fairs, 26, 59, 60, 61, 63, 65

Chilocco Indian Agricultural School, 151–52

Chimakum, 74

Chinook Jargon, 25, 130

Chivington, John, 91

Christianization, 38, 140–41, 143, 144, 182, 199; survivance, 191, 200–201

Chua (Rattlesnake), Mrs., *106*

churches, as community centers, 143–44

citizen's dress, *183*

citizenship, 38, 40

Civilization Division (BIA), 38, 39

Civilization of Indians law, 37

civilizing mission, 116, 193; bodily transformation and, 124–26; Christian, 38, 140–41, 143–44; of Indian Service, 135–36; Richard Henry Pratt and, 117–18; resistance to, 144–52; schools and, 120–23. *See also* allotment; education

Clallam. *See* S'Klallam

clambake, S'Klallam, 160, 188(n171)

clothing. *See* dress

collecting, collectors, 55–56

colonialism, 3, 34, 204; negotiation of, 194–95; and survivance, 30–31, 189

Comanche, 117

commercialization, handicrafts and dances, 54

commodities, 176; Indian arts and crafts as, 54–55

communities: interactions with, 119–20; maintaining identity of, 173–74; protection of, 155–56; transformations of, 135–36

community centers, churches and schools as, 143–44

Concho (Okla.), 92, 131

Conn, Steven, 203

conservatives, 153; community protection, 155–56

contact zone, 195; Indian school system, 196–97

Continental Congress, 37

contracts, 39

Cooking Utensils, in Winter Count, *18*

corn grinding, Hopi, 45, *107*, 108

corn growing, 12, 48

Courts of Indian Offenses, 173

coyotes, in Winter Count, *15*

crafts, 60; commercialization of, 54–55. *See also* beadwork

Crane, Francis, 6

Crane, Mary, 6
Crazy Horse, 81; death of, 21
Cree, 14, 19
Criscoe, Ms., *139*
Crook, George, 86
Crooked Wrist, in Winter Count, *11*
Crow, in Winter Count, *11, 13, 16, 18, 19, 22, 23*
Crow Creek Reservation, 155
Crow Dog, 22
culture: adaptation, 158–59; comparisons, 47; evolution, 44; retaining, 179–80
curio collecting, 55
curricula, at Indian schools, 61, 62, 79, 126–27, 131–35
Curtis, Edward, 26–27
Curtis, Mr., 20
Cushing, Frank H., 56
Custer, George Armstrong, 21, 81
Cut Meat Reservation, 123
Cut Meat Station, beef rationing, *171*
Cyrus, 130

Dakota, Winter Count, *8–24*. *See also* Lakota Sioux
dances, 22, *51*, 54; on Rosebud Reservation, 88–89
Darlington, Brinton, 92
Darlington Agency, 92, 169
Dartmouth College, 37
day schools, 39, 83, 92, 98, 119, 155; assimilationist structure of, 120–23; Hopi, 103–4; S'Klallam, 4, 36, 42, 73–77, 81
Deadwood, 21, 23
dealers, 56
deaths, in Dakota Winter Count, *9, 10, 11, 12, 13, 14, 15, 16, 17, 18, 19, 20, 22, 23, 24*
Denver Museum of Nature and Science, 7
Dewey, John, 206
Dexter, Willie, *74*
disease, 39; among Dakota, *10, 11, 16, 17*
disobedience, Chilocco Indian Agricultural School, 151–52
Dodge City (Kans.), 70
dolls: Cheyenne-Arapaho, *181, 182*; Seminole, *113*
domestic arts, training in, 131, *132*
domesticity, 131
dress: and identity, *122, 124, 126, 128, 133, 137, 183*; resistance through, *145, 152*; traditional, 176, *177–79*
drownings, in Winter Count, *13*
drum, Lakota Sioux, *33*
Dunbar, John, 84

Eagle Feather, Edna, *139*
eagle feathers, in Bratley collection, *46*
Eaglehorn, Fannie, 194
Earlocker, Katherine, 93, *139*
Eastern Pequot, hybridity of, 199
economics, and education, 136–37
education, 3, 110, 116, 180, 203; assimilation through, 54, 118–23, 189; BIA programs, 60–64; changes in, 205–6; Cheyenne and Arapaho, 92–93; Christian reformers and, 140–41; and economic advancement, 136–37; and employment, 137–38; federal policies and funding, 37–40; Hopi attitudes toward, 206–8; Lakota Sioux, 21, 82–83; purpose of, 25, 193; and race, 40–41; resistance to, 144–52, 194–95; support for, 152–55
Education Aid Association, 71
Education Division (BIA), 39
Eells, Edwin, 73
Elk, Solomon, *144*, 173, 200
Elk Looks Back, Bessie, *86, 121, 124, 132*
Elk Looks Back, Emma, *86, 121, 124, 132*; writing lesson by, *128*
Elk Looks Back, Levi, *124*
Elk Stands Looks Back, 21
Elk Teeth, Chief, 65, 120, *147*
Elk Teeth, Jossie, *124*
Elk Teeth, Nat, *86, 124*
Elk Teeth, Rosa, *86, 121*
emigrants, on Platte River, *19*
employment, by Indian Service, 137–40, 195
English language: at Hopi, 207; at Indian schools, 128–30
entertainment, 58. *See also* fairs
epidemics, in Winter Count, *11, 16, 17*
Episcopalians, 140, 143
Episcopal Missionary Society, Lakota Sioux school, 82–83
ethnographies, 47, *48*
ethnology, Lewis Henry Morgan and, 44
evangelism, Protestant, 141
Ewing, Henry P., 96
exhibits: of Bratley's collection, 49, 50; at world's fairs, 26, 61–62
expansionism, American, 59

fairs, exhibitions at, 59–64
families: nuclear, 116, *117*; resistance by, 152, 153
Farr, William E., 26, 34, 125
Fast Dog, 23, *147*
Fast Dog, Mercy, 172

Fast Dog, Sage, 172
Fellows, Corabelle, 123, 193
Finger, Bob, 149
First Mesa, 104, 106, 108, *165*
First White (First Good White Man), 9
flags: American, *174*, 191–92; ceremonial, *18*
Flanders, Elizabeth, 194
Florida, Bratley family in, 110–12
Foot, Eddie, *86, 124*
Foot, Jessie, *124, 145*
Foot, Nellie, *86, 121, 124, 132*
football, 133–34
Forsyth, N. F., 26
Fort Huachuca, 150
Fort Marion, 118
Fort Robinson, 21
Four Ways, 20
freighting, 169
frontier, settlement of, 68–69
Fulton, Lloyd, 208

Gamble campaign, 159
gambling games: Cheyenne and Arapaho, 94, 95; S'Klallam, *160*
gardens, 131–32, *136*
gender roles, Plains tribes, 168, 171
genocide, cultural, 31
George, Eddie, 146
George, Ted, 146
Ghost Dance, 23
gift giving, giveaways, 174–76; communal, 119, *120*
goats, at Hopi, *110*
Goes-to-War, 28
Gold's Curiosity Shop, 55
Gonzalez, Patricia, 128, 140
Good Bear, Paul, 93, *139*
Good Bird, Gracie, *86, 121, 124, 132*
Good Bird, Stella, *86, 124*
Good Bird, Willie, *86, 122*
Good Kill, Alice, *122*
Gover, Kevin, 204
Grand Canyon, 50, 53, 97, *103*
Grand Ronde Reservation, agriculture, 169–70
Grant, Ulysses S., 38, 140
Great Sioux Reservation, 81; schools on, 82–83
Greiffenstein's Trading Post, 37
Grey Eagle Tail, 14; book cover from, *201*
Grey Eagle Tail, John, *147*
Grey Eagle Tail, Paul, *122*
grinding tools, S'Klallam, *43*
Groves, Mary Elizabeth. *See* Ranson, Mary Elizabeth Groves

Hailmann, William N., 79, 130
hair cutting, 180; at Havasupai, *133*;
    at Hopi, 125–26; Lakota Sioux,
    146, 147–48
hairstyles: butterfly whorl, *107, 127*;
    choices in, 202
Hallowell, Irving, 190
hammers, S'Klallam granite, *42–43*
Hampton Institute, 39, 40, 118, 136–37,
    155
hangings, 24
Harris, Fannie, 93
Harvard Peabody Museum, 43, 60
Hastings, Mary Emma. *See* Bratley,
    Mary Emma Hastings
hatbands, beaded, *182*
Havasupai (Havasu'Baaja), 7, 95–96,
    117, 168, 196; agriculture, 161–62,
    193; basketry, *100, 163*; resistance
    by, 150–51
Havasupai Agency and Reservation,
    99, 101, *193*; Bratleys at, *96, 98*
Havasupai Day School, *95, 96, 98,
    99, 133*
Hayes, Rutherford B., 95
Hayt, Ezra, 92
Heard Museum, *Remembering Our
    Indian School Days* exhibit, 203
Henry, Richard, 74
Henry, Willie, 74
High Back Bone, *19*; Winter Kill
    depiction of, *20*
Highland School, 70
High Pipe, 153; family of, *154*
High Pipe, Cathleen, 176, 180
High Pipe, Luella, 208
High Pipe, Sarah, 208
High Pipe, Travis, 143, 153, 168
Hoag, Enoch, 92
Ho-Chunk, survivance, 197–98
Hoelscher, Steven D., 197
Hollow-Horn Bear
    (Matȟóȟéȟloǧeča), 85–86, *87*
Holy Medicine, Alice Rowles, 153
homemaking, training in, 131, 132
homesteads: in Florida, 111; in
    Kansas (Section 36), 69–70, 72
Honavi, Ruth, *107, 127*
Hopi, 7, 25, 27–28, 30, 31, 47, 56, 101, 103,
    106, 120, 158, 170; attitudes toward
    education, 206–8; corn grinding at,
    45; hair cutting at, 125–26; objects
    made by, *49, 58, 105*; Protestant
    churches at, 143–44; religious
    traditions of, *173, 182, 185, 186*;
    resistance on, 149–50; subsistence
    practices of, *48,* 162, 164–67;
    wedding practices of, *156, 157*

Hopi Boarding School, 103
Hopi Indian Agency, 101
Hopi Mission, 143–44
Hopi Snake Dance, 27
Horn, *147*
horses, *10*; federal issues of, *20, 23*;
    Plains tribes and, 171–72; thefts
    of, *18, 19*
houses, on Rosebud Reservation,
    172–74
Howling Buffalo, Armin Jean, 131
Howling Wolf, 118
Hoyt, J. L., 49
Hume, Annette Ross, 56
Hume, Charles, 56
hunting practices, Plains tribes,
    170–71
Hutchinson, Elizabeth, 54, 55

icehouse, Lakota Sioux, 134–35
icons, traditional, *151, 182, 184,* 199,
    200
identities: Anglo-American, 124;
    dress and, *126, 128, 137*; hair
    cutting and, 147–48; maintaining
    traditional, 173–74, 179–80; Plains
    tribes, 171; team sports and, 134;
    traditional subsistence and, 160,
    165
ideographs, in Swift Bear Winter
    Count, 8–24
imprisonment: of Hopi resisters,
    149–50; of parents, 146, 148
Indian Appropriation Act, 168–69
"Indian Beliefs" (Bratley), 50
Indian corners, 55–56, *57, 58*
Indian craze, 25, 54, 57–58; collecting
    and tourism, 55–56
Indian Messiah, 23
Indian problem, 116
Indian Reorganization Act, 206
Indian Residential Schools, Truth
    and Reconciliation Commission,
    202–3, 204–5
Indian schools, 27, 37, 38–39, 54,
    75, 80, 206, 209; assimilationist
    structure at, 120–28, 189, 193; ath-
    letics at, 133–34; as contact zone,
    196–97; curricula, 61, 79, 126–27;
    employment at, 137–40; on Great
    Sioux Reservation, 82–83; at Hopi,
    103–4; and Indigenous identities,
    179–80; language use at, 128–31;
    military-style system at, 118–19;
    paternalism of, 62–63; resistance
    to, 144–53, 194–95; on Rosebud
    Reservation, 84, 86–89; voca-
    tional curricula at, 131–33, 134–35;

White children in, 110, *111. See also
    various schools by name*
Indian Service. *See* Bureau of Indian
    Affairs; Indian schools
Indian Wars, 192
individualism, 141
industrial training, 131–32
insurgents, treatment of, 149–50
interviews, 34–35
Iron Horse, 22
Iron Shell, Chief, 85
issues, federal, *17, 20, 21, 23, 24,* 92, 119

Jack, Wilson, 74
Jackson, Helen Hunt, 55–56
Jamestown (Wash.), 75
John, Louise, 74
John, Peter, 74
Jones, Clara, 179; basketmaking, *182,
    185*
Jones, Gene, 179, *182, 185*
Jones, Jacob, 74
Jones, William A., 120, 153
Jumping Bull, 14

Kansas, 37; Bratley family in, 41–42,
    68–70, 98–99, 101, 110
Kansas State Fair, 49
Kaskaskia, 37
katsinas, depictions of, *49*
Kayu (Watermelon), *47*
Keam, Thomas, 167
Keams Canyon, 150
Keppler, Joseph "Udo," 56
Kicking Bear. *See* Wright, James G.
killings, Winter Count records of, *9,
    10, 11, 12, 13, 14, 15, 16, 17, 18, 19, 20,
    21, 22, 23, 24*
Kills Plenty, George, *86,* 124
Kills Plenty, James, *147*
Kills Plenty, Lucy, *86, 122, 124*
Kiowa, 117
kivas, Hopi, *185, 186*
Kuwanwisiwma, Leigh J., 143–44,
    182, 207, 208
Kwaazi (Little Rabbit), *47*

labor, 132; Cheyenne and Arapaho,
    168–69; Hopi shared, 162, 164;
    paid, 137–38
Lakota Sioux (Sicangu Oyate), 29,
    37, 47, 64, *121, 126, 137, 143, 153, 159,
    161, 163, 171, 183, 191*; beadwork,
    151, 182, 184; bison as icon, 199,
    200; drum, *33*; giveaways, *120*;
    houses, 172–73; icehouse, 134–35;
    polygamy, *174, 175*; resistance,
    146–48, 151; on Rosebud

Reservation, 82–89; sales of traditional objects, 167–68; traditional dress, *145*, *177–79*; Winter Count, 7, *8–24*

landscape, Bratley's observation of, 51–53

language use, 143; English, 128–30; tribal, 130–31

leadership, tribal, 155

Learning to Do by Doing Chart Company, 72

lectures, Bratley's, 49–50

Leesummit School, 70

Left Hand, 154

leggings, Lakota Sioux, *151*

Lemhi, 145

Lenoman, Officer, *98*

lightning, 24

Lightning Hawk, in Winter Count, 22, *24*

literacy, historical, 204

Little Beaver, in Winter Count, 9, *10*

Little Big Horn, Battle of, 81

Little Chief, 93

Little Dog, Leland, 89, 143, 147, 153, *172*, 180, *196*

Little Man, Chief, *15*

Little Raven, Chief, 93, *94*, 154

Little Thunder, 15

Lomayestewa, Lee Wayne, 105, 120

London world's fair, 59

Lonetree, Amy, 203; on survivance, 197–98, 202

Lower Cut Meat camp, 14, 20, 23, 153

Lower Cut Meat Creek Day School, *24*, *161*, *209*; Bratleys at, *57*, 84, *86–89*; curricula at, 126–27; resistance at, 146–47; students at, *121*, *122–23*, *124*, *125*, *139*; vocational training at, 131, *132*

Mabel, *107*

Magee, Thomas B., 26

mail carrier, Hopi, 27–28, *31*

Makes Enemy, 180, 202

Manakaja, Chief, *196*

manhood, American notions of, 132–34

Markowitz, Harvey, 141

Matȟóȟéȟloǧeča (Hollow-Horn Bear), 85–86, *87*

McCleave, Christine Diindiisi, 205

McClintock, Walter, 26

McCracken, Krista, 203

medicine arrow, *15*

Meek, Leah, *139*

Meek, Willie, 93, *139*

Meriam Report, 206

metalworking, training in, 132

metates and manos, Hopi, *107*, *108*

meteors, in Swift Bear's Winter Count, 12, *14*

Miami (Fla.), Bratley family in, 110–12

Miami River, 111

Miles, John D., 92–93, 168

Milk Camp Day School, 148

Miniconjou, 19

missions, missionaries, 38, 42, *104*, *141*, 143, 155, 182

Mennonite Church, 143, 182

moccasins, Lakota Sioux, *176*

Mohawk, 199

Moqui. *See* Hopi

moral code, American Protestant, 141

Morgan, Lewis Henry, 44

Morgan, Thomas J., 39, 54, 60, 61–62

Mormons, and Hopi, 101, 103

Mosquida, Fred, 130–31

Mud Hole, Chief, *29*

mules, 19, 20

Mules Father, in Winter Count, *16*

names, naming, at Indian schools, 123–24, *125*

National Cowboy & Western Heritage Museum (Oklahoma City), Lakota Winter Count in, 7, *8*

National Museum of the American Indian (NMAI), 203

Native Americans, 41, 54; and fair exhibitions, 26, 59–65. *See also various groups; tribes*

Navajo Agency, 103

na'ya, 162, 164

neck piece, Lakota Sioux, *146*

New, Charles, *86*, *124*

New, Thomas, *124*, *145*

NMAI. *See* National Museum of the American Indian

nostalgia, imperial, 54

Odell, Ms., *139*

Oglala Sioux, 83, 138, 155, 180

Oklahoma, 91

Old Hawk, 14

Omaha, 20

Omaha (Nebr.), 50, *51*

One Ear Horse, 24

Oneida, 37

One Wood, *147*

One Wood, Tommy, *124*

Oraibi, 101, *150*, 182

Oraibi Day School, 103

oral history, S'Klallam, 46–47

Ortiz, Fernando, 190

Otterman, Allen, *86*, *122*, *124*

Otterman, Chief, *147*

Otterman, Edith, 176

Otterman, Maggie, *86*, *121*, *124*, 172

Otterman, Tommy, *86*, *124*

pageants, 173

Pail in His Hand, *10*

Paints Himself Yellow, *16*

parades, 173, *174*

parents, resistance by, 145, 146, 147–48, 152

parfleche, Lakota Sioux, *90*

paternalism, 62–63, 140–41

Patsy, Francis, 74

Pavatya, Tommy, *170*

Pawnees, Winter Count depictions of, *9*, *10*, *14*, *15*

Pawnee Tom, 14

Peabody Museum (Harvard), 43, 60

performances, public, 173–74

persistence, 116; cultural, 157–67, 180–85

Philadelphia, 59

photography, 34; Bratley's, 25, 56; power of, 28, 30; survivance and, 197–98, 202; types of, 26–27

piki bread, 164, *166*

Pine Ridge Agency, 23

Pine Ridge Reservation, 79, 138

Plains tribes, 167, 168; adoption of American flag, *191–192*; beef rations, *170–71*; and horses, 171–72. *See also various tribes*

Platte River, emigrants on, 19

plays, 54, 173

Plenty Coup, 172–73

Plenty-Holes, Sammy, 122–23

Plenty Holes, Silas, *86*

Point Julia day village (Wash.), 75

Polacca, 207

Polacca, Lyman, 106–7

Polacca Day School, 58, 103, 207; students at, *104*, 125–26

police, Lakota Sioux, 24, *138*

polygamy, Lakota Sioux, 174, *175*

Pompadour, 19

Pony, Nancy, *86*

Port Gamble, 75, *76*, 77

Port Gamble Day School, 4, 36, 42, 81, *129*; Bratley at, 73–77; dissension and resistance at, 145–46

pottery, Hopi, *105*, *106*, *156*, *157*

pouches, Lakota Sioux, *142*, *184*, *200*

Powell, John Wesley, 43

Powiky, Sam, 27–28, *31*

Pratt, Mary Louise, on contact zones, 195–96

Pratt, Richard Henry, 21, 41, 134; and resistance leaders, 117–18
prejudices, 37
progressives: Cheyenne and Arapaho, 153–55; community protection, 155–56
projectile points, 41, 42, 168
propaganda, for Indian school system, 54
Protestants, 143; civilizing mission, 140–41
Pulls the Arrow Out, 23, 147
Puyallup (Wash.), Port Gamble Day School at, 73–77

Quaker Church, 92, 140
quillwork, Lakota Sioux, 199–200, 201

rabbit stick, Hopi, 164–65
rabies, in Winter Count, 15
race, and education, 40–41
Ranson, Della. See Bratley, Della Ranson
Ranson, Mary Elizabeth Groves, 77
Ranson, William H., 70, 77
rations: beef, 170–71; dependence on, 92, 167; federal, 17, 20, 21, 23, 24, 119
Rattlesnake Elk, in Winter Count, 18
Real Bull, 94
reconciliation, 34, 204
Red Cloud, 12, 20, 21, 81, 82
Red Cloud Agency, 20
Red Hill (Okla.), 198
Redland (Fla.), 111
Red Leaf, in Winter Count, 17, 19
Reel, Estelle, 39, 41, 54, 61, 131, 132, 136, 138
religious beliefs: Hopi, 173, 182, 185, 186; Lakota Sioux, 143, 200–201
Remembering Our Indian School Days: The Boarding School Experience (exhibit), 203
reparations, 205
repatriation, 205
reservations, 21; cultural adaptation on, 158–59. See also by name
residential schools (Canada): effects of, 204–5; and Truth and Reconciliation Commission, 202–3
resiliency, 179
resistance, 159, 180, 182, 185, 194–95; leaders of, 117–18; punishment for, 149–50; against schooling, 144–49, 150–52
restorative justice, 34
Revolutionary War, 37

Ritter, Ms., 103
Robinson Museum (Pierre, SD), 7
Rolls Off, 23
Rosebud Agency, 22, 23, 84
Rosebud Reservation, 47, 64, 82, 90, 119, 120, 126, 136, 140, 159, 161, 163, 171, 174, 175, 183, 191, 194, 208; acculturation, 191–92; Christian evangelism, 141, 142, 144; day schools on, 83–85; Della and Jesse Bratley at, 45, 46, 78, 86–89, 177–79; establishment of, 81–82; houses on, 172–73; Hollow-Horn Bear at, 85–86; icehouse at, 134–35; Lower Cut Meat Creek Day School at, 84, 121, 122–23, 124, 125, 139, 145, 209; resistance on, 146–48, 153
Row of Lodges, 154
running, runners, Hopi, 165, 166, 167

saddle, elk horn, 123
St. Francis Mission School, 208
St. Louis World's Fair, 59–60; BIA exhibit at, 63–64
salmon fishing, 159–60
salvage paradigm, 43, 44–45
Sand Creek massacre, 91
Santa Fe, 55
savagery, 41, 122
sawmills, at Port Gamble, 76
Scabby Creek, 22
scalpings, in Winter Count, 11, 16, 18
"School for the Prophets," 118
schools, 21, 70, 75, 110. See also Indian schools
Search the Enemy Out, 19
Search the Enemy Out, Cora, 122, 124
seasonal mobility, of Plains tribes, 171, 172
Seatkin, Julia, 74
Second Mesa Day School, 103
self-government, tribal, 206
self-support: as goal, 38–39, 41; traditional handicrafts and, 54
Seminole, 7, 63; doll, 113
Setzer, F. M., 93
sewing, training in, 131, 132
sheep, at Hopi, 110
Sherburne, J. H., 26
Sherman Institute (Riverside), 150
shooting stars, in Swift Bear's Winter Count, 12, 14
Short Woman, 83
Shoshone, depicted in Winter Count, 11, 12, 14, 20
Show, 20
Shuplo, 30

Sicangu Oyate (Sicangu Lakota), 82. See also Lakota Sioux
Sikyátki, 108
Silliman, Stephen W., 198–99
Single Wood, 19
Sioux, treaties, 21, 82; See also Dakota; Lakota Sioux
silversmith, Hopi, 158
Sitting Bear, 23
Sitting Bear, Freddie, 86, 124
Sitting Bull, 14, 22, 81
Six More Crows, 22
S'Klallam, 4, 7, 75–76, 141, 188(n171), 208; basketmaking, 182, 185; objects collected from, 42–43; oral history of, 46–47; and Port Gamble Day School, 36, 74; resistance by, 145–46; teaching English to, 129–30; traditional cultural practices, 159–60, 179
Skokomish, 74
Skokomish Reservation, 75
Skookum John, 77
sla-hal, 160
Sleeping Bear, Frank, 86, 124
Slow Fly, Alice, 145
Slow Fly, Sammy, 124
smallpox, among Dakota, 11, 16, 17
Smithsonian Institution, 7, 43–44
Snake Dance, Hopi, 106, 166
Social Darwinism, 40
social evolution, 107, 108, 110
Sol, Alice, 74
soldiers, 20, 21, 23
Sololk, 30
Sontag, Susan, 28
South Dakota, 21; Bratleys in, 84–89; Rosebud Reservation in, 81–84
Southern Cheyenne. See Cheyenne
Southeast Museum of the North American Indian, 6–7
Southwestern Business College, 70–71
spiritual practices: Hopi, 173, 182, 185, 186; Lakota Sioux, 143, 200–201
Spit (Wash.), 75–76, 77, 129
Spooner, Margaret, 139
Spotted Bear, in Winter Count, 20
Spotted Female Elk. See Big Foot
Spotted Horse, in Winter Count, 18
Spotted Penis, in Winter Count, 15
Spotted Tail, 21, 22, 153
Standing Bear, Luther, 122, 140
Standing Bull, 14
Standing Little Tail, 124, 145
starvation, of Dakotas, 10
Steed, George, 147
Steward, Raymond, 23

Stockbridge, 37
stock raising, 168–69
stone tools, collection of, 41–42
Stuart, Paul, 116–17
students, *139, 171*; bodily transformations of, *121, 122–23, 124–25, 127–28,
  133*; curricula, 126–27; hair cutting,
  125–26; language use, 128–31; naming of, 123–24; resistance by, *145–53*
subsistence, traditional practices,
  159–62
Sullivan, Kelly, 130
Sun Dance, 143; federal ban on,
  173–74
Supai (Ariz.), 95
survival, 179, 197
survivance, 30–31, 32, 197–98; Hopi,
  206–8; material evidence of,
  198–205
sweatlodge, Lakota Sioux, *163*
Swift Bear, Winter Count of, *8–24*
syncretism, 192

Tagg, John, 28, 30
Tawaquaptewa, 150
Tayloe, Edward C., 148
Taylor, Mittie, 93
Ten Crows, 22
Tewa, Snake Dance at, 106
Third Mesa, *150*
Thorney, in Winter Count, 19
Thorpe, Jim, 134
Three Stars, Clarence, 21, 138
Thunder bird, 24
Tie Knot in His Penis, *14*
tipis, *172, 173*; play, *180, 182*
Tom, at Port Gamble Day School, *74*
Tom, Eliza, *74*
tourism, 192; ethnographic, *55, 56*
traders, White, *9, 10, 11*
transculturation, 190, 191, 194, 195
Trans-Mississippi and International
  Exposition (Omaha), 50, *51*
TRC. *See* Truth and Reconciliation
  Commission
treaties, 21, 37, 74, 82, 91
Treaty of Fort Laramie, 82, 86, 91
Treaty of Point No Point, 74
Treaty of the Little Arkansas, 91
tribal councils, 159
tribe, 206; as community, 116, 117,
  119–20

Truth and Reconciliation Commission (TRC; Canada), 34–35,
  202–3, 205
Truxton Canyon Boarding School,
  96
Tulalip Indian Boarding School, 179;
  basketmaking at, *182, 185*
Turning Eagle, *20, 23, 146–48*
Turning Eagle, Kittie, *86, 121, 124, 146,
  147, 148*
Tuscarora, 37
Tuskegee Institute, 40
twins, *47*

Underwater, John, *86, 122, 124*
Underwater, Minnie, *86, 124*
Underwater, Policeman, *86*
US Congress, on Indian education,
  37, 38, 118–19
US Department of the Interior, 38
US Department of War, 38
US government: assimilation poli-
  cies, 36, 37–41, 190–93, 204
universalism, 40
University of Manitoba, Truth and
  Reconciliation Commission
  research center, 203
Upper Brulé Sioux Nation. *See*
  Lakota Sioux
Upper Cut Meat, 20
utensils, beaded, *179*
Utes, 12, 155–56, 171

values, Indigenous, 174, 176
violence, in school settings, 24,
  146–48, 185, 194, 196–97
Vizenor, Gerald, 30–31, 197
vocational training, at Indian
  schools, 131–32
Voth, H. R., 182

wagons, Plains tribes' use of, *172, 173*
Walapai, 96
Walnut Canyon, 108, *109*
Walsh, William, 140, 155–56
warfare, Lakota (Dakota), *9, 10, 11, 12,
  13, 14, 15, 18, 20*
Washington, DC, 17, 207
Wa-sku-pi, in Winter Count, 12
Watonga (Okla.), *51, 198*
Wazazia band, 153
wealth, and polygamy, 175

weaving, Hopi, *186*
wedding practices, Hopi, *156, 157*
Western Navajo Boarding School,
  103
Whirlwind Soldier's Camp School,
  84–85
White, Ms., *139*
White Cloud, in Winter Count, 22,
  24
White Face Bull, 149
Whitehat, Clare, 127–28
Whiteman, Chester, 92
Whiteman, Marie, 95, 134
White Shield, 154
White Wolf, 14
*Wi-jn-jon, Pigeon's Egg Head (the
  Light) Going to and Returning
  from Washington* (Catlin), 26
Wilson, Horace, 96
Wilson, Tama, 96
Winter Count, Chief Swift Bear's,
  7, 8–24
Wichita (Kans.), Bratley family in, *58,
  69–70, 72, 98, 110, 112*
Wisconsin, 68
Wisnowski, Joshua, 160
With Horns, *147*
With Horns, Harry, *124, 145, 177–78*
With Horns, Hattie, *86, 124*; primer,
  62
Wood, Lee, *86, 124*
Wood, Tommy, *86*
World's Columbian Exposition, 59,
  60, 61, 63
world's fairs, exhibits at, 26, 59–64
Wounded Heel, *11*
Wounded Knee massacre, 23, 122–23
Wright, Grace, 93
Wright, James G. (Kicking Bear), 23,
  83–84

Yankton Agency, 22
Yellow Cloud, *147*
Yellow Ear, 154
Yellow Face, *11*
Yellow Horse, 154
Yellowman, Gordon, 131, 152, 208
Yellow Robe, Chauncey, 19; dual
  portrait of, *27, 201–2*
Yellow Robe, Chief, 13, 19, 23, *27*
Yellow Robe, Samuel, *86, 124*
Yunosi, *168*